LIVES OF FAMOUS CHRISTIANS

Lives of Famous Christians

A Biographical Dictionary

Tony Castle

SERVANT BOOKS
Ann Arbor, Michigan

Published by Servant Books
P.O. Box 8617
Ann Arbor, Michigan 48107

Printed in the United States of America
ISBN 0–89283–380–7

88 89 90 91 92 10 9 8 7 6 5 4 3 2 1

This work was originally published in Great Britain by
Hodder and Stoughton Limited.

#17916872

Abbot, Edwin (1838–1926)

Anglican schoolmaster and scholar who was headmaster of the City of London School for twenty-four years (1865–1889). He resigned to devote himself to theological study and writing aimed at the general public.

Abbot, Ezra (1819–1884)

United States Protestant biblical scholar who contributed widely to reviews and journals on New Testament textual criticism. His principal single production was *The Authorship of the Fourth Gospel* (1880), defending the Johannine authorship.

Abbot, George (1562–1633)

Archbishop of Canterbury. From an early date he supported the Puritan cause, which brought him into conflict with, among others, William Laud. In 1609 Abbot was made bishop of Lichfield and Coventry, in 1611 archbishop of Canterbury. In 1621 he accidently shot a gamekeeper; a commission met to consider if he was fit for the primacy. King James exercised his casting vote in his favour. Although Abbot crowned Charles I, he was continually in disagreement with the king and was suspended from his functions for a while in 1627.

Abelard, Peter (1079–1142)

Philosopher and theologian. Of Breton origins, Abelard showed early signs of a lively and independent mind. As a lecturer he stimulated and inspired large numbers of students, but his stubborn independence angered his elders. His career was cut short by the tragic consequences of his love affair with Héloise, niece of Fulbert, a canon of Notre Dame. Abelard retired to the monastery of Saint-Denis, and Héloise became a nun. His popular success as a theologian brought attacks from other theologians, particularly on his teaching about the Trinity. Later Abelard became abbot of Saint-Gildas de Ruys in Britanny (1125–1132) but his reforming zeal offended the community. About 1140 St Bernard of Clairvaux denounced some of Abelard's teaching to the bishops of France; several selected passages were condemned at the Council of Sens. Abelard and St Bernard were eventually reconciled. Abelard was enthusiastically devoted to the search for the truth, but his considerable influence upon the shape of Western theology was more through his lectures than his writings.

Adam of Marsh (d. c. 1258)

An English Franciscan theologian, friend of Robert Grosseteste and Simon de Montfort; his influence was felt on the political and social life of the period, and respect for his scholarship won him the title 'Doctor Illustris'.

Adam of St Victor (d. between 1177–1192)

Educated at Paris c. 1130, he entered the abbey of Saint-Victor and is famous for writing a number of musical sequences used in the Roman liturgy.

Adam, Karl (1876–1966)

Catholic theologian who was ordained to the priesthood in 1900. After pastoral work he taught at the University of Munich, then at Strasbourg (1918) and finally at Tübingen. His writings, projecting a liberal and modern outlook to orthodox theology (the best-known example is *Das Wesen Des Katholizismus,* 1924) had a great influence, especially among the educated laity.

Adamson, Patrick (1537–1592)
Archbishop of St Andrews, Scotland, who was involved in a long controversy with the Presbyterian party in the Scottish Kirk. His writings and oratory caused much hostility and he was excommunicated by the Synod of Fife (1586). Having lost the favour of King James I he ended his days in poverty.

Adrian (also Hadrian)—There were six popes of this name, the most noteworthy being:

Adrian I (d. 795)
Pope from 772, who fought against the heresy of adoptionism, and is remembered for his working relationship and rapport with Charlemagne. Their relationship symbolised the medieval ideal of state and church working together in a united Christendom.

Adrian IV (c. 1100–1159) (originally Nicholas Breakespear)
The only Englishman to become pope, he originated from Abbot's Langley, Hertfordshire. Educated in France, he became an Augustinian monk and abbot in 1137, and while on a trip to Rome, retained in papal service, was elevated to cardinal c. 1150. As pope (1154) he crowned Frederick I (Barbarossa) and continued a stormy relationship with him; he is said to have granted the overlordship of Ireland to Henry II of England, but the document concerned, *Laudabiliter,* is now believed to be a forgery.

Aelfric (c. 955–c. 1010)
Abbot of the Benedictine community at Eynsham, Oxfordshire, and the greatest scholar of the English Benedictine re-

vival, accorded the title 'the Grammarian'. His *Catholic Homilies,* sermons based on the church fathers, were cited by the sixteenth-century Reformers, especially in defence of their eucharistic teaching.

Aelred of Rievaulx, St (c. 1110–1167) (also Ailred)

Spiritual writer and outstanding Cistercian abbot. Brought up in the court of King David I of Scotland, he became a Cistercian monk at Rievaulx Abbey, Yorkshire, where later, in 1147, he became abbot. Adviser to both kings and bishops, he is best remembered for his influential spiritual writings, his most important being the *Speculum Caritatis* ('Mirror of Love').

Affre, Denis-Auguste (1793–1848)

Archbishop of Paris, famous for his reforming spirit, who fearlessly opposed King Louis-Philippe (1843 ff) and welcomed the establishment of the Second Republic (1848). Grieved by the bloody insurrection of the Parisian workers, known as the June Days, he was accidently shot dead while trying to negotiate with them.

Agapetus—There were two popes of this name. The first

with the title 'saint', was pope from 535 to 536 and traveled to Constantinople where he deposed the patriarch for his Monophysite beliefs.

Agatha, St—See St Agnes.

Agnes, St (b. c. 304)

As with St Agatha, also a virgin martyr, little reliable information is known of her life. Both were reputed to be beautiful Christian young women who refused to abandon their faith and were exposed and tormented in brothels (Agnes in Rome and Agatha in Palermo). Their sufferings ended in martyrdom.

Agricola, Johann (c. 1494–1566) (original name Schneider)
Friend and follower of Martin Luther who studied theology under Luther at Wittenberg and introduced the Reformation to Frankfurt and Eisleben. He espoused antinomianism, which brought him into conflict with Luther.

Aidan, St (d. 651)
Monk of Iona, missionary in Northumbria and the first bishop of Lindisfarne. From his monastic centre at Lindisfarne Aidan evangelised northern England, founding churches and monasteries. He was renowned for his learning and charity.

Alain (or Alan) of Lille (c. 1128–1203)
Theologian, so celebrated in his day as to be called 'the Universal Doctor'. His work *The Art of the Catholic Faith* reveals the mystical slant of his theology. When he moved from teaching in Paris to Montpellier, he combated the Catharist heresy. In later life he joined the Cistercians at Citeaux.

Alban, St
The first British martyr. According to the Venerable Bede he was a pagan serving in the Roman army who, after conversion, sheltered a fugitive priest. Disguised in the priest's clothes, he was arrested and put to death in the priest's place. It is not clear whether this took place during the persecution of Septimius Severus (c. 209) or that of Diocletian (c. 305).

Albertus Magnus, St (c. 1200–1280) (Albert the Great)
Dominican philosopher, theologian and scientist. After studying in Italy and Germany, he was sent to Paris to lecture on the Bible and theology, one of his pupils being Thomas Aquinas, and there the newly translated works of Aristotle greatly influenced him. He was bishop of Regensburg (1260–1261) and preached a crusade (1263–1264) on the order of Pope Urban IV, but he received the appellation 'Great' for his huge contri-

bution to medieval learning. He was canonised and proclaimed a doctor of the church in 1931.

Alcock, John (c. 1430–1500)
Educated at Cambridge, where he later founded Jesus College; after ordination he rose rapidly in various posts to become successively bishop of Rochester (1472), Worcester (1476) and Ely (1486); for a time he was also chancellor of England. His most important work was *The Hill of Perfection* (1497).

Alcuin (c. 732–804)
Educator, poet, deacon and inspirer of the Carolingian renaissance. Born and educated at York, where he became master of the cathedral school, in 781 he met Charlemagne and accepted his invitation to found an educational centre at Aachen. This centre suffused learning and culture throughout Europe, Alcuin being the foremost among many eminent scholars. His influential writings included history, poetry, educational manuals and theology (an attack upon the adoptionist heresy), but lacked originality. He made important reforms in the liturgy and left more than three hundred Latin letters. Although he had a reputation for sanctity he was never proposed for canonisation.

Aldhelm, St (c. 639–709)
Abbot of Malmesbury (675), poet and first bishop of Sherborne (705). While little is certain about the details of his life, he was highly regarded as the most learned teacher of his time and as a pioneer in Latin verse among the Saxons.

Alexander—Eight popes had this name, the most noteworthy being:

Alexander III (1105–1181) (born Orlando Bandinelli)
Canon lawyer and lecturer at Bologna who rose rapidly to cardinal in the church and then opposed the growing power of

Frederick Barbarossa. As pope (1159) he was a vigorous defender of papal authority, opposing not only Barbarossa but also Henry II of England over the Thomas à Becket affair.

Alexander of Hales (c. 1186–1245)
Philosopher and theologian, accorded the title 'Doctor Irrefragabilis'. He originated from Halesowe, West Midlands, but studied and taught at Paris, where he lived most of his life. He joined the Franciscan order (1236) and founded a Franciscan school of theology. He began a *Summa Theologica* which was completed by his followers.

Alexander, Michael Solomon (1799–1845)
First Anglican bishop of Jerusalem. Born a strict orthodox German Jew; at twenty-one he came to England and was converted to Christianity. After ordination he worked for the conversion of Jews, first in Danzig (1827–1830) then in London (1830–1841)—he became the first bishop of Jerusalem in 1841.

Alford, Henry (1810–1871)
Scholar of New Testament Greek and dean of Canterbury who went from a fellowship at Cambridge to pastoral posts. Remembered for his edition of the Greek New Testament (1849–1861) and several well-known hymns, including 'Come, ye thankful people, come'.

Alfred the Great (849–899)
Saxon king of Wessex (from 871) who saved England from conquest by the Danes and, himself an educated man, was successful in promoting a great revival of learning. He translated many Latin works, including spiritual classics, and founded several monasteries, although his monastic reforms did not receive support.

Allen, Richard (1760–1831)

First United States black bishop of the African Methodist Episcopal church. Born of a slave family, he was converted to Methodism at seventeen and permitted to preach when twenty-two. After buying his freedom in 1786 he joined the Methodist church in Philadelphia, but, unhappy with restrictions placed upon him, in 1787 he founded his own independent church for blacks. He was officially ordained (1799) and after the foundation of the African Methodist Episcopal church he was chosen as its first bishop in 1816.

Allen, William (1532–1594)

English cardinal and scholar who inspired the Roman Catholic Douai version of the Bible. A fellow of Oriel College, Oxford, he refused to acknowledge Elizabeth as head of the English church and was ordained a priest on the continent. He founded colleges for the training of priests to work on the English mission, at Douai (1568), Rome (1575–1578) and Valladolid (1589). He lost the support of many English Roman Catholics for his championing of the cause of Philip II of Spain and his Armada.

Aloysius Gonzaga, St (1568–1591)

Son of the Marquis of Castigilione, he was destined, after education as a page, for military service. Experiencing a vocation to the religious life, after great family opposition and poor health, he joined the Jesuits (1585). With a reputation for personal austerity and care for the poor, he worked among the plague victims of Rome and died of the disease. He was canonised in 1726 and declared patron of Catholic youth.

Alphege, St (954–1012) (also known as Aelfheàh or Elphege)

Archbishop of Canterbury and martyr. Benedictine monk and anchorite who was chosen abbot of Bath then, in 984, bishop of Winchester; in 1005 he became archbishop of Canterbury. When the Danes sacked Canterbury they seized him for ransom but because he would not permit his poor tenants to be taxed to raise the money, the Danes pelted him with ox bones and killed him. From earliest times he was venerated as a martyr.

Ambrose, St (c. 339–397)
Bishop of Milan, and biblical critic. Son of the praetorian prefect of Gaul, he was himself governor of Aemilia and Liguria and only a Christian catechumen when, by popular acclaim, he was chosen as bishop of Milan. As a famous preacher and champion of orthodoxy he combated Arianism and paganism and stoutly upheld the independence of the church from state interference. He is remembered for his vital part in the conversion and baptism of St Augustine, his literary works and works of theology, particularly *De Sacramentis* and *De Officiis Ministrorum.*

Ambrose, Isaac (1604–1664)
A Lancashire Anglican priest, educated at Oxford, who became a Presbyterian (1641) and ministered in the Leeds area, but became caught up in the Civil War, twice being imprisoned by the Royalists. He published many religious titles, the most famous of which, *Looking unto Jesus* (1658), sprang from his own deep interior life.

Ames, William (1576–1633)
English Puritan moral theologian and controversialist who supported strict Calvinism in opposition to Arminianism. Compelled to leave England (1610) he settled in Holland and wrote and lectured in theology, particularly moral theology. Considered one of the greatest Calvinist theologians, his best-known work is *De Conscientia et ejus Jure vel Casibus* (1632).

Amsdorf, Nikolaus von (1483–1565)
German Protestant Reformer, theologian and friend of Martin Luther who sought to retain the purity of Luther's teaching in the face of liberalising elements.

Andrewes, Lancelot (1555–1626)
Anglican theologian, court preacher and bishop of Winchester. An esteemed scholar, he served in several parishes from 1589 before becoming successively bishop of Chichester (1605), Ely (1609) and Winchester (1619). He sought to defend and advance Anglican doctrine, criticising both Puritan and Roman Catholic teaching. In his time he was renowned for his preaching (some of his sermons were published as *Ninety-Six Sermons* in 1629), and his most famous book, *Preces Privatae* (1648), a collection of prayers, was still respected three hundred years later.

Anselm, St (c. 1033–1109)
Archbishop of Canterbury and founder of scholasticism. From Aosta, Italy, he became a Benedictine monk (1063) at Bec, France, where he became prior and abbot in 1078, by which time he was renowned as a leader and original thinker; from which period date his *Monologium* and *Proslogium*. Named archbishop of Canterbury (1093) he became involved in the investiture controversy which led to exile from England (1103–1106). In his last two years he was engaged in a conflict with the see of York over primacy. The greatest of his many theological works, *Cur Deus Homo* ('Why Did God Become Man?'), is a classical presentation of the satisfaction theory of the atonement; he is also remembered as the originator of the ontological argument for God's existence. He was declared a doctor of the church in 1720.

Ansgar, St (c. 801–865) (also Anskar)
French Benedictine monk and outstanding missionary in northern Europe. He worked first in Denmark (826–829),

then Sweden, being the first to introduce Christianity to the country (829–831). Recalled, he was appointed the first bishop of Hamburg (832). He initiated missionary work to all the Scandinavian countries and was accorded the title 'Apostle of the North'. Despite the ravages of the Northmen, he combated the slave trade and converted Erik, king of Jutland (854). He was canonised shortly after his death and declared patron saint of Scandinavia.

Anthony of Kiev (d. 1073) (also Anthony of Pechersky)
The founder of monasticism in Russia. Introduced to the solitary life at a Greek Orthodox monastery on Mt Athos, he returned to Kiev and settled in a cave on Mt Berestov. This became a centre which grew into a community and there the 'Monastery of the Caves' was founded. This institution exerted a great influence upon the Russian Orthodox church—for example, by the year 1250 fifty of its monks had become bishops.

Anthony of Padua, St (1195–1231) (originally Ferdinand de Bulhoes)
Born at Lisbon, he joined the Augustinian canons (1210) transferring to the Franciscan order (1221) in the hope of finding martyrdom as a missionary to the Moors. Illness forced him to return from Morocco and he was unexpectedly asked to preach at an ordination, revealing himself to be an eloquent preacher of great learning. He was sent to preach all over Italy with sensational success. After a number of teaching appointments he settled at Padua, where his fiery sermons denouncing corruption and wrongdoing resulted in a reformed city. He was particularly devoted to the care of the poor, and even in his own lifetime was credited with being a worker of miracles.

Antony of Egypt, St (250–356)
First Christian hermit and monk, founder of Christian monasticism. After distributing his family inheritance (269) he de-

voted himself to a solitary life of asceticism. About 285 he sought greater solitude on Mt Pispi, by the Nile. After twenty years he emerged to organise and write a rule for the colony of ascetics that had developed around his retreat. He went twice to Alexandria, first in 311 to encourage the Christian community then suffering persecution and second (about 355) to support his friend Athanasius in his stand against Arianism.

Aphraates (early fourth century) (also Afrahat)

Earliest Syriac Christian writer. Knowledge of his life is limited, but it seems he was a monk who became a bishop, writing under the pseudonym of 'the Persian Sage'. Between 336 and 345 he composed twenty-three biblical commentaries (inaccurately called 'Homilies') which are the earliest writings we have, casting invaluable light upon the simple presentation of Christian teaching at that time.

Aquaviva, Claudio (1543–1615)

Son of the Duke of Atri, he joined the Society of Jesus in 1567 and rose swiftly to become the Jesuits' youngest (and many have considered, the greatest) father general of the order. His remarkable leadership gifts were severely tested in a number of crises, and under him the Society more than doubled its numbers and widened its influence, particularly in missionary work.

Arminius, Jacobus (1560–1609) (originally Jacob Harmensen)

Celebrated theologian and minister of the Dutch Reformed church who could not accept the strict Calvinist teaching on predestination and consequently developed a system of belief later named after him (Arminianism). He was educated at Leiden, where he later returned (1603) as professor of theology; later still he taught at Basel, then Geneva. The latter part of his life was dominated by controversy, particularly with the zealous Calvinist, Francis Gomar.

Arnauld, Antoine (1612–1694) (also Arnault)

French philosopher and leading theologian of the Jansenist movement. Student of the Sorbonne, in law and theology, he was ordained a priest in 1641 and deeply associated himself with the Jansenist centre at the convent of Port-Royal. His book *De la fréquente communion* (1641) caused a storm and he was forced to withdraw from public life and the faculty of the Sorbonne. In his voluminous writing he defended Jansenism and attacked Calvinism. He finally settled in Brussels, where he died.

Arnauld, Jacqueline Marie Angélique (1591–1661)

Known as 'Mère Angélique', abbess of Port-Royal convent. Sister of the above, she was committed to religious life at seven and took the veil in 1600, becoming abbess in 1602. After a conversion experience in 1608 she threw herself into the reform of her community and the new austere life attracted a big following. Directed by Francis of Sales for a time, later (1635) she turned to Jansenism and the convent of Port-Royal became an enthusiastic centre of the movement.

Arndt, Johann (1555–1621)

Lutheran theologian and mystical writer. Pastor of Badeborn (1583–1590) he was compelled to move on, first to Quedlinburg, then Brunswick, by the Calvinist hostility. Best remembered for his widely read and much appreciated *Four Books on True Christianity* (1606–1610), which were the inspiration of many Protestant and Catholic devotional works.

Arnold, Matthew (1822–1888)

Poet and literary critic whose criticism covered not only literature but also theology, history and science. Educated at Oxford (1841–1844) he spent the greater part of his working life as a government inspector of schools (1851–1883). Besides poetry, e.g., *Poems* (1853) and *New Poems* (1867), he published religious works, e.g., *St Paul and Protestantism* (1870) and *God and the Bible* (1875).

Arnold, Thomas (1795–1842)

Headmaster of Rugby School and father of the above. After studying at Oxford, where he proved to be a fine classical scholar, he was ordained and, in 1828, became headmaster of Rugby. He gradually raised the school to be a great public school much in demand. He developed a system of education firmly based upon a religious foundation; among other things he encouraged a prefect system which became the model of most English secondary schools. The Arnold tradition at Rugby had a wide and lasting effect upon English secondary education.

Asbury, Francis (1745–1816)

English Methodist lay preacher who volunteered for service in North America, where his unstinting efforts (he averaged five thousand miles a year on horseback), and leadership as the first United States consecrated bishop of the Methodist Episcopal church, assured the continuance of the church in America.

Athanasius, St (293–373)

Theologian, bishop of Alexandria and champion of orthodoxy. As secretary to Alexander, bishop of Alexandria, he attended the Council of Nicaea (325), having written his famous treatise *De Incarnatione* some seven years earlier. He succeeded as bishop (328) and from Nicaea to the end of his life he was the champion of the Council's decrees and its struggle against Arianism. His Arian enemies forced him into exile (336), to flee to Rome (339), and caused the enmity of the emperor Constantius (356) and a second exile (365); but he never gave up the struggle and he brought about the final triumph of the Nicene party at the Council of Constantinople (381). Beside his important anti-Arian writings he also left letters and *The Life of St Antony*.

Athanasius the Athonite, St (c. 920–c. 1003)

Originally named Abraham, he left urban monastic life in Constantinople and founded the first communal monastery on Mt Athos (961), which was already populated with scattered hermits. Despite fierce opposition he succeeded in his foundation, including the writing of a rule, with the support of the emperors Nicephorus Phocas and John Tzimisces.

Athanasius I (1230–1310)

Monk and patriarch of Constantinople who opposed the work for reunion between the Eastern and Western Churches of the Second Council of Lyons (1274). His own severe reforming measures for his clergy failed and brought about his resignation.

Athenagoras (second century)

Greek Christian philosopher and apologist. Believed to be a converted Platonist philosopher from Athens, he addressed his *Embassy for the Christians* (c. 177) to the Emperor Marcus Aurelius, answering current calumnies against the Christians, viz. atheism, cannibalism and incest. It is not certain that *On the Resurrection of the Dead,* although ascribed to him, is his work. An able apologist, he was the first to apply Neoplatonic concepts to interpret Christianity.

Augustine of Canterbury, St (d. 604 or 605) (also called Austin)

First archbishop of Canterbury. While prior of St Andrew's, Rome, he was dispatched with about forty monks by the pope, St Gregory the Great, to evangelise the English (596). Although the group desired to turn back, Gregory encouraged them on and they landed in Kent in 597, being well received by King Ethelbert I of Kent. Within a few months the king and thousands of his subjects embraced Christianity and a centre was established at Canterbury. Augustine was consecrated archbishop and he sent for more missionaries. He was not so successful in building a relationship with the Celtic church already existing in Wales and the north. By the time of his death a Benedictine monastery and a cathedral were founded at Canterbury and bishops had been consecrated for Rochester and London.

Augustine of Hippo, St (354–430) (Latin name Aurelius Augustinus)

Bishop of Hippo and a doctor of the church. Born in North Africa of a pagan father and a devout Christian mother, Monica, he was educated as a Christian, but abandoned his faith and lived an immoral life, which he recounts in his *Confessions* (400). He taught rhetoric at Tagaste, Carthage, Rome (383) and Milan (384), where he fell under the influence of Ambrose, bishop of Milan. He returned to the Christian faith at Easter 387. His mother, who had worked and prayed for his conversion, died (387) on the way back to North Africa; at Tagaste he founded a monastic community, but accepted priestly ordination (391) and eventually the see of Hippo in 396. His penetrating understanding of Christian doctrine, and brilliant exposition, was expressed in two hundred treatises, three hundred letters and nearly four hundred sermons, as valuable today as they have been throughout the centuries. He had embraced the Manichaean heresy in his youth, but as bishop he led the church's fight against that heresy, Donatism and Pelagianism. After his *Confessions,* one of Christianity's great spiritual classics, his best-known work is the *City of God* (413-426), published in twenty-two books. He died while the Vandals were besieging Hippo.

B

Baader, Franz Xaver von (1765–1841)
Roman Catholic layman from Munich, influential theologian who contributed in 1815 to the Holy Alliance, a security pact between Russia, Austria and Prussia. He is now considered one of the founders of modern ecumenical activity.

Bach, Johann Sebastian (1685–1750)
German composer who, from 1723 until his death, was cantor at the Thomas School, Leipzig. It is to this period that his chief religious works belong. Originally written for and used by the German Lutheran church, the music is now more usually performed outside divine worship.

Bacon, Roger (c. 1214–c. 1292)
A Franciscan philosopher who, with great energy, after studying in England (probably at Oxford) and at Paris, described futuristic mechanical inventions (flying machines, motorised ships, etc.) and sought to reform the study of theology. A man of wide vision, Roger was commissioned by his friend, Pope Clement IV, to write an encyclopaedic work on the relationship of philosophy to theology, called *Maius Opus* (1267). He suffered imprisonment for his unconventional opinions after Clement's death.

Baillie, John (1886–1960)
Sometime professor of divinity at the University of Edinburgh and principal of New College; writer and author of the popular *A Diary of Private Prayer*.

Baillie, Robert (1599–1662)
Presbyterian minister and theological scholar; he led the Scottish movement to reject (1637) for Scotland the Church of England's Book of Common Prayer.

Baillie, Robert (c. 1634–1684)
Scottish Presbyterian executed for allegedly conspiring to assassinate King Charles II (the evidence was inconclusive). From 1676 Baillie had become associated with the struggle to free Scottish Presbyterianism from the control of the Anglican Church of England.

Baius, Michael (1513–1589)
Flemish theologian whose work on grace and justification, together with that of Jan Hessels, was censured by ecclesiastical authorities; his system of thought, Baianism, is often considered one of the foundations of Jansenism.

Baker, Augustine (1575–1641)
A convert to Roman Catholicism who became a Benedictine monk and an important writer on ascetical and mystical theology. Although his teaching was not new and was based upon his personal experience, it was vigorously attacked. Baker's spiritual writings were the fruit of his work as spiritual director to the English Benedictine nuns at Cambrai, France. After his death from the plague his better-known writings were collected and published in *Sancta Sophia* (1657) ('Holy Wisdom'). He also conducted important research into the history of the Benedictine order in England.

Baldwin of Canterbury (d. 1190)

Cistercian monk who, although elected archbishop of Canterbury, was constantly opposed by the monks of Christ Church, Canterbury. A scholar and writer who took part in one of the Crusades, it is said that he died of grief at the lack of discipline of the Christian armies.

Ball, John (d. 1381)

A priest, and one of the leaders of the Peasant Revolt in England; excommunicated for teaching Wycliffite doctrines on ownership and property. Ever popular with the people for his continual preaching on the equality of persons, he was executed as a traitor under King Richard II.

Baraga, Frederic (1797–1868)

Pioneer missionary and first bishop of Marquette, Michigan. Inspired by the Redemptorist, Fr Hofbauer, he renounced his inheritance and was ordained (1823) in Yugoslavia; he volunteered for the American mission and worked energetically and successfully among the Ottawa and Chippewa Indians. Appointed vicar apostolic of Upper Peninsula Michigan, he traveled widely, raised funds and recruited priests and sisters. When he was made bishop (1857) he transferred the see to Marquette (1866). His voluminous writings are of great historical interest and his grammar and dictionary of the Indian languages were the first to be published.

Barat, St Madeleine-Sophie (1779–1865)

Daughter of a French cooper, but well educated by her priest brother, Louis, Madeleine-Sophie desired to enter a Carmelite convent as a simple lay sister. Joseph Varin, superior of the Sacred Heart Fathers, encouraged her to lead a small community of women dedicated to the Christian education of girls. This led to the formation of the Society of the Sacred Heart, a congregation of religious sisters which, due to Mother Barat's efforts, became established in twelve countries, including the

United States. She was elected superior general for life, and the rules of the Society were adopted in 1815. She was beatified in 1908 and declared a saint of the Roman Catholic church in 1925.

Barbara, St
A virgin martyr who, in the third century, according to legend, was tortured and condemned to death by the authorities. On her refusal to abandon her Christian faith, her pagan father was ordered to kill her, which he did but, according to the legend, he was afterwards immediately struck by lightning. There is no evidence to support this spurious legend of the seventh century.

Barberi, Dominic (1792–1849)
Of peasant origins, Dominic entered the Passionist order as a lay brother, but in 1818 he was ordained a priest. He lectured and taught at several places in Italy up to 1841, when a longtime desire to work as a missionary in England became a reality. He was given a house in Aston, Staffordshire as a missionary base. In 1845 he received John Henry Newman into the Roman Catholic church. Despite much abuse and opposition, Dominic persevered with his preaching and made many converts. By the time of his death in 1849, he had established four Passionist houses in England. He was beatified by the Roman Catholic church in 1963.

Barbon, Praise-God (c. 1596–1680)
Nicknamed 'Barebone' or 'Barebones', Barbon was a sectarian preacher from which the Cromwellian 'Barebones Parliament' derived its name.

Barclay, Robert (1648–1690)
Scottish Quaker writer and apologist. Robert was born at Gordonstoun, Morayshire, and at nineteen followed his father into

the Society of Friends. In 1673 he published his *Catechism and Confession of Faith,* followed in 1675 by his principal work, his *Apology.* This early exposition of the Society's teaching defined Quakerism as a religion of the 'inner light'. He defended his teachings against Roman Catholic and Protestant attacks. Through his friendship with the Duke of York (later King James II) he was able to be of assistance to William Penn and to promote the establishment of Quaker settlements in the New World.

Barclay, William (1907–1978)
Popular New Testament scholar and prolific writer of sixty religious books. Highly regarded as a spiritual guide and mentor to tens of thousands of Christians.

Barnes, Ernest William (1874–1953)
Anglican bishop of Birmingham and leader of the Modernist movement in the Church of England; renowned as a pacifist during World War II. Bishop Barnes was very opposed to the Anglo-Catholic wing of the Church of England and he was vociferous in his attacks upon ritualistic practices. His scientific approach to Christianity brought him into conflict with his fellow bishops; his book *The Rise of Christianity* (1947) was condemned by the archbishops of Canterbury and York.

Barnes, Robert (c. 1495–1540)
English Protestant martyr who helped to spread Lutheranism in England. Originally prior of the Austin friars at Cambridge, due to the influence of Thomas Bilney he embraced the teachings of the Reformers and left England in 1528 for Germany, where he formed a lasting friendship with Martin Luther. Thereafter he traveled to and fro between England and Germany. A little more than a month after his protector, Thomas Cromwell, fell from favour, he was burnt as a heretic with two other Lutherans.

Barnett, Samuel Augustus (1844–1913)
Anglican priest and social reformer who, for twenty-one years as a parish priest, devoted himself to the cultural and religious improvement of the East End of London. From 1884 to 1896 Barnett was the first warden of Toynbee Hall. Through his pastoral concern, teaching and writing he worked for the reform of social conditions through the application of Christian principles. To foster the study of social problems Barnett House was founded at Oxford to his memory.

Baronius, Caesar (1538–1607)
Church historian and apologist for the Roman Catholic church. He joined the Oratory of St Philip Neri and later succeeded him as superior. Hailed in Roman Catholic circles as the 'father of ecclesiastical history', his major massive work *Annales Ecclesiastici* is now recognised as biased, but acclaimed for its enormous accumulation of sources. He ended his life as a cardinal and the librarian of the Vatican.

Barrow, Henry (c. 1550–1593)
Congregationalist martyr and separatist. As a lawyer he had been converted from a dissolute life to the life of a strict Puritan. Friendship with John Greenwood, the separatist, led Barrow to the advocacy of separate and autonomous local churches. Greenwood and Barrow were imprisoned for their beliefs and later died together on the scaffold.

Barth, Karl (1886–1968)
One of the most influential Protestant theologians of modern times. Barth studied theology at Berne, Berlin, Tübingen and Marburg. His pastoral work began at Geneva (1909–1911) but it was while he was pastor at Safenwil for ten years that he wrote his sensational commentary *The Epistle to the Romans* (1918). Subsequently he held the chair of theology at Göttingen, Münster and Bonn. While at the latter Barth started

work on his seminal four-volume work, *Die Kirchliche Dogmatik* ('Church Dogmatics'). His opposition to the rise of National Socialism and his work for and promotion of the anti-Nazi Confessing Church led to his suspension from his post at Bonn, when he refused the oath of allegiance to Hitler. As a Swiss subject he was able to accept the chair of theology at Basel, where he continued until his retirement in 1962.

Bartolomeo, Fra (1472–1517) (also called Baccio della Porta)

Florentine painter who was the most prominent exponent of the classical idealism of the High Renaissance style. An admirer of the Florentine Dominican reformer Savonarola, after Savonarola's death Bartolomeo joined the Dominican order in 1500. He became a friend of Raphael and was also influenced by Bellini and Michelangelo. All his work was religious, from the early *Annunciation* (1497) to his gentle *Pieta* (1515).

Basil the Great, St (c. 329–379)

One of the great fathers of the church, brother of St Gregory of Nyssa and St Macrina. After the best possible education available at the time, Basil withdrew from the world to a hermit's life near Neocaesarea. He returned to public life at the call of his bishop, Eusebius of Caesarea, in Cappodocia, to join in the battle against Arianism. He was ordained priest to help Eusebius and in 370 succeeded him as bishop; this office he held until his death. In 371 he came into conflict with the emperor Valens, who divided Basil's province. Basil was renowned in his own lifetime for his learning, eloquence and personal sanctity. His exceptional organising ability left a lasting imprint upon the shape and form of Eastern monasticism and his charitable foundations to help the needy survived several hundred years. Not long after his death he was declared a saint and a little later a doctor of the church.

Baur, Ferdinand Christian (1792–1860)

German Protestant theologian and scholar who initiated the Protestant 'Tübingen School' of biblical criticism. Educated at Tübingen, Baur first taught at the seminary at Blaubeuren before becoming professor of theology at Tübingen, where he remained until his death. A disciple of F.D.E. Schleiermacher, he was also influenced by Hegel's conception of history. Baur applied Hegelian principles to the New Testament pastoral letters and the life and teaching of St Paul (his two-volume book, *Paul the Apostle of Jesus Christ*, 1873 and 1875). Later in life Baur concentrated upon church history, taking ten years (1853–1863) to write his five-volume work *History of the Christian Church*. At first his pioneering work was rejected but later it was accepted as an important contribution to biblical scholarship.

Baxter, Richard (1615–1691)

Moderate Puritan minister who had a profound influence upon the Protestantism of seventeenth-century England. Largely self-educated, he was ordained into the Church of England in 1638, but two years later he rejected the current understanding of episcopacy in the Church of England and allied himself with the Puritan cause. From 1641 to 1660 he conducted a ministry at Kidderminster that was a model of pastoral care. His preaching drew large crowds and people traveled far to seek his spiritual counsel, yet throughout he suffered continual ill health. He served briefly as a chaplain to the parliamentary forces during the Civil War but his moderation sought continual reconciliation; in 1660 Baxter helped in the restoration of the monarchy. His fight for moderate dissent in the Church of England and the refusal of a bishopric brought him persecution for his views and imprisonment in 1685. He left nearly two hundred writings, all reflecting his deep piety and moderation.

Baylon, St Paschal (1540–1592)

Spanish shepherd youth, self-taught, who after much persistence was admitted as a lay brother into the Franciscan order.

He served, for most of his life, as a porter at various Spanish friaries and won renown for his piety and care of the sick and needy. Baylon defended the Catholic teaching on the Eucharist in public debate and consequently after his canonisation by the Catholic church in 1690 became patron of eucharistic confraternities and congresses.

Beaton, David (1494–1546)
Cardinal archbishop of St Andrews, and papal legate in Scotland from 1544. Trusted counselor of King James V, after whose death Beaton made a bid for the regency; although he failed in this he secured considerable influence over the regent, the Earl of Arran, and due to his efforts English attempts to subjugate Scotland failed. Beaton had a popular reformer, George Wishart, who was also politically involved, executed. In revenge a band of Protestant nobles assassinated him.

Beauduin, Lambert (1873–1960)
Belgian Benedictine liturgist and founder of Chevetogne; one of the original founders of the liturgical movement. In 1924, when Pope Pius XI encouraged the Benedictines to pray and work for Christian unity, Beauduin founded a monastery of Union, now at Chevetogne. His approach to the problems of unity did not win approval until the pontificate of John XXIII.

Becket, St Thomas (c. 1118–1170)
Educated in Paris, after three years as a city clerk Thomas was taken into the household of Archbishop Theobald of Canterbury. After ordination to deacon he was appointed archdeacon of Canterbury in 1154; the following year Henry II chose him as his chancellor. Thomas enjoyed the close friendship of the king, sharing his interest in hunting and the pomp of royal occasions. He very reluctantly accepted the see of Canterbury in 1162, changing his lifestyle and becoming devout and austere. Thomas resigned the chancellorship and soon found himself in conflict with the king.

Thomas resisted Henry's attempts to take the trial of criminal clerks away from the church courts. As a result of a series of reprisals by the king, Thomas was summoned to trial, but fled the country and appealed to the pope. After the threat of an interdict on England a reconciliation between king and archbishop was affected. Becket returned to his see and popular acclaim. A fresh disagreement brought hasty words from the king which sent four knights to Canterbury, and Thomas was murdered in his cathedral on 29 December 1170. Universal indignation swept Europe; miracles were recorded at Thomas's tomb and a cultus rapidly developed. In 1173 Pope Alexander III canonised him.

Bede the Venerable, St (672/673–735)

As an orphan at the age of seven, Bede was placed in the charge of the Benedictine monastery at Wearmouth, later transferred to Jarrow, under the care of St Benet (Benedict) Biscop. Apart from one visit to Lindisfarne and York, Bede spent the whole of his life at the Jarrow monastery. He devoted himself to the study of Scripture and teaching and writing. His early books appear to have been written for the pupils at the monastery school. His *De Temporibus* ('On Times') was for the clergy to help them calculate the date of Easter. In his own life, and through the middle ages, Bede was renowned for his Scripture commentaries. However, his fame in more recent centuries has rested upon his *Ecclesiastical History of the English People*. Of special interest is his method of dating events from the time of Christ's birth (AD), a method which became commonly accepted through the popularity of his writing. The title 'the Venerable' was bestowed within a hundred years of his death; Bede was formally canonised and declared a doctor of the church in 1899.

Beecher, Henry Ward (1813–1887)

American liberal Congregational minister who, through his social concern and oratorical skill, became one of the most influential Protestant preachers of his time. He vehemently opposed slavery and supported most liberal causes of the time—women's suffrage, evolution, scientific biblical criticism, etc. His later years were overshadowed by unproven charges of immoral affairs.

Beecher, Lyman (1775–1863)
Revivalist Presbyterian minister and father of a celebrated United States family. Pastor at Lichfield and Boston, he turned his attention to the west and became president of the new Lane Theological College, Cincinnati, Ohio (1832–1850). Although he was tried for heresy, he was acquitted and was respected for his stand against rationalism.

Bell, George Kennedy Allen (1881–1958)
Ordained in 1907 to the Anglican priesthood, he then became curate at Leeds. After four years as a lecturer Bell became secretary to Archbishop Randall Davidson, later in 1924 dean of Canterbury and finally bishop of Chichester in 1929. His great interest, dating from 1919, was the ecumenical movement. He supported the Confessing Church in Germany in its struggle against Hitler's regime. Through his German contacts he was instrumental in securing asylum in England for many Jews and non-Aryan Christians. During World War II he was outspoken in his condemnation of the saturation bombing by the Allies of German cities; he also opposed Britain's decision to make nuclear weapons. His European connections facilitated the first meeting of the World Council of Churches in 1948; he presided as chairman of its central committee from 1948 to 1954 and as honorary president until his death in 1958.

Bellarmine, St Robert (1542–1621)
One of the most enlightened Jesuit theologians of the Counter-Reformation period and widely recognised as one of the most saintly. After entering the Society of Jesus in 1560, he was

ordained in 1570. There followed twenty-nine years as a lecturer in theology during which he proved himself a vigorous
and successful opponent of Protestant doctrine. Bellarmine was
made a cardinal in 1599, but his great love of the poor
prompted him to give away everything he owned and he died a
pauper. He was canonised in 1930 and declared a doctor of the
Roman Catholic church the following year.

Belloc, Hilaire (1870–1953)

French-born poet and Roman Catholic writer and essayist,
regarded as one of the most versatile of English writers of the
early twentieth century. Educated at the Oratory School, Birmingham, and (after military service in the French army) at
Balliol College, Oxford. In 1906 Belloc was elected as the
Liberal MP for Salford; his individualism and liberalism cut
short a political career, but he teamed up with G.K. Chesterton, who illustrated his satirical novels. He is best remembered
for his light verse, but his interests and the breadth of his
writing were wide, including humorous verse for children,
history, biography, sailing and travel. The best example of the
latter was his *Path to Rome* (1902), but his chief work was on a
topic dear to him, *Europe and the Faith* (1912). His ardent
profession of his faith shone through virtually everything he
wrote.

Benedict—There were fifteen popes titled Benedict, from
Benedict I (d. 579) to Benedict XV (d. 1922). Probably the
most noteworthy were:

Benedict XII (d. 1342) (original name Jacques Fournier)

The third pope to reign at Avignon, from 1334 to 1342.
Benedict devoted himself to the reform of the church and its
religious orders. A Cistercian monk, graduating in theology at
Paris, he first served as an abbot, then bishop and cardinal in
1327. His ability as a theologian recommended him to his
fellow cardinals, and as pope he immediately settled a theologi-

cal dispute about the Beatific Vision (direct supernatural knowledge or vision of God) and set about a rigorous reform of the religious orders. This latter met fierce opposition and most of his reforming work was undone after his death.

Benedict XIV (1675–1758) (original name Prospero Lambertini)

After a succession of appointments in Rome, Lambertini was chosen for the papacy; his intelligence and moderation won the admiration and respect not only of all Christians but also of the philosophers of the Enlightenment. Benedict showed real interest in scientific learning and in the Papal States, encouraged agricultural reform, free trade and reduced taxation. He was conciliatory in his relations with the secular powers and as a scholar in his own right wrote seminal books, the most important being on the canonisation of saints. Benedict also founded a number of academies in Rome and laid the groundwork for the present Vatican museum.

Benedict XV (1854–1922) (original name Giacomo Della Chiesa)

After studying in Rome, Giacomo entered the papal diplomatic service. Pius X made him archbishop of Bologna and, in 1914, a cardinal. Elected pope a month after the outbreak of World War I, he devoted himself to the relief of distress and the maintaining of a strict neutrality. Benedict worked hard to get both sides to state their aims, so these might be reconciled. Neither side cooperated; both accused him of favouring the other side, and took no serious note of the peace plans Benedict proposed. (Had they done so several million lives would have been spared.) The Italian government, belligerent towards the Catholic church, prevented the participation of the papacy at the Versailles Peace Conference. His last years were spent in readjusting the organisation of the Roman Catholic church in the wake of the disastrous conflict, and in the promotion of missionary work.

Benedict (Benet) Biscop, St (c. 628–689/690)

Of noble birth, a thane of King Oswy of Northumbria, Biscop
Baducing (his original name) came under the influence of St
Wilfrid and, after two journeys to Rome, embraced the religious life in 666, taking the name Benedict. In 669 he was
appointed abbot of the monastery of St Peter and St Paul,
Canterbury (later St Augustine's), and, after a fourth journey
to Rome, founded the Benedictine monastery of St Peter at
Wearmouth; in 682 a sister foundation was made at Jarrow,
dedicated to St Paul. His repeated (five) journeys to Rome
resulted in the introduction into England of glass windows,
stone churches, and many manuscripts and paintings. His
most celebrated pupil was the Venerable Bede. Crippled about
686, he remained bedridden until his death. From his monastic foundations came a British tradition of learning and artistic
achievement that was a strong influence throughout the northwest of Europe.

Benedict of Nursia, St (c. 480–c. 547)

Founder of the Benedictine monastic way of life (based upon
his celebrated rule); regarded as the father of Western monasticism and founder of the monastery at Monte Cassino. Benedict was born at Nursia and educated at Rome, where the
permissiveness of the age prompted him to withdraw (c. 500)
to a cave at Subiaco, about forty miles from Rome. After three
years of solitude he became abbot of a local monastery, but his
reforming zeal met with resistance and after an assassination
attempt he returned to his cave. Disciples flocked to him and
with them he founded twelve monasteries composed of twelve
monks at each under Benedict's overall charge. As a result of
the jealous intrigues of a local priest, Benedict left Subiaco
with a small band of followers and settled on the summit of a
steep hill at Cassino, halfway between Rome and Naples.
None of the dates of Benedict's life are certain, but he was
buried at Monte Cassino in the same grave as his sister, St
Scholastica, who had founded a convent nearby. As a tribute

to the work of evangelisation and civilisation of the Benedictine order through Europe in the Middle Ages, Pope Paul VI proclaimed Benedict the patron saint of Europe in 1964.

Bengel, Johann Albrecht (1687–1752)
German Lutheran biblical scholar. He worked on classical and patristic literature, but his chief work of importance was as the founder of Swabian Pietism and as a New Testament textual critic. His approach to New Testament exegesis is accepted as the beginning of modern scientific work in biblical studies.

Benson, Edward White (1829–1896)
Anglican priest, educator and, from 1883, archbishop of Canterbury. He served first as an assistant master at Rugby School, Warwickshire, then in 1859 as headmaster of the New Wellington College, Berkshire. When the new diocese of Truro, Cornwall, was established Benson was consecrated as its first bishop. He was enthroned as archbishop of Canterbury in 1883, and his period of office is memorable for the revival of the court of the archbishop of Canterbury to pass judgment upon ritual charges brought against Edward King, the bishop of Lincoln. Benson's interest in the study of St Cyprian contributed to a renewal in patristic scholarship and his influential *Cyprian* (1897) was published posthumously.

Benson, Richard Meux (1824–1915)
Anglican priest; vicar of Cowley. Inspired by John Keble he founded the Society of St John the Evangelist (the Cowley Fathers) in 1865. His sermons and writings reveal a deep spirituality.

Benson, Robert Hugh (1871–1914)
Son of E.W. Benson; ordained to the Anglican ministry, in 1894 he joined the Community of the Resurrection at Mirfield. In 1903 he was received into the Roman Catholic church; the remainder of his life was devoted to preaching and

writing. Benson is particularly remembered for his vivid religious novels, e.g., *By What Authority* (1904) and *Come Rack! Come Rope!* (1912).

Beran, Josef (1888–1969)
Cardinal archbishop of Prague, interned in 1949 by the Communist regime in Czechoslovakia for forbidding to allow his clergy to participate in political life. He was released and left Czechoslovakia in 1965.

Berengar of Tours (c. 999–1088)
After studying under the celebrated Fulbert at Chartres, Berengar returned to Tours, where he became head of the school there. His fame rests upon his very independent challenge to the current theological view of the Eucharist, particularly the theory of transubstantiation as handed down in the teaching of Paschasius Radbertus. His views were criticised and condemned by successive popes, and contemporary theologians vied with one another to argue against him. He ended his days in ascetic solitude. His teaching was clearly expressed in his *De Sacra Coena* and he forced the church to re-examine its eucharistic teaching.

Berkeley, George (1685–1753)
Philosopher and Anglican bishop; educated at Trinity College, Dublin, and after traveling abroad and attempting to found a missionary college in America, appointed bishop of Cloyne in 1734. As a philosopher he arrived at a radical theory of perception, and it is for his metaphysical doctrine that he is celebrated.

Bernadette of Lourdes (1844–1879)
Marie-Bernarde Soubirous (affectionately known by her family as 'Bernadette') was the eldest child of an impoverished miller and was always frail in health. Between 11 February and

18 July 1858, in a shallow cave on the bank of the river Gave, near Lourdes, she had a series of eighteen visions of a beautiful young woman. Her identity was revealed with the words, 'I am the Immaculate Conception'. The appearances of the Virgin Mary were accompanied by supernatural occurrences, some taking place in the presence of many witnesses. Bernadette suffered severely for some years from the suspicious disbelief of others, but steadfastly defended the genuineness of the visions. She eventually joined the Sisters of Notre Dame at Nevers where she lived a self-effacing life, loved for her kindliness and holiness, in spite of constant ill health. She died in agony, cheerfully accepting her sufferings. She was declared a saint by the Roman Catholic church in 1933, not for her part in the Lourdes apparitions but for the remarkable sanctity of her later life.

Bernanos, Georges (1888–1948)
French Roman Catholic novelist and writer, regarded as one of the most original and independent of his time. For Bernanos the supernatural world was very real and always close at hand. The constant theme of his many novels was the struggle between the forces of good and evil for man's soul. This is perfectly exemplified in the most celebrated of his novels, *The Diary of a Country Priest* (1936).

Bernardino of Siena, St (1380–1444)
Of noble birth, at twenty-two Bernardino entered the Observants, a strict branch of the Franciscan order. Deeply disturbed by the breakdown in morals and the lawlessness of the time, he set about the regeneration of the age with preaching tours, which resulted in the reform of many cities and won him a great reputation as an eloquent preacher. He sought to bring about moral reform through inculcating a deep personal love of Jesus Christ and he was an energetic promoter of devotion to the Holy Name of Jesus. He was canonised in 1450.

Bernard of Clairvaux, St (1090–1153)

Of noble parentage, Bernard decided at twenty-two to become a Cistercian monk and took with him thirty young men, including his brothers and uncles. His abbot at Citeaux sent him off after three years to found a new monastery at Clairvaux; this quickly became a centre of the Cistercian order, famous throughout Europe. For ten years Bernard endured great hardships as he struggled to combine a mystical calling with service to others. The most active period of his life was from 1130 to 1145, when due to his reputation for holiness he was in constant demand, called to assist the pope at the time, preach the Second Crusade and serve on various civil and ecclesiastical councils. But Bernard always remained the ascetic Cistercian monk drawn to mysticism; his *De Diligendo Deo* was one of the most influential and outstanding books on mysticism to come from the Middle Ages. He was canonised in 1174 and declared a doctor of the church in 1830.

Bernard of Cluny (c. 1140) (also known as Bernard of Moval or Morlaix)

A monk of the Abbey of Cluny of whom little is known. Famous in his time as a preacher and writer, he is best remembered now for *De Contemptu Mundi* ('Condemning the World'), a poem of three thousand lines in which he attacks the monastic disorders of his age and stresses the transitory nature of life on earth. The poem is the source of many famous hymns, e.g., 'Jerusalem the Golden'.

Bernard of Montjoux, St (d.c. 1081)

As vicar general of the Aosta diocese in the Italian Alps, Bernard was concerned for travelers through two passes and established hospices to care for them. The dogs used by the hospices—and in time the passes themselves—were named after him.

Bersier, Eugène (1831–1889)

Writer and minister of a congregation of the Free Reformed church in Paris, Eugène worked for church unity and wrote on church history and liturgy.

Bertold von Regensburg (c. 1220–1272)

Famous German Franciscan preacher who used his eloquence to insist that true repentance comes from the heart and all else are merely outward symbols.

Bérulle, Pierre de (1575–1629)

Cardinal, reformer and statesman who, as a prominent leader of the 'French School' of spiritual thought, played an essential role in reviving Catholicism in seventeenth-century France, principally by his teaching and by founding the Oratory (a congregation of priests without vows) which in turn founded seminaries and improved the standard of preaching.

Bessarion, John (1403–1472) (originally Basil)

Byzantine scholar and cardinal; a major contributor to the revival of Greek studies in the West; an ardent supporter of the reunion of the Eastern and Western churches.

Bessette, André (1845–1937)

Born near Montreal, Canada, at twenty-five André joined the Congregation of the Holy Cross and spent the next sixty-seven years in menial tasks. His heroic virtue and reputation for healing drew millions to Montreal to see him. His devotion to St Joseph occasioned the building of St Joseph's Oratory, Montreal, the most popular shrine in North America. He was honoured with the title 'Blessed' in 1982 by Pope John Paul II.

Beza, Theodore (1519–1605)

French Calvinist theologian, author and Bible translator. After studying law and publishing Latin verse, in 1548 Beza had a conversion experience and joined John Calvin at Geneva. On

Calvin's death he succeeded him as leader of the Swiss Calvinists; he published a life of Calvin in 1564. Beza's Bible commentaries were widely read in his time and his Greek editions and Latin translations of the New Testament were basic sources for the later Geneva Bible and the Authorised Version. In 1581 he donated the Codex Bezae (probably fifth century) to the University of Cambridge. Beza is considered Calvin's equal in the establishment of Calvinism in Europe.

Bilney, Thomas (c. 1495–1531)
Protestant martyr. At Cambridge he is believed to have converted Hugh Latimer to the doctrines of the Reformers. Arrested in 1527 for heresy, he recanted, but in 1531, for spreading ideas critical of the hierarchical structure of the church and the cult of the saints, he was burnt at Norwich.

Binney, Thomas (1798–1874)
English Congregational minister who worked to obtain reunion with the Church of England. He introduced the chanting of psalms into Congregational worship as one step towards this. He wrote *Twenty-Four Reasons for Dissenting from the Church of England* (1848).

Birinus, St (d. 649 or 650)
Consecrated a bishop in Genoa, Birinus landed in Wessex and converted the local king. He was the first bishop of Dorchester and is regarded as the apostle of the West Saxons.

Bishop, Edmund (1846–1917)
Lay liturgist and historian. His early working years were spent in government posts, but after his reception into the Roman Catholic church in 1867, he sought admittance into the Benedictine order. Poor health frustrated his desire and he devoted his life to studying and writing on liturgy, especially from a historical angle. His best-known work was *The Genius of the Roman Rite* (1899).

Blackburn, Gideon (1772–1838)

American Presbyterian clergyman and pioneer missionary to the Cherokee Indians. After preaching, teaching and introducing new agricultural methods to the Indians, Blackburn withdrew because of failing health. Taking up education, he founded a theological college that was subsequently named after him.

Blair, James (1656–1743)

Scottish Episcopalian minister who emigrated to America after being deprived of his Edinburgh parish for refusing the oath supporting the Roman Catholic Duke of York as heir to the throne. In Virginia he founded a college, which is now the second-oldest institution of higher education in the United States.

Blaise, St (d.c. 316)

Little is known of his life, but according to tradition Blaise was of noble birth, and bishop of Sebastea. During the emperor Licinius's persecution, the local governor of Armenia hunted down Blaise, who had become a hermit, and executed him. The blessing of throats associated with St Blaise arose from the miracle he is said to have worked in saving the life of a child choking to death on a fish bone.

Blake, William (1757–1827)

Apprenticed at fourteen to an engraver, Blake used his talent throughout his life in illustrating his own writings and poetry and that of others. His early work also brought an appreciation of Gothic art, with which spirit he became imbued. In 1778 Blake became associated with the followers of the mystical sect of Swedenborg, but he was personally opposed to dogma and asceticism; his visionary genius developed a boundless sympathy with all living things. Blake's great allegorical poem *Jerusalem* took ten years to complete; his greatest work of art, the illustrations for the Book of Job, was completed just a year or two before his death.

Blastares, Matthew (fourteenth century)
Greek Orthodox monk and theologian whose system of church and civil law influenced Slavic legal codes. Blastares is best known for his alphabetical handbook of church law.

Bloomfield, Charles James (1786–1857)
Anglican bishop of London who worked for clerical reform and was a zealous church builder. He enjoyed a wide reputation as a classics scholar.

Blondel, Maurice (1861–1949)
Devout French Catholic philosopher whose *L'Action* (1893) gave birth to his 'Philosophy of Action', from which he developed a Christian philosophy of religion. Many later books amplified his original thought. For some years he was associated with the Modernist movement in the Roman Catholic church.

Blosius, Franciscus Ludovicius (1506–1566)
Benedictine monastic reformer and spiritual writer. His concern for monastic renewal shone through his writings; his mystical writing was more popular, in his day, than *The Imitation of Christ*.

Bloy, Leon (1846–1917)
Fervent Roman Catholic French novelist who, principally through his writings, preached that spiritual renewal was to be attained through suffering and poverty. He made an impact upon many of his contemporaries, e.g., Maritain, Huysmans and Rouault.

Blumhardt, Johann (1805–1880)

Protestant evangelist whose preaching and ministry, attended by miraculous healing, drew large crowds to Möttlingen in Württemberg. The latter part of his life was spent at Bad Boll, near Göppingen, where an influential centre of missionary work developed.

Boehme (Bohme) Jacob (1575–1624)

Lutheran philosophical mystic who claimed that he was personally illuminated to write. His mystical experiences occurred while he was following the trade of shoemaker, but when published in 1612, in *Aurora*, the local Lutheran pastor condemned the book. He was forbidden to write, but in 1619 he defied the ban, describing his mysticism in alchemical terms. His works included *The Way to Christ* (1622), *The Great Mystery* and *On the Election of Grace*.

Boethius, Anicius Manlius Severinus (c. 480–c. 524) (St Severinus)

Scholar, philosopher and statesman; consul under the emperor Theodoric the Ostrogoth. His most famous book, *De Consolatione Philosophiae* (written in prison), argues that the soul can attain to the vision of God through philosophy. This and other philosophical works had a profound influence in the Middle Ages, particularly upon Aristotelian studies. He also wrote a number of short theological treatises. Known also as St Severinus (canonised in 1883), his arrest and execution for treason by the Arian emperor brought him recognition as a martyr for the orthodox Christian faith.

Bolland, Jean (1596–1665)

Little is known of Bolland's life. A Jesuit ecclesiastical historian, he was chosen to continue the project of Rosweyde, whose idea was to compile the *Acta Sanctorum,* an exhaustive collection of the lives of the Christian saints using the best historical methods. Bolland (and those after him called

Bollandists) traveled widely, combing through and examining all existing records. Work on the *Acta* has continued into the present time.

Bonar, Horatius (1808–1889)
Scottish Presbyterian minister whose poems, hymns and prayers were popular during the nineteenth century.

Bonaventure, St (c. 1217–1274)
Giovanni di Fidanza was an Italian by birth, but was educated in theology at the University of Paris, where later he was head of the Franciscan school, having become a Franciscan in 1244. In 1257 he was elected minister general of his order, due to his personal holiness and his defence of the order. Bonaventure wrote several spiritual books and an officially approved *Life of St Francis*. Created a cardinal in 1273, he was a leading figure at the Second Council of Lyons, and died before the end of it. Bonaventure made a real impact upon the theology of his day and his spiritual books had a lasting influence. Declared a saint in 1483, he was made a doctor of the church in 1589.

Bonhoeffer, Dietrich (1906–1945)
Lutheran theologian and pastor. Bonhoeffer received his theological education at Tübingen, Rome and Berlin, and subsequently lectured in theology at the Union Theological Seminary, New York, and at the University of Berlin. From the start Bonhoeffer was opposed to the Nazi movement and sided with the Confessing Church, for whom he headed a new seminary at Finkenwalde. For his association with the resistance to Hitler and a link with the failed assassination attempt on the Führer, he was arrested in 1943 and hanged at Flossenbürg in 1945. In his theological thought, which matured while he was in prison, he sought to speak in a secular way to secular society about God; this comes across in *Letters and Papers from Prison* (1953). Bonhoeffer had an enduring interest in ecumenism

and a link with the United Kingdom through his friendship with Bishop Bell of Chichester.

Boniface, St (c. 675–754)

Often known as 'the Apostle of Germany', Wynfrid or Wynfrith was born in Devon, England. From an early age he was in the care of the Benedictine order, which he joined and in which he was ordained a priest. His first attempt in 716 to evangelise the Frisian Saxons met with no success, and he traveled to Rome where he was given papal authority; his second missionary journey, in 719, met with considerable success. He was recalled to Rome and consecrated a missionary bishop. From 725 to 735 he worked with success in Thuringia. After organising the church in Bavaria, he was entrusted with a complete reform of the Frankish church (740–747). Consecrated archbishop of Mainz about 747, he was martyred by pagan Frisians on Pentecost Day 754.

Boniface—Nine popes bear this name; two, Boniface I and Boniface IV, were honoured with the additional title of 'Saint'.

Bonner, Edmund (c. 1500–1569)

An outstanding Oxford lawyer who from 1532 to 1543 served Henry VIII on various foreign missions, supporting the king in his antipapal measures. Bonner was made bishop of London in 1540 but, during the reigns of Edward VI and Elizabeth I, would not impose Protestant doctrine and worship. As a result he was deprived of his see and imprisoned from 1549 to 1553. Under Mary Tudor he was restored to his bishopric but was rebuked by Mary's government for his reluctance to prosecute Protestants in London. He was deprived again of his see by Elizabeth I and spent the last ten years of his life in the London Marshalsea prison.

Booth family—The family associated with the foundation and development of the Salvation Army.

William Booth (1829–1912)
Apprenticed to a pawnbroker at the age of thirteen, William became a Methodist about the same time. In 1844 he had a conversion experience and two years later became a revivalist preacher. In 1855 he married Catherine Mumford. Leaving the Methodist church, which was unhappy with his style of evangelisation, he founded his own revivalist movement in the East End of London, combining evangelism with social service; later, in 1878, this was called the Salvation Army. As the movement spread General Booth spent more and more time traveling and organising. In his book *In Darkest England,* and in *The Way Out,* he outlined remedies for the social ills of his time.

Catherine Mumford Booth (1829–1890)
Wife of William Booth, but a famous preacher in her own right. The author of *Female Ministry,* she promoted the idea that the sacraments are unnecessary for salvation.

William Bramwell Booth (1856–1929)
Succeeded his father as leader of the Salvation Army; he broadened out the Army's Youth Service.

Evangeline Cory Booth
Led and developed the Salvation Army in the United States.

Borgia, St Francis (1510–1572)
The fourth Duke of Gandia, Borgia held various appointments in the court of Charles V of Spain. After the death of his wife, Eleanor, in 1546, he entered the Society of Jesus. He was a friend and adviser of St Ignatius Loyola and St Teresa of Avila.

Through his efforts and reputation for piety the Society of Jesus spread through Europe. He was also responsible for the foundation of many schools and colleges. He became the third father general of the order.

Borromeo, St Charles (1538–1584)

Created cardinal archbishop of Milan at the age of twenty-two, Charles was concerned for the need of reform in the Roman Catholic church and took a prominent part in the reforming Council of Trent. At its close he threw himself energetically into the implementation of its decrees. Considered a model bishop, he regularly visited the thousand parishes in his diocese, lived simply and won the admiration of all during the plague of 1576-1578 for the courageous care he gave his flock. His reforming zeal met with opposition, and an assassination attempt was made on his life. He was canonised by the Roman Catholic church in 1610.

Bosco, St John (1815–1888)

Of peasant origins, after ordination John worked in a Turin suburb providing for the needs of boys and young men. He opened workshops, schools, a boarding house and, in 1859, founded the Society of St Francis of Sales (Salesians) to care for the hundreds of youths that looked to him. The work of the Salesians had spread to many countries by the time of his death.

Bossuet, Jacques-Bénigne (1627–1704)

Ordained a priest in 1652, Bossuet has been accepted as one of the greatest preachers of all time. As bishop of Meaux he taught the French Dauphin and became famous for his funeral orations, his fight against Jansenism and his clash with Fénelon over mysticism and Quietism. His later writings, *Meditation sur L'Évangile* and *Élévations sur les mystères,* rank as French spiritual classics.

Boulter, Hugh (1672–1742)
English archbishop of Armagh, Ireland, and virtual ruler there representing the Protestant interest and ascendancy. He believed England's interests in Ireland were threatened by the large Roman Catholic majority, so he applied the penal laws with energy and Catholics were deprived of the vote. He was noted for his generosity to the poor.

Bourdaloue, Louis (1632–1704)
Famous French Jesuit preacher whose sermons on moral matters were a regular and beneficial part of the court of Louis XIV from 1670 onwards. He earned the title of 'king of preachers and preacher of kings'.

Bourgeois, Louis (b.c. 1510-d. after 1561)
Protestant Huguenot composer who wrote many melodic settings to the psalms, which appeared in the Genevan Psalter. He owed much to his close friendship with John Calvin.

Bourne, Francis (1861–1935)
Cardinal archbishop of Westminster who proved a strong and resolute leader of English Catholics and, during World War I, a patriotic Englishman.

Bousset, Wilhelm (1865–1920)
Biblical scholar and theologian; cofounder of the so-called 'History of Religions school'. In his principal work, *The Religion of the Jews in New Testament Times,* he investigated the relations between later Judaism and the early Christian church.

Bradford, John (c.1510–1555)
Protestant martyr. Bradford studied law first, then changed to theology. His strong preaching encouraged Nicholas Ridley, bishop of London, to take him as secretary. Imprisoned under Mary Tudor, he was eventually burnt at Smithfield for his Protestant beliefs.

Bradwardine, Thomas (1290–1349)

Chaplain to King Edward III, theologian and mathematician; his principal work, *De Causa Dei contra Pelagium* (1344), won him the title 'the Profound Doctor'; consecrated archbishop of Canterbury while in Avignon, he died of the Black Death before being enthroned.

Brady, Nicholas (1659–1726)

Anglican priest and poet who graduated and first worked in Ireland but whose later life was spent in the pastoral ministry in England. Brady, with Nahum Tate, was author of a metrical version of the psalms, licensed in 1696.

Brainerd, David (1718–1747)

Presbyterian missionary to the Seneca and Delaware Indians of New York and New Jersey. Famous for his diary, published posthumously, which aroused wide interest in missionary work to the American Indians.

Brant, Joseph (1742–1807)

Mohawk Indian chief, with the Indian name of Thayendanega, and fearless military ally of Britain in the War of Independence. Effective Christian missionary, he helped in the translation of the Book of Common Prayer and the Gospel of St Mark into Mohawk.

Bray, Thomas (1656–1730)

Anglican clergyman who founded the Society for Promoting Christian Knowledge (SPCK) in 1698, and in 1701 the separate Society for the Propagation of the Gospel (SPG). Selected by the bishop of London to represent him in the colony of Maryland, Bray recruited missionaries and launched a free library scheme. By 1699 there were thirty, the SPCK being founded to support the libraries, which Bray also introduced into England. The latter part of his life was occupied in pastoral work as vicar of a London parish.

Brebeuf, St Jean de (1593—1649)

French Jesuit priest who dedicated his life to the conversion of the Huron Indians in Canada. Despite much opposition and danger, he converted many thousands of Indians until he was captured by the Iroquois tribe and cruelly tortured to death. Known for his holiness and courage, Jean was canonised by the Roman Catholic church in 1930.

Brendan, St (c. 484—c. 577)

Also known as Brendan the Voyager, or the Navigator. Little is known for certain of his life; he was reputedly born near Tralee, County Kerry, became a monk and was ordained a priest. He is credited with founding many monasteries in Ireland and Scotland. A noted traveler and voyager, he was immortalised in an Irish epic of the ninth century (*Navigatio Brendani*) which describes his intrepid voyages of discovery in a leather craft.

Brenz, Johannes (1499—1570)

After studying theology at Heidelberg, Brenz was ordained priest in 1520, but by 1523 he had stopped celebrating mass and begun to support the work of the Reformers. In his book *Syngramma Suevicum* he expounded Luther's doctrine on the Real Presence in the Eucharist. He helped in the reconstitution of the University of Tübingen and was the author of two catechisms and several books.

Brewster, William (1567—1644)

At Scrooby, Nottinghamshire, where he had spent his early life, Brewster first became a Puritan leader. He migrated to Holland, where he printed Puritan books; he accompanied the *Mayflower* pilgrims in 1620 and was the real religious leader, dominating the formation of doctrine and worship.

Bridget of Ireland, St (d.c. 524) (also known as Bride or Brigit)

Although she is one of the patron saints of Ireland and ever popular there, little is known of Bridget's life, apart from legend and folklore. Born of a noble father and slave mother, she was later sold to a Druid whom, tradition says, she converted. After she was restored to her father, a match was made for her with the king of Ulster. Her piety won her release and a grant of land at Kildare, where she is said to have founded the first convent in Ireland. She is also credited with founding other communities.

Bridget of Sweden, St (c. 1303–1373)
Patron saint of Sweden and founder of the Brigittine order of sisters; a mystic whose published revelations were influential in the Middle Ages.

Brooks, Phillips (1835–1893)'
United States Episcopal clergyman who won an international reputation as a preacher. Pastor in Philadelphia and Boston (his ministry there lasted twenty-two years), in 1891 he was consecrated bishop of Massachusetts. Widely known as the composer of the carol, 'O Little Town of Bethlehem'.

Brother Laurence—See Herman, Nicholas.

Browne, Robert (c. 1550–1633)
Puritan separatist church leader, one of the original founders of the French church movement among Nonconformist Christians. He led a separatist church at Norwich in 1580, and for this and similar activities he was imprisoned thirty-two times and exiled in 1582. He made submission to the Church of England in 1584 and accepted ordination for the Anglican church. He finished his days in a pastoral role, but he exercised a great influence upon early Congregationalism.

Browne, Sir Thomas (1605–1682)
Physician and author who is best known for his book *Religio Medici* (1642), which describes his religious outlook and expressed a religious tolerance unknown at the time; the book was read throughout Europe.

Brownson, Orestes Augustus (1803–1876)
Roman Catholic writer. Largely self-educated, Brownson became a prolific writer on theological, sociological and philosophical subjects. Before becoming a Roman Catholic (1844) he served as a Universalist minister (1826–1831), a Unitarian and pastor of his own religious foundation (1836–1842). He published *Brownson's Quarterly Review* (1844–1875) and his autobiography, *The Spirit-Rapper* appeared in 1854.

Brunner (Heinrich) Emil (1889–1966)
Ordained in the Swiss Reformed church, Brunner worked first as a pastor then, from 1924 to 1953, as professor of systematic and practical theology at the University of Zurich. He conducted many lecture tours in the United States, and his many books helped to shape the course of modern Protestant theology. He was one with Karl Barth in opposing theological liberalism but opposed him on the degree of knowledge of God attainable from creation.

Bruno of Cologne, St (c. 1030–1101)
Ordained at Cologne, he was made head of the cathedral school of Reims; among his pupils was the future Pope Urban II. Offered the see of Reims, he retired instead with six companions to Chartreuse, near Grenoble, where he founded the Carthusian order. In 1090 Pope Urban II summoned him to Rome as an adviser, but soon afterwards he retired to a desert in Calabria and founded another monastery, where he died.

Bruno of Querfurt, St (c. 974–1009) (also known as Boniface)
Missionary to the Prussians; a bishop martyred with eighteen companions in Poland after much success preaching to the Magyars.

Bruno the Great, St (925–965)
Youngest son of the emperor Henry I, he became archbishop of Cologne in 953 and as such exercised considerable influence over his brother, the emperor Otto, in furthering peace and learning.

Bryan, William Jennings (1860–1925)
Lawyer from Illinois, who became a dynamic Democratic politician, and championed many liberal causes, e.g., women's suffrage. He ran for president three times and served as Secretary of State under President Wilson. In contrast his deeply held fundamentalism led to his involvement in the famous Scopes trial (*Creationism v. Darwinism*) at Dayton, Tennessee.

Bryennios, Philotheos (1833–1914)
Eastern metropolitan, theologian and church historian who in 1873, in Constantinople, discovered several early Christian documents, including the *Didache* and two epistles of St Clement of Rome.

Bucer, Martin (1491–1551)
As a Dominican monk Bucer became familiar with the teaching of Erasmus and Martin Luther. Released from his monastic vows in 1521, he preached Lutheranism, becoming leader of the Reformed church in Switzerland on the death of Zwingli. Bucer moved to England in 1549 and was appointed Regius professor of divinity at Cambridge, advising Cranmer on the Anglican Ordinal of 1550.

Buchman, Frank (1878–1961)
A Lutheran minister, he worked in a parish in Philadelphia but resigned in disillusionment. Buchman took up evangelical work among students and traveled widely. The Group movement developed, and as its leader he traveled around the world

and in 1938, in London, launched the Moral Rearmament movement.

Bugenhagen, Johannes (1485–1558)
A priest colleague of Martin Luther who organised the Lutheran church in north Germany and Denmark; the *Brunswick Church Order* was mainly his work.

Bulgaris, Eugenius (1716–1806)
Greek Orthodox theologian and scholar of the liberal arts who spread knowledge of Western thought throughout the Eastern Orthodox world.

Bulgakov, Sergius (1871–1944)
Russian theologian and priest who started his adult life as a religious sceptic active in Marxism. Disillusioned, he gradually found his way back to the church. Expelled from Russia, he became dean of the Orthodox Theological Academy at Paris from 1925. His involvement in the ecumenical movement and his theological writings ensured that he was well known throughout Europe and America.

Bull, George (1634–1710)
Anglican bishop and High Church theologian who attacked Protestant theories of justification on the one hand, and *The Corruptions of the Church of Rome* (his celebrated book of 1705) on the other.

Bullinger, Heinrich (1504–1575)
Convert from Roman Catholicism to the teaching of Zwingli, on whose death in 1531 he succeeded as principal pastor of Zurich. He helped draft the First Helvetic Confession of 1536, and the Second Confession of 1566 was his own work. He corresponded with Henry VIII and Edward VI of England; Elizabeth I sought his support with her own settlement of church affairs.

Bultmann, Rudolf (1884–1976)
New Testament scholar and theologian who studied at Tübingen, Marburg and Berlin; later he was appointed to teach at the Universities of Marburg, Breslau and Giessen before his appointment in 1921 as professor of New Testament studies at Marburg, where he stayed until 1951. Influenced by the German existentialist philosopher Martin Heidegger, Bultman published many works, developing from criticism to his position on the demythologising of the New Testament message.

Bunsen, Christian Carol (1791–1860)
Liberal Prussian diplomat, scholar and theologian; while in office representing his country in England he was instrumental in the scheme for a joint Lutheran-Anglican bishopric in Jerusalem. His writings were voluminous, the most important being *Signs of the Times* (1856), defending religious and personal freedom.

Bunting, Jabez (1779–1858)
Wesleyan Methodist minister who, as president of the first Wesleyan theological college, had the task of organising Methodism into a church, independent of the Church of England.

Bunyan, John (1628–1688)
Born of poor parents at Elstow, Bedfordshire, Bunyan fought for the parliamentary side in the Civil War; about 1649 he married, and his gradual conversion dates from this time. Recognised as a preacher among the Independents of Bedford, he spent most of the years 1660 to 1672 in Bedford gaol for holding unapproved services. There his writing began, which led to *The Pilgrim's Progress,* his autobiography *Grace Abounding,* and the allegory *The Holy War.* After release he worked among the Independents of Bedford.

Burgos, José (1837–1872)
Roman Catholic priest who spoke out against the oppressive power and privilege of church and Spanish rule in the Philippines; he was arrested and executed. This 'martyrdom', as it was considered locally, initiated a movement which eventually achieved Burgos's desired reforms and the overthrow of Spanish domination.

Burrough, Edward (1634–1663)
Quaker preacher who defended Quaker doctrines against, among others, John Bunyan; arrested in 1662 for holding illegal meetings, he was committed to Newgate prison, where he died.

Bushnell, Horace (1802–1876)
American Congregationalist and controversial theologian, pioneer of liberal theology in New England. His seminal books, which examined and re-explained theological language and concepts, were bitterly attacked, but had a lasting impact.

Butler, Alban (1710–1773)
English Roman Catholic priest who returned to his seminary, the English College, Douai, France, as lecturer. After extensive research throughout the continent he published (1756–1759) his classic *Lives of the Saints*. The four-volume work with more than sixteen hundred hagiographies went through many editions and has never been out of print. (It was revised and updated in 1956.) Butler worked for a while as a mission priest in the English Midlands; from 1766 until his death he was president of the English College at Saint-Omer.

Butler, Christopher (1902–1986)
Benedictine abbot, theologian and writer. He was a brilliant student at St John's, Oxford, finishing with three First-Mods., Greats and theology; he moved to Keble College as tutor and prepared for the Anglican ministry. In 1928 Butler became a

Roman Catholic and joined the Benedictine order; ordained in 1933 he became abbot of Downside in 1946. At the Second Vatican Council he made a creative contribution and was elected auxiliary bishop of Westminster in 1966. Considered the foremost English Roman Catholic theologian of modern times, he made a substantial contribution to ecumenism, particularly on the Anglican-Roman Catholic International Commission (ARCIC) for fifteen years.

Butler, Joseph (1692–1752)
English bishop, moral philosopher and preacher in the royal court. As an author he was influential in defending revealed religion against the rationalists of his time.

Byrd, William (1543–1623)
Organist first at Lincoln Cathedral and then, from 1572, at the Chapel Royal, London, where he shared duties with his teacher, Thomas Tallis. Although he was a Catholic this never prevented him from composing and playing for the established church. Considered the greatest English composer of the Shakespearean age, he wrote much secular as well as liturgical music.

C

Cabrini, St Frances Xavier (1885–1917)

The first American citizen to be canonised by the Roman Catholic church (1946), Frances was born in Lombardy, Italy. At the direction of her local bishop she founded, in 1880, the Missionary Sisters of the Sacred Heart, who devoted themselves to the education of girls. Pope Leo XIII directed her attention to the United States, where she and her sisters worked among the needy Italian immigrants. Mother Cabrini, as she was known, became a naturalised citizen of the United States in 1909. Despite constant bad health and innumerable obstacles she traveled widely in the United States and Europe, founding sixty-seven hospitals, schools, orphanages and convents.

Cabrol, Fernand (1855–1937)

Benedictine monk and abbot of St Michael's Abbey, Farnborough, Hants, who gained an international reputation as a liturgist and writer on the history of church worship.

Caedmon (658–680)

Little is known of his life except through the Venerable Bede, who tells how Caedmon, an illiterate herdsman at Whitby, had a dream in which he was told to sing of 'the beginning of things'. By virtue of his hymn of creation, Caedmon has the distinction of being the first Old English Christian poet.

Caesarius of Arles, St (c. 470–542)
Monk and abbot who in 503 became archbishop of Arles and a leading prelate of the Gallican church. Famed for his preaching, he energetically and decisively opposed semi-Pelagianism.

Caird, Edward (1835–1908)
Scottish philosopher (chief representative of the new Hegelian movement in British philosophy) and theologian. He wrote a critical review of Kant's philosophy and *The Evolution of Religion* (1893).

Caird, John (1820–1898)
Minister of the Church of Scotland, theologian and renowned preacher. Principal of Glasgow University, he followed, like his brother Edward, the New-Hegelian movement.

Cajetan, Thomas de Vio (1469–1534)
Entering the Dominican order in 1484, Cajetan taught theology and philosophy at Padua, Pavia and Rome. As master general of his order (1508–1518) and cardinal he urged church reform, particularly at the fifth Lateran Council (1512–1517). As papal legate in Germany, Cajetan met and reasoned with Martin Luther, and he opposed the divorce plans of Henry VIII of England. His profound commentary on Thomas Aquinas's *Summa Theologica* established his reputation as a scholar and founder of the revival of Thomism.

Calixtus (also Calistus or Calisbus)—There were three
popes with this name; the most significant was:

Calixtus I, St (d. 222)
Bishop of Rome from c. 217, he appears to have started life as a slave. Denounced as a Christian, he was sent to the Sardinian

mines. After regaining his freedom he was elected pope. Attacked by a theologian, Hippolytus, he was accused of Modalist doctrines; Calixtus, however, condemned Sabellius, the principal exponent of the Modalist heresy.

Calixtus, Georg (1586–1656)
German Protestant theologian who persistently attempted, from 1613, to develop a theology which would reconcile Lutherans, Calvinists and Catholics. He expanded his system, given the name 'Syncretism', in many writings.

Calvin, John (1509–1564)
French theologian and one of the most important figures of the Protestant Reformation. After studying theology at Paris and law at Orleans, and the publication of his book *De Clementia*, Calvin had a religious experience in 1533 and broke with the Catholic church. As a preacher and organiser he worked to found the Reformation at Geneva. Driven out of the city for three years, Calvin settled at Strasbourg, where he was pastor and lecturer. His master work, the *Institutes of the Christian Religion*, was published in 1536.

In 1541 he returned to Geneva and devoted the next fourteen years to the establishment of a theocratic regime on the Old Testament model. His opponents were tortured and executed. Calvin's Scripture commentaries date from this period as does his treatise on predestination. His mastery of the city by 1555 left Calvin free to devote more time to the spread of Reformed Protestantism in other countries. In 1559 the Academy of Geneva was founded to continue his teaching. Simple and austere in lifestyle, Calvin was a reticent man and little is known of his personal life. His wife died in 1549 and his only child died at birth in 1542. His great intellectual ability and charismatic leadership account for his enormous impact upon the course of Western church history.

Camillus de Lellis, St (1550–1614)

Founder of the Ministers of the Sick. Camillus began life in Bucchianico, Italy, and served as a mercenary in the Venetian army against the Turks. A compulsive gambler, he lost all his money and became a labourer. After conversion in 1575 he worked, despite an incurable disease in his legs, as a nurse at St Giacomo's hospital in Rome. Under St Philip Neri's guidance he grew to great holiness and was ordained priest in 1584. Camillus was resolved to found an order to be totally devoted to the care of the sick, with a fourth vow to care for all, especially those who were plague-stricken. His order was revolutionary in its methods, for example, in providing the first medical corps for troops in battle; the separation of those with contagious diseases; well-aired wards, etc.; and above all for providing a caring which embraced the physical and spiritual needs of patients. Despite several painful illnesses Camillus continued caring for the sick until his death. He was canonised in 1746.

Campbell, Alexander (1788–1866)

Founder of the Disciples of Christ (Churches of Christ) or 'Campbellites'. Son of Thomas Campbell, a Presbyterian minister who emigrated to the United States, Alexander took the leadership of his father's reform movement, opposed both to speculative theology and emotional revivalism. He founded, in 1840, Bethany College and remained its president until his death. A prolific writer, he also founded and edited the *Christian Baptist*.

Campbell, Thomas (1763–1854)

Presbyterian minister of Irish origin who emigrated to the United States in 1807 and founded the Christian Association of Washington, Pennsylvania. He assisted his son, Alexander, in the foundation of the Disciples of Christ (1832).

Campion, Edmund (1540-1581)

Son of a London bookseller, Campion was teaching at Oxford University when he was ordained a deacon for the Anglican church in 1569. A crisis of conscience led him to be received into the Catholic church. Traveling to Rome, he entered the Society of Jesus and was ordained in 1578. He joined the first Jesuit mission to England in 1580, preaching extensively, especially in the London area and Lancashire. The secret publication of his *Ten Reasons* (1581), defending the Catholic position, occasioned one of the most intensive manhunts in English history. He was betrayed at Lyford, near Oxford and imprisoned in the Tower of London. When he would not renounce his Catholicism he was tortured, then hanged, drawn and quartered at Tyburn on 1 December 1581. In 1970 he was canonised as one of the forty English and Welsh martyrs.

Canisius, St Peter (1521-1597)

Educated at the University of Cologne, Peter became a Jesuit in 1543 and taught in various universities and founded colleges in six places. He lectured widely against Protestantism and composed several catechisms, the most famous of which was published in 1554 and ran through four hundred editions in 150 years. More than any other Catholic theologian, Canisius delayed the advance of Protestantism and advanced the Counter-Reformation in southern Germany. In 1580 he settled in Fribourg and founded a Jesuit college, which became the University of Fribourg. He was canonised in 1925 and declared a doctor of the church.

Cantelupe, St Thomas de (c. 1218-1282) (also known as Thomas of Hereford)

English reforming bishop of Hereford whose reforming spirit and ascetical life recommended him to King Edward I as confidential adviser. A dispute with John Peckham, archbishop of Canterbury, sent Thomas to Rome to plead his cause, where he died.

Capgrave, John (1393–1464)

English historian and theologian who lectured at Oxford University; ordained priest, he later became a hermit of the Augustinian order. He is credited with many theological works and is especially remembered for his *Life of St. Katharine*.

Carey, William (1761–1834)

Northamptonshire shoemaker, almost entirely self-taught, who left Anglicanism to become a Baptist in 1783; he became a preacher and pastor and moved to a ministry at Leicester. Three years later, in 1792, he published his famous *Enquiry* into Christian's missionary obligation. This led to the formation of the English Baptist Missionary Society. In 1793 Carey left for Calcutta to fulfil a lifelong call. In five years he had translated the New Testament into Bengali and had visited two hundred villages. He moved to Serampore, which became his base. His prodigious work of translation continued and included the whole of the Bible in Bengali (1809) and parts of it in twenty-four other languages. His call to mission and his personal example touched the conscience of British Christians and inspired a renewed drive for mission.

Carlile, Wilson (1847–1942)

After a career in business, Carlile was accepted for ordination by the Anglican church in 1880. In 1882 he founded the Church Army. He continued to help with its administration until his death.

Carpenter, William Boyd (1841–1918)

Anglican priest and prolific writer who established a reputation as a preacher, winning the admiration of Queen Victoria, who appointed him first Royal chaplain then bishop of Ripon. He was responsible for the foundation of Ripon College, Oxford.

Carroll, Charles (1737—1832)
Lawyer and Federalist politician who always signed himself 'Carroll of Carrollton', (after his estates in Maryland). Educated by the Jesuits, he was the longest-living patriot leader of the American Revolution and the only Roman Catholic to sign the Declaration of Independence.

Carroll, John (1735—1815)
Born in Maryland, but educated in Flanders, Carroll entered the Society of Jesus in 1753. He returned to Maryland in 1774 as a missionary, and ten years later became Superior of the Missions; subsequently he was the first Catholic bishop in America, consecrated in 1789 for the see of Baltimore.

Carstares, William (1649—1715)
Scottish Presbyterian theologian and statesman who was imprisoned for plotting to overthrow Charles II; later became William of Orange's chaplain and adviser. In 1703 he was made the principal of Edinburgh University and moderator of the established Church of Scotland.

Cartwright, Peter (1785—1872)
Most famous of the nineteenth-century Methodist circuit riders in Kentucky. He was an outspoken preacher, whose *Autobiography* (1856) gives an insight into the lives and travels of the itinerant preachers of the period.

Case, Shirley Jackson (1872—1947)
Canadian-United States theologian and educator. Dean of the University of Chicago Divinity School (1933—1938). His work on the interaction between Christianity and society provided principles for those engaged in the 'social gospel'.

Casel, Odo (1886—1948)
Benedictine monk and liturgist of international repute and influence. He studied and wrote widely on the theological

aspects of liturgy. Casel was one of the forward-looking litur-gists who prepared the way for the liturgical reforms of the Second Vatican Council.

Cassander, Georg (1513–1566)

Catholic theologian who sought, through his prolific writings, to draw Catholics and Protestants together. In 1564 the em-peror Ferdinand I called upon Cassander to assist in an official attempt at reconciliation, but his tireless efforts were not ap-proved of by either side.

Cassian, John (c. 360–435)

Probably of Roman birth, Cassian became a monk and was trained by monks in Egypt; he was ordained deacon by John Chrysostom. Nothing is known of the years 405–415, but immediately after that period he founded the Abbey of Saint-Victor at Marseilles. His writings, reflecting what he had learnt in Egypt, influenced all Western monasticism. He is honoured as a saint in the Eastern church.

Caswall, Edward (1814–1878)

Anglican priest who converted to the Roman Catholic church in 1847 and, after his wife's death in 1850, joined John Henry Newman's Oratory at Edgbaston. His fame rests upon his many popular hymns for Catholic usage and his successful translations of Latin hymns still in popular use.

Catherine, St (1522–1590)

Baptised Alessandra dei Ricci, she entered the Dominican con-vent at Prato at thirteen and was prioress there for the last thirty years of her life. Famous for her stigmatisation, the ecstasy she was rapt in for twenty-eight hours each week for several years, and her reputation for sanctity. Canonised by the Roman Catholic church in 1746.

Catherine of Alexandria, St (d.c. early fourth century)
Her historicity is doubtful. Despite great devotion to her during the Middle Ages, and many popular legends, nowhere is Catherine mentioned before the ninth century. According to legend she was an exceptionally learned young girl of noble family who opposed the persecution of Christians by the emperor Maxentius. She defeated eminent scholars sent to argue with her; arrested, she was tortured on a spiked wheel that broke (hence the Catherine wheel), and she was finally beheaded. The legend alleges that the body was taken by angels to Mt Sinai, where it was supposed to have been found in 800; there the great monastery of St Catherine still stands.

Catherine of Genoa, St (1447–1510)
Originally Caterina Fieschi, of a distinguished family, she was married at sixteen and led an unhappy life, until her conversion after a mystical experience in 1473. She gave herself to selfless care of the sick and her husband was subsequently converted. They agreed to live in continence, the husband joining the Third Order of St Francis. Catherine underwent a series of remarkable mystical experiences. Her spiritual teaching was contained in *Dialogo* and *Trattato del Purgatio*, published after her death.

Catherine of Siena, St (1347–1380)
Born Caterina Benincasa, from her earliest years she lived a devout and mortified life and began to have visions. At sixteen she joined the Third Order of St Dominic and gave herself to prayer and the service of the sick. Her evident holiness and mysticism won her many followers. When Florence was placed under an interdict by Pope Gregory XI, Catherine went to Avignon to mediate and promote a crusade. With others she worked for the pope's return to Rome, and after the return she was invited to Rome as an adviser. She worked hard to have Urban VI accepted as the true claimant to the see of Rome. Catherine's spirituality and remarkable spiritual gifts contin-

ued to attract a large following. Her mystical experiences and teaching were recorded in her *Dialogo,* which, with over 350 letters and four treatises, is our chief source of her spirituality. Canonised in 1461, Catherine was declared a doctor of the church in 1970.

Caton, William (1635–1665)

Under the influence of George Fox, Caton became a Quaker and an itinerant preacher and missioner. He traveled through France and Holland where he was not always well treated. His *Journal* is still read in Quaker circles.

Caussade, Jean Pierre de (1675–1751)

Jesuit spiritual writer and preacher. His influence made mysticism once more acceptable after the Quietist period. His best-known work in the English language is *Abandonment to Divine Providence,* but there were also letters of spiritual direction and *An Instruction* on prayer.

Cecilia, St (second and third century)

Virgin martyr and patroness of music. Although one of the most famous of the Roman martyrs, her historicity is doubtful. According to a fifth-century legend she was of noble birth and married against her will to Valerian, a pagan, whom she converted together with his brother. They were martyred before Cecilia, who gave away all she had to the poor and then faced death by suffocation. When this failed she was beheaded. She is the patroness of church music.

Cedd, St (d. 664)

Brother of St Chad, and brought up with him at Lindisfarne under St Aidan. He worked among the people of Mercia and then of Essex and was consecrated bishop of the East Saxons in 654. He founded monasteries at West Tilbury, Bradwell-on-Sea and in Yorkshire at Lastingham, where he died of the plague.

Celestine—Five popes share this title; those of note were:

Celestine I, St (d. 432)

Pope from 422 to 432. He energetically fought against the heresy of Pelagianism, sending Germanus of Auxerre to Britain to deal with it; he wrote to Gaul against the semi-Pelagianism of Cassian and condemned Nestorianism at a Roman synod in 430.

Celestine III (c. 1106–98)

Friend of Peter Abelard and Thomas à Becket, he was known for his moderation and patience. Elected pope at eighty-five years of age, he had continual difficulties with the German emperor Henry VI, who oppressed the church in Germany and, among other things, imprisoned King Richard the Lionheart.

Celestine V, St (c. 1215–1296)

Formerly a Benedictine monk, he became a hermit with a wide reputation for austerity and sanctity, and founded the Celestines, a group of hermits. Elected pope when nearly eighty in 1294, he abdicated after a few months when he realised his incapacity for the post. His successor, Boniface VIII, had him imprisoned, where he died.

Chad, St (d. 672)

Brother of St Cedd and pupil of St Aidan of Lindisfarne. Succeeded Cedd as abbot of Lastingham and was soon afterwards irregularly consecrated bishop of the Northumbrians. When St Wilfred returned Chad accepted the irregularity, stepped down and was sent instead as bishop to the Mercians, with his see at Lichfield. He founded monasteries at Lindsey and Barrow and is credited with the conversion of the kingdom of Mercia.

Challoner, Richard (1691–1781)

Born of Presbyterian parents, Challoner became a Roman Catholic before the age of fourteen, when he went to Douai in Flanders, to train for the priesthood. He remained there after ordination, becoming vice-president. In 1730 he was sent to London to support the small, harassed Catholic community. He was consecrated bishop (*in partibus*) of Debra and assistant to Dr Petre, the vicar apostolic, whom he succeeded in 1758. He was the author of many books, including the ever-popular prayer book *The Garden of the Soul* (1740) and *Meditations for Every Day of the Year* (1753); both were frequently reprinted. He revised the Douai-Rheims version of the Bible and his historical works, including *Britannia Sancta* (1745), were well researched.

Chalmers, James (1841–1901)

Scottish Congregationalist member of the London Missionary Society; exploring the southwest Pacific, he was known as 'the Livingstone of New Guinea'. He tried to form an indigenous church but was killed by local tribesmen.

Chalmers, Thomas (1780–1847)

Presbyterian minister, theologian, social reformer and philanthropist. Famed as a preacher, on becoming minister at the largest and poorest Glasgow parish, St John's, Chalmers concerned himself with the problems of the poor. In 1823 he became professor of moral philosophy at St Andrews and, in 1828, professor of theology at Edinburgh. He was the acknowledged leader of the Evangelical party in the Church of Scotland, advocating the parishioners' right to choose their own minister. On 18 May 1843 the 'Disruption' occurred when 203 commissioners walked out of the general assembly of the Church of Scotland. Chalmers became the first moderator of the new Free Church of Scotland. He was subsequently chosen as principal of the New College at Edinburgh, for ministerial training.

Chanel, St Peter Mary (1803–1841)

French priest of humble origins who, after pastoral work, joined the Marist order in 1831. In 1836 he was sent as a missionary to the New Hebrides in the Pacific and worked with success on the island of Futuna. He was murdered there by a chief when he discovered his son wanted to be baptised. He was canonised in 1954 as the first martyr of Oceania.

Chantal, St Jane Frances de (1572–1641)

Married in 1592 to the Baron de Chantal, who was killed in a hunting accident in 1601, and left a widow with four children, Jane Frances placed herself under the spiritual direction of St Francis of Sales in 1604. In 1610, with her family provided for, she founded, with St Francis, the Visitation Congregation of sisters. Francis died in 1622 and her son was killed in battle in 1627. During the plague of 1628 she turned her convent into a hospital. At her death the Visitation Congregation had eighty-six houses. She was canonised in 1767.

Chapman, John (1865–1933)

Biblical and patristic scholar who converted from Anglicanism to the Roman Catholic church in 1890. Two years later he joined the Benedictine order. When the community on Caldey Island joined the Catholic church in 1913, Chapman was sent as superior. He became abbot of Downside Abbey in 1922. His works on Scripture were seminal, and his *Spiritual Letters* (1935) has proved to be a book of lasting value.

Charles I (1600–1649)

King of Great Britain and Ireland from 1625; Charles inherited from his father a firm belief in the divine right of kings. His authoritarian rule, at a time when aspirations for greater political and religious freedom were riding high, occasioned the Civil War. One result of the king's surrender in May 1646 was the disestablishment of the Church of England. His resolve not to surrender his principles led to his illegal execution, considered by many as a martyrdom. Churches have been dedicated to King Charles the Martyr and for nearly two hundred years the day of his death was honoured by the Church of England.

Charron, Pierre (1541–1603)
Famous French preacher, theologian and philosopher. His works *Les Trois Vérités* (1593) and *De la sagesse* (1601) made a major contribution to the new thought of the seventeenth century. Charron is noted for his sceptical tendency coupled with a traditional Catholicism.

Chemnitz, Martin (1522–1586)
Lutheran theologian who was one of the principal influences in consolidating and defending Luther's doctrines after his death, so much so that he was called 'the second Martin'. Refusing many important posts offered to him, Chemnitz spent most of his life in pastoral work and writing. Two of his principal works were the defence of Luther's teaching on the Real Presence in the Eucharist and an attack upon the decrees of the Council of Trent.

Cheney, Charles Edward (1836–1916)
Ordained a priest in the Protestant Episcopal church of the United States, Cheney signed the 'Chicago Protest' against the 'unprotestantising' of the church; and, after a conviction before an ecclesiastical court, helped to found the Reformed Episcopal church, in which he served as a bishop.

Chesterton, Gilbert Keith (1874–1936)
Literary critic, poet, novelist and essayist. Chesterton was a master in the use of paradox, and used it to debunk Victorian pretensions. His voluminous works were enhanced by his interest in theology. Before turning from Anglicanism to Roman Catholicism in 1922, he published *Heretics* (1905) and *Orthodoxy* (1908); after his conversion there was an edge to his contro-

versial works, *The Catholic Church and Conversion* (1926), *The Everlasting Man* (1925), etc. His fiction is still well received, but his fame as a novelist rests principally upon his sleuth series, the Father Brown stories.

Cheverus, Jean-Louis Lefebvre de (1768–1836)
French priest who fled the French Revolution and on arrival in Boston, served Indian missions, showing remarkable courage and charity during the yellow fever epidemic of 1798. In 1808 Cheverus was consecrated the first Roman Catholic bishop of Boston. He returned to France in 1823 and became archbishop of Bordeaux; he was elevated to cardinal in the year of his death.

Christopher, St (fl. c. third century)
Although one of the most popular of saints, there is no certainty that he existed; for this reason he was dropped from the Roman Calendar in 1969. Tradition has it that he was martyred in Lycia under the emperor Decius, about AD 250. There are many later legends about him, including the familiar story that represents Christopher as a giant who, after conversion, dedicated his life to transporting travelers across a river. One day a little child asked to be carried across. In mid-stream the burden became very heavy; the child was none other than the Christ-child and his care for the world (Christopher comes from the Greek, 'Christ-bearing').

Chrysostom, St John (c. 347–407)
As a hermit-monk, John lived the austere Pachomian rule for eight years, which damaged his health. After his ordination in 386, his bishop instructed him to devote himself to preaching, which he did with such great talent for twelve years that he won the title 'Chrysostom' or 'golden-mouthed'. Against his wish, in 398 he was consecrated patriarch of Constantinople, and his reforming zeal and plain-speaking pleased the common people and angered the wealthy. Powerful opponents had

John convicted on false charges at the Synod of the Oak (403). Deposed from his see, Chrysostom was banished twice from Constantinople (403 and 404). His death was hastened in exile by an enforced march in severe weather conditions. While not an outstanding theologian, Chrysostom's fame rests upon his preaching (many scriptural homilies and sermons have survived) and his literal exegesis of the Bible, which was opposed to the allegorical sense popular at the time.

Church, Richard William (1815–1890)

Anglican priest, fellow of Oriel College and subsequently rector of Whatley in Somerset, who worked to allay the outcry against his friends in the Tractarian Movement. Dean of St Paul's Cathedral from 1871, he wrote several biographies and his *Oxford Movement, Twelve Years 1833–1845* is regarded as the best record and judgment of the time.

Clare, St (1194–1253)

Influenced by St Francis of Assisi, Clare refused to marry as her parents wished and instead joined Francis. He placed her first in a Benedictine monastery then, when other women joined her, set up their own religious house, with Clare as abbess. So the Poor Clare order began, and was soon housed at San Damiano, near Assisi, living in the 'privilege of perfect poverty'. Many daughter houses sprang up throughout Europe in the thirteenth century. Famed for miracles during her life and after, Clare was canonised two years after her death.

Clarke, Samuel (1675–1729)

Chaplain in turn to the bishop of Norwich and, in 1706, Queen Anne, Clarke was not only a theologian but also a philosopher and exponent of the physics of his friend, Isaac Newton. In 1712 he caused a stir with his apparently Unitarian book, *Scripture Doctrine of the Trinity*. His condemnation was sought, but Clarke promised to write no more on the subject. His philosophical writings and correspondence brought him in touch with the philosophers Hume, Locke and Leibniz.

Claudel, Paul Louis Charles (1868–1955)
French poet, playwright and giant of French literature in the early twentieth century. His writing was achieved against the backcloth of an illustrious career in the French diplomatic service. Claudel served with distinction in the United States, the Far East and central Europe; he was French ambassador in Tokyo (1921), Washington (1927) and Brussels (1933). His sudden conversion to the Roman Catholic faith gave a unique dimension to his writing, particularly his plays, which reveal a grand design in creation, a movement from man's lusts and appetites to a redemptive consecration of the world to Christ.

Clement—Fourteen popes shared this title, the most noteworthy being:

Clement I, St (Clement of Rome) (pope from 88–97 or possibly 92-101)
Probably the third bishop of Rome after St Peter. It is feasible that he is the Clement referred to in Philippians 4:3. Certainly Irenaeus of Lyons speaks of him as a contemporary of the apostles. There is spurious Clementine literature, but the authorship of the *Letter to the Church at Corinth* (c. 96) is confidently ascribed to Clement. Many third- and fourth-century Christians accepted it as part of Scripture.

Clement VII (1478–1534)
Born Guilio de Medici; despite being illegitimate, he became archbishop of Florence and a cardinal in 1513, and pope ten years later. Of unreproachable character, Clement was, however, personally weak and vacillating; he became caught up in the ambitious struggles of the emperor Charles V and Francis I of France. When Rome was sacked in 1527, Clement was imprisoned for seven months, during which Henry VIII of En-

gland asked for an annulment of his marriage to Catherine of Aragon. Clement vacillated, finally (in 1533) finding that Henry's marriage was valid. Henry's Act of Supremacy, declaring the kings of England to be heads of the English church, followed. Clement's indecisiveness allowed the Protestant movement to sweep Europe. To his contemporaries Clement appeared as a Renaissance prince concerned with the patronage of the arts.

Clement of Alexandria, St (c. 150–c. 215)
Of Greek origin, Clement became a pupil and convert of Pantaenus, who was leader of the catechetical school of Alexandria. While there Clement wrote his principal works, among them *An Exhortation* and *The Instructor*. He succeeded Pantaenus as head of the school in AD 190. During the persecution conducted by the emperor Severus (201–202) Clement fled to Jerusalem and took refuge with his friend Alexander, bishop of Jerusalem.

Clifford, John (1836–1927)
Baptist minister and social reformer who started work at ten in a lace factory; after a conversion experience Clifford prepared for the Baptist ministry. His congregation at Paddington, London, became so large that a chapel at Westbourne Park was built and opened in 1877. In 1888 Clifford became president of the Baptist Union; theologically liberal, he defended the Union against Spurgeon's charges of heresy. Champion of the working classes, he came to national attention in 1902 with his passive resistance to Balfour's Education Act. Clifford served as president of the National Free Church Council (1898) and was the first president of the Baptist World Alliance.

Clitherow, St Margaret (1556–1586)
Wife of a butcher of York, Margaret was an Anglican who converted to Roman Catholicism in 1574. She was repeatedly

fined and imprisoned for nonattendance at the Anglican church. Margaret allowed the Catholic Mass to be said secretly in her home and provided a hiding place for priests. During a sudden raid on 10 March 1586 she was seized and charged with the capital offence of harbouring priests. At her trial Margaret refused to plead to save her children being forced to witness against her. For this she was crushed slowly to death with an eight-hundred-pound weight. Hence she won the title 'the martyr of York' and was canonised as one of the forty martyrs of England and Wales in 1970.

Cocceius, Johannes (or Koch) (1603–1669)
Biblical scholar and theologian of·the Reformed church who was a leading exponent of covenant theology. Prolific writer, his collected works were published as *Opera Omnia* in twelve volumes.

Coffin, Henry Sloane (1877–1954)
United States educator and Presbyterian minister who was known for his preaching, applying Christianity to social problems. Coffin also sought to raise the standard of theological education. Moderator of the general assembly of the Presbyterian church of the United States of America (1943–1944).

Colenso, John (1814–1883)
Anglican clergyman and mathematics teacher at Harrow who in 1846 became vicar of Forncett St Mary, Norfolk. In 1853 he was appointed the first bishop of Natal, where he was very pastorally involved with his Zulu congregation. In response to their needs he questioned the literal truth of the Pentateuch and followed an earlier critical book on Romans with work on the Pentateuch. His very liberal views led to his excommunication by the archbishop of Cape Town. Colenso appealed to London and the judicial committee of the Privy Council, who decided in his favour. A schism followed, led, after his death,

by his daughter, Harriette. Colenso always retained the affection of his people. The schism was finally ended in 1911.

Colet, John (1466–1519)
Dean of St Paul's who preached against the clerical abuses of his time and as one of the chief Tudor humanists promoted Renaissance culture in England. A friend of Erasmus and Thomas More, he never lost their support although he was several times suspected of heresy. From his father he inherited a fortune which he used, in part, to found St Paul's School.

Collier, Jeremy (1650–1726)
Anglican priest who wrote in support of King James II and was imprisoned on suspicion of treason. He became the bishop of the nonjurors (those clergy who refused the oath of allegiance to William and Mary in 1689) and wrote and preached against the current immorality of the stage.

Colman of Lindisfarne, St (c. 605–676)
Monk of Iona who succeeded St Finan as bishop of Lindisfarne (661). In the clash between Celtic and Roman liturgical customs Colman supported the Celtic at the Synod of Whitby (664) while St Wilfred spoke for the Roman usage. The synod decided in favour of the Roman and Colman resigned his see and retired to Iona. In Scotland he founded several churches and journeyed to Ireland, where he built monasteries at Inishbofin and Mayo.

Columba (Columcialle), St (c. 521–597)
Of noble Irish family, ordained a priest (c. 551), Columba founded churches and monasteries in Ireland before building a monastery on Iona (c. 563) and setting out with twelve companions to convert Scotland, founding churches and monasteries in many places. As an abbot and missionary he has been credited with doing more than any other to convert Scotland to Christianity.

Contarini, Gasparo (1483—1542)
Theologian and humanist scholar who began as a diplomat; as. an advocate of reform and reconciliation he worked for an agreement with the Lutherans on justification. Although only a layman, he was elevated to cardinal and contributed to the preparatory work for the Council of Trent.

Conwell, Russell Herman (1843—1925)
Lawyer, publisher, educator and clergyman; Conwell was converted from atheism while recovering from a serious wound received during the American Civil War. He became a very successful Baptist minister in Philadelphia, where he founded Temple University and three hospitals. He won world fame and great wealth through a lecture, 'Acres of Diamonds' (theme: opportunity lies in your own backyard), which he delivered approximately six thousand times. It was also published.

Cornelius à Lapide (1567—1637)
Flemish Jesuit and professor of biblical studies at Louvain and Rome. His celebrated series of biblical commentaries appeared gradually over a period of thirty years. These won acclaim and enduring popularity for their clarity and depth of scholarship.

Cosin, John (1594—1672)
While a chaplain at Durham Cathedral (1619) Cosin wrote, at the request of King Charles I, a daily prayer book, *Collection of Private Devotions*. Exiled during the Puritan Commonwealth government, he was made bishop of Durham at the Restoration. His literary works were controversial and as a liturgist he promoted a scholarly approach to worship which established him as one of the fathers of Anglo-Catholicism.

Cosmas & Damian, Saints (trad. d. c. 303)
Brothers who have been accepted since the fifth century as the patron saints of physicians. Little is known for certain of their

lives or martyrdom. Tradition records that they were Christian physicians who would accept no money for their services. They were said to have been tortured and beheaded for their faith during the persecution of Diocletian.

Cottolengo, St Joseph (1786–1842)

Born near Turin, where he later worked as a pastoral priest, he was one day called to attend a poor dying woman, only to discover that there were no facilities for the poor. Joseph opened a small house ('Piccola Casa') which quickly expanded to cope with the need. His caring widened to include the aged, deaf, blind, crippled and insane. His 'Piccola Casa' grew into a great sprawling medical institution. To minister to the various patients and needs he founded fourteen different religious congregations of religious sisters, brothers and priests. He was canonised in 1934.

Cotton, John (1585–1652)

Escaping the persecution of Nonconformists by the Church of England, Cotton became the New England Puritan leader. Within the First Church of Boston, from 1633–1652, Cotton was regarded as the spiritual leader and teacher.

Court, Antoine (1695–1760)

French minister of the Reformed church and itinerant preacher who devoted his life, from the age of twenty-one, to the restoration of Protestantism in France.

Couturier, Paul Irénée (1881–1953)

French priest and educator who dedicated the latter part of his life to work for Christian unity. He popularised and extended the idea of an annual Week of Prayer for Christian Unity (18–25 January); from 1939 the octave was observed as the Week of Universal Prayer. Through interdenominational conferences, vast correspondence and the writing of innumerable tracts, Couturier did more than any other Roman Catholic to further Christian unity over a period of twenty years.

Coverdale, Miles (1488–1568)
After ordination in 1514 Coverdale became an Augustinian friar; absorbing Lutheran opinions, he left the order and preached against images and the Mass. Forced to reside abroad, he produced the first complete English translation of the Bible. On his return to England he edited the Great Bible (1539). After Henry VIII's death he was made bishop of Exeter in 1551. Exiled again under Queen Mary, on his return he assisted at the consecration of Matthew Parker as archbishop of Canterbury, but felt unable to resume the see of Exeter. For the remainder of his life he was the leader of the Puritan movement.

Cox, Richard (c. 1500–1581)
Dean, first of Christ Church, Oxford, then of Westminster Abbey, he made important contributions to the Prayer Books of 1549 and 1552. A zealous supporter of the Reform in England, he was imprisoned and then exiled during Queen Mary's reign. On his return he was briefly bishop of Norwich, then of Ely.

Cranmer, Thomas (1489–1556)
Educated at Cambridge and ordained in 1523, he caught the attention of Henry VIII by his support for the king's royal divorce plans. He secretly married Margaret Osiander in 1532, while on a mission for Henry. In 1533 he was appointed archbishop of Canterbury and the same year annulled Henry's marriage to Catherine of Aragon; in the following years he invalidated Henry's second, fourth and fifth marriages. In 1547, after Henry's death, Cranmer acted as counselor to Edward VI and proceeded to Protestantise the Church of England and promote its union with the Reformed churches of Europe. He promoted the publication of an English Bible and

was largely responsible for the Prayer Books of 1549 and 1552. Tried for treason when Mary Tudor came to the throne, his life was spared by the queen. However, he was imprisoned and tried for heresy. After several recantations, which he later renounced, he died courageously at the stake on 21 March 1556.

Cromwell, Oliver (1599–1658)
Elected MP for Cambridge, Cromwell's religious fervour sustained him in his political struggles as a leader of the Puritan party. He viewed the Civil War as a religious struggle, his own role as God's instrument. Captain at the battle of Edgehill, he was second-in-command of the new Parliamentary Army at the battle of Marston Moor. Cromwell supported the Independents against the Presbyterians and worked for the execution of Charles I. He used his New Model Army to crush an Irish revolt and the Scots, and in 1653 he dismissed the Long Parliament. As lord protector of the Commonwealth he ruled from 1653 and attempted to instil 'true godliness' in England. On his death Cromwell was buried in Westminster Abbey but at the Restoration his body was disinterred and dishonoured.

Crowther, Samuel (c. 1809–1891)
Sold into slavery at twelve, but rescued by the British; Adjai's name was changed and he was educated at a mission school. The Church Missionary Society ordained him and sent him to his own Yoruba country (modern Nigeria). Crowther accompanied several expeditions in the Niger territory, for which he was consecrated as the first African bishop in 1864.

Cruden, Alexander (1701–1770)
Of Scottish Presbyterian upbringing, Cruden was famed for his eccentricities, bordering on insanity, and his *Concordance* of the Bible.

Cullen, Paul (1803–1878)

Ordained priest in Rome (1829), he stayed there as rector of the college, returning to Ireland as archbishop of Armagh in 1850. He was appointed the First Irish cardinal in 1866 and played an important part in the First Vatican Council.

Cuthbert, St (634–687)

A monk of the monastery of Melrose from 651, Cuthbert became prior and, on Colman's resignation of the see of Lindisfarne, he and his abbot, Eata, took responsibility for Lindisfarne. They implemented the Roman liturgy as decreed by the Synod of Whitby. Cuthbert retired as a hermit in 676 but, nine years later, took Eata's place as bishop of Lindisfarne. There followed two years of intense missionary activity. Due to Viking incursions Cuthbert's body was not given a permanent resting place until 999, in Durham Cathedral.

Cyprian, St (c. 200–258)

Thascius Caecilianus Cyprianus was converted from paganism about 246 and two years later was elected bishop of Carthage. During the Decian persecution of 250 he hid and returned to Carthage in 251. He became involved in a dispute over rebaptism with Stephen, bishop of Rome. A new persecution broke out under the emperor Valerian. At first Cyprian was merely banished, but later, in 258, he was arrested and martyred at Carthage, becoming the first martyr-bishop of Africa. His theological writings were popular and of some lasting importance. His collected letters, some sixty-five of them, reveal Cyprian as an ideally pastoral bishop.

Cyril of Alexandria (376–444)

Born at Alexandria, nephew of the patriarch Theophilus, Cyril succeeded his uncle on his death in 412. He immediately waged war upon Novatianism and had the Jews expelled from the city. In 430 he became embroiled with Nestorius and worked for his condemnation, which occurred at the Synod of

Rome in 430 under Pope Celestine. In 431 Cyril presided over the third General Council at Ephesus, which again condemned Nestorius. A brilliant theologian, Cyril wrote important treatises that clarified the church's teaching on the Trinity and the incarnation. His writings have remained famous for their accurate thinking and precise exposition. He was declared a doctor of the church in 1882.

Cyril of Jerusalem, St (c. 315–386)
As bishop of Jerusalem from 349, Cyril developed the idea of the Holy City as a centre of pilgrimage. For opposing Arianism Cyril was three times banished from his see. His work, the twenty-three *Catecheses* (c. 350), lectures for catechumens preparing for baptism, cast light on the method of preparation for baptism then customary.

Cyril, St (826–869) and Methodius, St (c. 815–885)
These brothers are always taken together; both were scholars and theologians in their own right, but together won the title 'the Apostles of the Slavs' for their joint missionary work among the Danubian Slavs. In their work they broke with custom and introduced a Slavonic liturgy and translated the Bible into Slavonic, having specially invented a Slavid alphabet. Conflict arose with the German bishops over the use of the vernacular for the liturgy. Cyril's death spared him the later harassment that Methodius experienced.

D

D'Ailly, Pierre (1350–1420)

French theologian and bishop who was influenced by the teaching of William of Ockham in his theology, which in turn influenced Luther and other Reformers. He worked for the healing of the Western Schism, seeking ways of reconciling the factions. His celebrated *Tractatus super Reformatione Ecclesiae* suggested reforms later adopted by the Council of Trent.

Damasus, St (c. 304–384)

Elected pope in 366, Damasus was energetic in suppressing various heresies. With the help of his secretary, St Jerome, he promulgated a canon of sacred Scripture and commissioned Jerome in 382 to revise the biblical text (known as the Vulgate).

Damien, St Peter (1007–1072)

Zealous reformer who first lived a hermit's life, then preached with great effect against contemporary abuses. Reluctantly made bishop of Ostia and then cardinal (1057), he advised and served three successive popes, acting as their reconciling emissary. Damien's prolific writings denounced simony and promoted clerical celibacy. His life was an inspiring example of voluntary poverty.

Damien, Father (1840–1889)

Born Joseph de Veuster, of a Belgian family, he joined the Picpus Fathers in 1860 and requested to be sent to the Pacific Islands. After nine years of missionary work he asked to be allowed to devote himself to the lepers abandoned on the island of Molokai. In appalling conditions he ministered to the needs of six hundred lepers, singlehanded, for ten years. He contracted leprosy in 1885 and for the last six years he was joined by a few priests and nuns. His body was taken back to Belgium in 1936 to an acclaim denied him in life.

Dante, Alighieri (1265–1321)

The greatest Italian poet, prose writer, moral philosopher and political thinker. His Christian epic *The Divine Comedy,* inspired by his love for Beatrice, is.one of the landmarks in the literature of the world.

Darboys, Georges (1813–1871)

Archbishop of Paris and upholder of the Gallican tradition and episcopal independence, which brought him into conflict with Pope Pius IX. At the First Vatican Council he opposed the defining of papal infallibility, considering it inopportune. His concern for the destitute during the siege of Paris (1870–1871) was exemplary, but he was deliberately shot by the Communards, with four of his priests, on 24 May 1871.

D'Arcy, Martin Cyril (1888–1976)

Jesuit philosopher and theologian who was master of Campion Hall, Oxford, from 1933 to 1945 and provincial of the English Jesuits from 1945 to 1950. He was a prolific writer and exponent of Catholic philosophy and theology; his best-remembered works were *The Nature of Belief* (1931) and *The Mind and Heart of Love* (1945).

Davenport, Christopher (1598–1680)

Converted from Anglicanism to the Roman Catholic faith, he entered the Franciscan order and became dedicated to trying to reconcile the Thirty-Nine Articles of Anglicanism with Roman Catholic theology. He served as chaplain to the queens of Charles I and Charles II.

David, St (c. 520–c. 600)

Patron saint of Wales of whose life no reliable account exists. Legend has it that he was of noble family and, after ordination to the priesthood, adopted a severe form of monastic life, eventually founding twelve monasteries. Chosen bishop, he transferred his see from Caerleon to Mynyw (now St David's). The Synod of Victory is said to have been summoned by David. It supposedly defeated the Pelagian heresy in Britain.

Davidson, Randall Thomas (1848–1930)

Educated at Harrow and Oxford, and ordained in 1875, he became chaplain to the archbishop of Canterbury, A.C. Tait, and won the trust of Queen Victoria. Bishop of Rochester in 1891 and Winchester in 1895, he succeeded Frederick Temple as archbishop of Canterbury in 1903. Respected as a moderate, Davidson steered the Church of England through a difficult period and his service to his church and nation was recognised on his retirement when he was made Baron Davidson of Lambeth.

Davies, Samuel (1723–1761)

American Presbyterian preacher who, in Virginia, helped lead the religious revival known as 'the Great Awakening'. The power of his preaching was experienced not only in the United States but also on a trip to Scotland and England. He is also remembered as the first American hymnwriter of note.

Day, Dorothy (1897–1980)
Social reformer from New York City, remembered for her work among the American poor, particularly in the cities, where she founded houses of hospitality. She originally trained as a nurse but then worked as a journalist and was the co-founder of the influential *Catholic Worker* newspaper (1930).

Dearmer, Percy (1867–1936)
Hymnologist and writer who popularised and adapted medieval church music for use in Anglican worship. As a vicar of Hampstead he applied the ideals he set out in his *The Parson's Handbook* (1899). He wrote on a wide range of subjects and was also coeditor of various collections of hymns and religious music.

Delehaye, Hippolyte (1859–1941)
Belgian Jesuit priest who joined the Bollandists and spent his life studying and writing the lives of the saints. In 1912 he became president of the Bollandists; he wrote copiously and contributed regularly to the *Acta Sanctorum*.

De Lisle, Ambrose Lisle March Phillips (1809–1878)
Converted to Catholicism in 1824, he retained links with his Anglican past and, as a writer, worked for the reunion of Canterbury and Rome. His substantial gift of land, near Leicester, to the Cistercian order made the foundation of Mount St Bernard Abbey possible (1835–1844).

Denck, Hans (c. 1495–1527)
German reformer who theologically opposed Lutheranism, becoming an Anabaptist; for his beliefs he was forced to wander Europe. His life and beliefs were markedly influenced by the mystic, Johann Tauler.

De Nobili, Robert (1577–1656)

Jesuit missionary to India who adopted the mode of life of the
Brahmins in order to win converts. His methods were investigated, but he was permitted to continue and it is believed he
made a hundred thousand converts. His gifts as a linguist are
evident from his many religious and devotional works in San-
skrit, Tamil and Telugu.

Dibelius, Martin (1883–1947)

German New Testament scholar and one of the originators of
form criticism; he was also an enthusiastic supporter of the
ecumenical movement, being a leader of the Faith and Order
Commission. His most influential publication was *From Tradition to Gospel* (Eng. trans. 1934).

Dibelius, Otto (1880–1967)

German Lutheran bishop of Berlin (1945) who had been a
supporter of the Confessing Church and an outspoken opponent of Nazism. Against atheistic communism he presented
the same opposition; in 1954 he became president of the
World Council of Churches.

Dionysius, St (c. 250) (also known as St Denis)

Dionysius is the patron saint of France and, according to Gregory of Tours's (sixth century) history of France, he was the
first bishop of Paris and suffered martyrdom under the emperor Valerian.

Dionysius, St (d. 268)

Little is known of the life of this pope, bishop of Rome from
259; he had succeeded Sixtus II, who had been martyred.
Caught up in the subordinationism controversy, there was also
'the affair of the two Dionysii', when he was in dispute with
Dionysius, bishop of Alexandria.

Dionysius Exiguus (c. 500–c. 560)

Theologian and monastic expert on canon law and ecclesiastical chronology. In 525, at the request of Pope St John I, he worked out the Christian calendar still used today. Unfortunately he wrongly dated the year of Christ's birth. Also credited to him is a vast collection of church laws and council decrees.

Dionysius the Carthusian (1402–1471) (Denys van Leuven or Denys Ryckel)

Member of the Carthusian order who wrote Old and New Testament biblical commentaries; these and his theological works were very popular in the fifteenth and sixteenth centuries. As a mystic he was one of the luminaries of the Rhenish school of spirituality and his *De Contemplatione* was considered a spiritual classic.

Dionysius the Great, St (d. c. 264)

Bishop of Alexandria and theologian who opposed Sabellianism and who suffered persecution under Valerian. Accused of tritheism, he was in conflict with the pope of the same name; however, cleared of heresy, his teaching on the Trinity was later vindicated by the church.

Dodd, Charles Harold (1884–1973)

Educated at Oxford and Berlin, Dodd was ordained in 1912 for the Congregational ministry. From 1915 he lectured successively in New Testament studies and divinity at Oxford, Manchester and Cambridge. His seminal works, e.g., *The Parables of the Kingdom* and *History of the Gospel,* put forward his 'realised eschatology' thesis. Dodd also defended the historical value of the fourth Gospel and from 1950 was director of the *New English Bible* project.

Doddridge, Philip (1702–1751)

English Nonconformist minister in Leicestershire who is re-membered for the large number of hymns he wrote, and for his scheme to distribute Bibles at home and abroad, which makes him one of the pioneers of Nonconformist missionary work.

Dollinger, Johann Joseph Ignaz von (1799–1890)

German Roman Catholic church historian and theologian who, in his middle years, grew distrustful of the influence of the pope. He refused to accept the First Vatican Council (1871) decree on the infallibility of the pope and for the rest of his life supported the Old Catholic church movement in Germany.

Dominic, St (1170–1221)

Of Spanish birth, in 1199 he joined a community of canons in the diocese of Osma, leading an austere life of discipline; he was sent on a preaching tour among the Albigensian heretics and displayed great courage. In 1214 Dominic founded a new order, the order of Friars Preachers (Dominicans). He traveled widely, preaching and establishing the order. Dominic led a simple austere life, his heroic sanctity leading to his canoni-sation in 1234.

Donne, John (1572–1631)

A chequered career in law, as a 'gentleman adventurer' on a military expedition, as a secretary to Sir Thomas Egerton, etc., preceded ordination to the Anglican ministry in 1615. In 1621 he was installed as dean of St Paul's Cathedral, London, and became established as an eminent and popular preacher, a particular favourite at court. Donne was a leading poet of the seventeenth century English 'Metaphysical school'. His secular poetry dates from his youth and his religious poetry from the troubled middle years.

Dositheus (1641–1707)
Theologian of the Greek church, and important church politician, who from 1669, as patriarch of Jerusalem, stoutly supported Eastern Orthodoxy over the claims of Rome. To prevent Protestantism influencing the Greek church he called the important Synod of Jerusalem in 1672. His extensive writings were to support his resistance to both Roman Catholic and Protestant influences upon the Orthodox church.

Drexel, Katherine (1858–1955)
Daughter of a United States financier, she inherited a vast fortune on the death of her parents and she used it and dedicated her life to the welfare of American Indians and blacks. In 1891 she founded the Congregation of Blessed Sacrament Sisters, who worked in the schools (sixty-three by the time of her death) that she built. In 1915 she founded Xavier University in New Orleans for black girls.

Duchesne, Rose Phillipine (1769–1852)
French missionary sister who established the first Sacred Heart convents in the United States. After founding a Sacred Heart convent in Paris (1815) she led a group of nuns (1818) in pioneer missionary work west of the Mississippi. Schools were founded in Louisiana, and an academy and orphanage in St. Louis (1827). Mother Duchesne worked among the Potawatomi Indians at Sugar Creek, Kansas. Ill health drove her into retirement (1842) at her first foundation at St. Charles. Her sanctity of life led to her being beatified by Pope Pius XII in 1940.

Duff, Alexander (1806–1878)
Scottish Presbyterian missionary to India who, sent out as the first Church of Scotland missionary to Calcutta in 1830, joined the Free Church in 1843. His English school in Calcutta grew into a missionary college; when it was lost to him

because of the Disruption of 1843, he started again. He was moderator of the Free Church Assembly in 1851 and 1873.

Duns Scotus, John (c. 1265–1308)
Although he is regarded as the greatest medieval British philosopher and theologian, little is known of his life. He joined the Franciscan order and studied at Oxford and Paris. He was highly thought of as a scholar and lecturer, and his teaching marks him out as the leader of the Franciscan school of thought. 'Scotist' philosophy was taught alongside the 'Thomist' school in European universities. His most important publication is his *Commentary* on the *Sentences* of Peter Lombard.

Dunstan, St (c. 909–988)
Benedictine monk and abbot of Glastonbury, which he reformed and made famous for its learning. He served successive kings, eventually being elected archbishop of Canterbury; with the king, Edgar, he carried through sweeping reforms in state and church. He was also responsible for the restoration of monastic life in England.

Dupanloup, Felix (1802–1878)
French Catholic bishop of Orléans, noted for his promotion and defence of education. A liberal in thought and an innovator in educational methods, he defended papal temporal sovereignty but led the small group of bishops at the First Vatican Council who considered the declaration of papal infallibility as inappropriate at that time. He later accepted the Council's decrees.

Duperron, Jacques Davy (1556–1618)
Converted from Calvinism to Roman Catholicism, Duperron brought about the conversion to the Roman Catholic church of Henry IV of France in 1593. He was involved in conflict with the Huguenots and between the Gallicans and the Ultramontanists.

Du Plessis, David J. (1905–1987)
Pentecostal leader and ecumenist. Born in South Africa, he later worked in the United States. He began to preach at Pentecostal meetings early in life, later being ordained as an Assemblies of God minister. He was the first Pentecostal leader to work with the World Council of Churches. He attended the third session of the Second Vatican Council (1963) as an observer and served as a leader in the official Vatican-Pentecostal dialogue. In spite of opposition within his own church, he encouraged the charismatic movement in Protestant and Catholic churches from the 1950s.

Duplessis-Mornay, Philippe (1549–1623)
French statesman and leader of the Huguenots, he worked for the ideal of a united Protestant church and toleration for the Huguenots; he was successful in bringing about the Edict of Nantes in 1598.

Du Toit, Jakob Daniel (1844–1953)
Afrikaans biblical scholar, pastor and poet, who compiled a famous Afrikaans Psalter and translated the Bible into Afrikaans. His Calvinism and patriotism is revealed in his many poetic works.

Durie, John (1596–1680)
Scottish Protestant minister who devoted himself to the union of the Lutheran and Calvinist churches. In 1643 he was ordained priest in the Church of England, became a chaplain to the king and he espoused the royalist cause. Wavering in his allegiance eventually made him unacceptable to either party.

Duvergier de Hauranne, Jean (1581–1643) (also known as l'Abbé de Saint-Cyran)
One of the founders of the Jansenist movement, known for his remarkable erudition but hampered by an inability to communicate clearly. He sought to promote Augustinian thought in

opposition to the prevailing scholasticism and proposed the reform of Catholicism through Augustinian principles. His friendship with C. Jansen, his connection with the community at Port-Royal, and his evident power, led to the opposition of Cardinal Richélieu and imprisonment for five years.

Dwight, Timothy (1752–1817)

One of the most influential intellectual leaders of the new American republic. As an educator, minister and writer he helped to shape the educational pattern of New England. Many of his sermons were published and his ambitious poetic epic *The Conquest of Canaan,* in eleven volumes, was influential.

E

Eckhart von Hochheim (c. 1260–1327) (also known as Meister Eckhart)

Dominican theologian, preacher and mystic. He rose to the position of provincial of his order with the task of reforming the Bohemian religious houses. In Germany, from 1313, Eckhart was acknowledged as the finest preacher of his time and a mystic. His critics accused him of heresy and he appeared before the archbishop of Cologne in 1326. He appealed to the pope and the next year recanted. After his death twenty-eight propositions from his writings were condemned. Eckhart's mystical leanings and attempts to express the inexpressible seem to have occasioned the condemnation, but he succeeded in inspiring Tauler and Suso.

Edmund of Abingdon, St (c. 1180–1240) (also known as Edmund Rich)

He studied and later lectured at Oxford and Paris. Austere in lifestyle, he accepted the post of treasurer of Salisbury Cathedral and in 1233 he was elected archbishop of Canterbury. A saintly and attractive man of lofty ideals, he suffered, as archbishop, the opposition of the monks of Canterbury, and his own opposition to Henry III's policies led to a voluntary exile at Pontigny in France.

Edmund the Martyr, St (d. 869)

King of the East Angles; in 865 his kingdom was invaded by the Danes, who wanted Edmund to share his kingdom with their leader. He refused to associate with a pagan and was used by the Danes for target practice. Almost immediately he was honoured as a martyr. His body was moved in the tenth century to Bury St Edmund's, which promptly became a place of pilgrimage.

Edward the Confessor, St (1003–1066)

Of Saxon birth, but brought up and educated in Normandy, Edward succeeded his half-brother, Hardicanute, to the English throne in 1042. His reign appeared peaceful but there were continual internal struggles between the Saxons, led by the influential Earl Godwin, and Edward's Norman friends and advisers. He showed more interest in religious matters than affairs of state, acting more like a monk than a king. Edward was particularly concerned with the building of the great abbey church of Westminster, where he was buried. He was canonised in 1161.

Edwards, Jonathan (1703–1758)

Brought up in a Puritan atmosphere, Edwards showed great interest in philosophy and science from an early age. His interest in stating Calvinism in contemporary philosophical terms grew from 1727, after a conversion experience. Ordained to the Congregational church at Northampton, Massachusetts, he led the religious revival called 'the Great Awakening', but some excesses and his own extreme Calvinism led to his dismissal from Northampton. In missionary work at Stockbridge he worked among the Indians and wrote his most important works, *Freedom of the Will* and *Original Sin*. In 1757 Edwards accepted the presidency of Princeton College (later University) but died shortly afterwards. He is considered the greatest theologian of American Puritanism.

Egede, Hans (1686–1758)
Norwegian Lutheran minister and missionary who was the first to preach the gospel to the Eskimos of Greenland. In Copenhagen he founded a seminary (1736) to train missionaries for work in Greenland.

Elias of Cortona (c. 1180–1235)
One of St Francis of Assisi's earliest companions, mainly responsible for the building of the basilica at Assisi. Third general of the Franciscan order, but disposed in 1239, and expelled from the order. He established a monastery of his own at Cortona.

Eliot, John (1604–1690)
Born in Hertfordshire, England, and educated at Cambridge, Eliot emigrated to Boston in 1631, and from his Puritan church at Roxburg conducted a mission to the Indians, winning the title 'apostle to the Indians'. He wrote a *Catechism* (1653) and a translation of the Bible for them.

Eliot, T.S. (1888–1965)
American-born British poet and critic, educated at Harvard, Paris and Oxford. Brought up a Unitarian, Eliot passed through an agnostic period, reflected in his early poetry. The poem which made him famous, *The Waste Land,* (1922) expressed his disenchantment with the post-war period and his own sense of emptiness. In 1927 Eliot became a British citizen and was confirmed in the Church of England, in which he took an Anglo-Catholic position, which is reflected in his later verse, particularly *Ash Wednesday* (1930) and *Murder in the Cathedral* (1933). As a playwright he had little success, except for *The Cocktail Party* (1950), but was highly regarded as a critic. His greatest poetry appeared in *Four Quartets* (1935–1942); Eliot won the Nobel Prize for Literature in 1948.

Elizabeth of Hungary (or of Thuringia), St (1207–1231)

Daughter of the king of Hungary, she was betrothed in infancy to Louis of Thuringia and married at fourteen. There followed six happy years of marriage until Louis died on the way to the Sixth Crusade. Elizabeth had already shown great interest in an ascetic life and, driven from court, she settled at Marburg, where she built a hospice for the poor. She devoted the rest of her life to the care of the needy and was canonised in 1235.

Elizabeth of France (1754–1794) (also known as Madame Elizabeth)

French princess, sister of King Louis XVI, who refused to escape and leave her brother and his wife, Marie Antoinette, at the French Revolution. She shared their imprisonment and death, and was notable for her courage and exemplary Christian virtue.

Embury, Philip (1729–1775)

Of Irish birth, Embury was converted by John Wesley and, after emigrating to America in 1760, became the first Methodist preacher in America and founder of the first Methodist chapel in New York.

England, John (1786–1842)

Irish-born and educated, England was consecrated the first Roman Catholic bishop of the American diocese of Charleston (North Carolina, South Carolina and Georgia). He published a catechism and a missal for Americans and founded the first American Catholic newspaper. England began two schools, founded religious orders to care for the needy, and was the first Roman Catholic clergyman to address the United States Congress (1826).

Ephraem Syrus, St (c. 306–373)

Celebrated Syrian writer, biblical exegete and doctor of the church. He lived most of his life in his native Nisibis (Turkey), but moved to Edessa in 363, where most of his works were written. A prolific writer of biblical commentaries and homilies, he was more of a preacher than a theologian. His works are in verse and he composed over seventy hymns for the liturgy; although he was a popular writer with his contemporaries, his writings are difficult for modern readers.

Epiphanius, St (c. 315–403)
Bishop of Constantia (Cyprus) from 367, he was dedicated to the spread of monasticism and the refuting of heresies. His major work, *Panarion,* gives an account of eighty heresies known to him and ends with a presentation of sound teaching.

Erasmus, Desiderius (c. 1466–1536)
Christened Herasmus, probably at Rotterdam, and educated in a humanist environment, he reluctantly entered the monastery at Steyn as an Augustinian canon. After he was ordained a priest, in 1492, he was allowed to leave his monastery as secretary to the bishop of Cambrai. There began a quest for learning which took Erasmus all over Europe from Italy to England. In the latter he developed lasting friendships with scholars like John Colet, John Fisher and Thomas More; and he benefited from the patronage of William Warham, archbishop of Canterbury. Released from his monastic vows in 1517, he continued to wander Europe, establishing himself as the great scholar and figure of the Northern Renaissance. He was very critical of the contemporary church, and his satirical writing paved the way for the Reformation. When it broke, both sides appealed to him for support. He was first believed to be in support of Luther, but eventually wrote against him and withdrew to the stability of the traditional church. However, after his death, his writings were forbidden by several of the popes. After his version of the Greek New Testament, his next important contribution was to make the works of the early Christian writers available and to promote patristic studies.

Erigena, John Scotus (c. 810–877)

Apart from his birth in Ireland and the patronage he secured of the West Frankish king, Charles the Bald, little is known of his life. Scotus was a deeply original philosopher, and a scholar of high repute, who took part in contemporary debates upon predestination and the Eucharist; he developed a theory of knowledge that was highly influential. His translation and commentaries of the works of the Pseudo-Dionysius were a great service to later scholars.

Erskine, John (1509–1591)

Educated at King's College, Aberdeen, Erskine, who was Lord of Dun, was a close friend of the Reformers George Wishart and John Knox. He acted as an intermediary between Mary Queen of Scots and the Reformers. Four times Erskine was elected moderator of the general assembly of the reformed Church of Scotland.

Ethelbert of Kent, St (d. c. 616)

King of Kent from c. 560, he is said to have extended his kingdom to south of the Humber. His marriage to the Frankish princess Bertha, who was a Christian, introduced Christianity into Anglo-Saxon England and Ethelbert was eventually converted. He welcomed St Augustine and his monks in 597 and gave his full support to Christianity, holding the distinction of being the first Christian king in England.

Etheldreda, St (d. 679)

Daughter of the Christian king of the East Angles who, although married twice, lived a life of consecrated virginity. Egfrid, her second husband, consented to her becoming a nun and she founded the double monastery (for men and women living separately in community) at Ely.

Eudes, St John (1601–1680)

Born in Normandy and educated at Caen by the Jesuits, John was ordained for the Roman Catholic priesthood in 1625. A gifted speaker, he devoted the next fifty years to preaching parish missions. In 1641 he established both a congregation of sisters (order of Our Lady of Charity) to care for delinquent girls and women, and an association of priests (the Congregation of Jesus and Mary) to prepare candidates for the priesthood. One of his greatest achievements was to provide a theological foundation to the contemporary devotion to the Sacred Hearts of Jesus and Mary, which he had promoted.

Eusebius—There are seven famous Christians of the early centuries of Christianity with this title.

Eusebius, St (fourth century)

Pope and martyr who died in 309 (or 310), buried in the catacomb of Callixtus, Rome.

Eusebius of Caesarea (c. 260–c. 340)

Educated by the scholar and martyr, Pamphibus, about 314 he became bishop of Caesarea. He was already an established scholar and writer when Arius propounded his views; Eusebius, always fearful of Sabellianism, tried to hold a middle course. Although suspected, he was exonerated of the charge of heresy. His Caesarean Creed, which he presented to the Council of Nicaea, was not preferred to the Nicene Creed. Remembered as a church historian—'Father of Church History'—his voluminous works were mainly of an apologetical nature. His principal work (originally in seven volumes, but later extended to ten), was his *Ecclesiastical History,* which is our principal source for the history of the Eastern church from apostolic times.

Eusebius of Dorylaeum (fifth century)

Bishop of Dorylaeum, he was ever the champion of orthodox teaching; even as a layman he was the first to publicly challenge the teaching of Nestorius. He suffered deposition by the 'Robber Synod' of Ephesus for challenging Monophysitism. The Council of Chalcedon reinstated him to his see.

Eusebius of Emesa (d. c. 359)

Bishop of Emesa, biblical exegete and scholar. Friend of the emperor Constantius, he was suspected of semi-Arian teaching and only fragments of his writings are extant.

Eusebius of Laedice (c. 264–269)

Eusebius risked his life to help Christian martyrs during the persecutions of Decius and Valerian; revered for his saintliness, he was persuaded to accept the see of Laodicea.

Eusebius of Nicomedia (d. c. 342)

Important Eastern bishop who was a proponent of the Arian heresy.

Eusebius of Samosata, St (d. c. 379)

Great opponent of Arianism who, as bishop of Samosata, was exiled for upholding orthodox beliefs.

Eutyches (c. 378–454)

Archimandrite at Constantinople whose fierce opposition to Nestorianism seems to have led him to be accused of the opposite heresy; his name has been given to the Eutychian heresy.

Evagrius Ponticus (346–399)

Ordained a deacon by St Gregory of Nazianzus, he was first a gifted preacher then a monk living in the desert in Egypt. Highly regarded in his day as a spiritual guide and one of the first monks to write about spirituality, his writings were a formative influence on later spiritual writers.

Eymard, St Peter Julian (1811–1868)
French priest who, after some years of pastoral work, joined the Marist order. His great devotion to the Blessed Sacrament resulted in the foundation of an order of priests and a separate order of nuns devoted to the perpetual adoration of the Blessed Sacrament. St Peter also wrote several books on the Eucharist. He was canonised in 1962 by Pope John XXIII.

F

Faber, Frederick William (1814–1863)

Born at Calverley in Yorkshire, Faber was educated at Harrow and Balliol College, Oxford. Originally of Calvinist background, at Oxford he worked with J.H. Newman on the *Library of the Fathers* and in November 1845, a few weeks after Newman, he was received into the Roman Catholic church. He founded a small community at Birmingham, but when Newman introduced the Oratory of St Philip Neri into England he joined that, becoming superior of the London house in 1849. The author of popular spiritual books, e.g., *Growth in Holiness* (1854), he is best remembered for his popular hymns, e.g., 'Hark, Hark My Soul', 'My God How Wonderful Thou Art', and others still in current use.

Fabiola, St (d. 399)

Of a wealthy Roman family, she divorced a vicious first husband, a move disapproved of by her local Christian community, and this led her to a life of atonement. Under the direction of St Jerome, Fabiola gave away her wealth and dedicated herself to the care of the sick, founding the first public hospital in Europe.

Falconieri, St Juliana (1270–1341)

Of a Florentine family, she rejected her family's marriage plans and became instead a tertiary of the Servite order at sixteen.

After her mother's death in 1304, she headed a group of women dedicated to prayer and charitable works and in time founded the Servite order of nuns.

Faulhaber, Michael (1869–1952)
Born at Heidenfeld, Germany, ordained for the priesthood in 1892, he lectured in Old Testament studies at the universities of Wurzburg and Strasbourg. He became archbishop of Munich in 1917 and cardinal in 1921. The Nazi movement was totally repugnant to him and he courageously opposed it every way he could. An attempt was made on his life in 1934 and his residence was attacked in 1938.

Felix, St (d. c. 647)
Born and ordained in Burgundy, he was consecrated the first bishop of the East Angles by archbishop of Canterbury. From his see at Dunwich, Suffolk, he spent seventeen years converting the heathen of East Anglia.

Felix of Valois, St (1127–1212)
A French hermit who in 1198 founded an order of monks called the Trinitarians who devoted their lives to the redemption of Christian captives of the Saracens.

Fell, John (1625–1686)
Educated at Christ Church, Oxford, he supported the Royalist cause during the Civil War and, ordained in 1647, kept the Church of England services alive in Oxford during the Commonwealth. After the Restoration he became bishop of Oxford, where he established the university press and worked hard to restore the standards and traditions of the university.

Fénelon, Francois de Salignac de la Mothe (1651–1715)
Educated for the priesthood at Saint-Sulpice, he was ordained about 1675 and in 1678 was appointed superior of the Nouvelles Catholiques (recent converts from Protestantism). Sent on missionary work among the Huguenots, he returned to

tutor Louis XIV's grandson. In 1688 Fénelon met and began his support of Madame Guyon. He became implicated in the charges of Quietism made against her. Writing a defence of Christian mysticism, he became involved in a bitter controversey with Bossuet. As a result he was exiled from the French court in 1697 and thereafter worked humbly in his diocese of Cambrai. Highly respected for his writings on education, Fénelon was, above all, a master of the spiritual life and a mystical theologian and writer to whom history has not been kind.

Ferrar, Nicholas (1592–1637)
Educated at Cambridge, Ferrar studied abroad and in 1618 joined the council of the Virginia Company, but six years later entered Parliament. Leaving public life he was ordained a deacon in 1626 and set up a Christian community of about thirty persons at Little Gidding in Huntingdonshire, where he remained leader until his death. The community was visited three times by King Charles I but, as with most of Ferrar's writings, it was destroyed by the Puritans in 1646.

Ferrar, Robert (d. 1555)
Bishop of St David's and a Protestant martyr who was condemned to death under Queen Mary for denying the Roman Catholic doctrine on the Eucharist.

Figgis, John Neville (1866–1919)
Anglican theologian and historian whose original thinking and writing on the relationship between church and state sounded the alarm on the dangers to religion and human freedom from the all-competent modern state.

Finney, Charles Grandison (1792–1875)
Lawyer from Connecticut who, after conversion at twenty-nine, became a full-time Presbyterian evangelist. He led many highly successful revivals in the New York area and from 1837 became Congregational minister at his own church, the Broad-

way Tabernacle, Oberlin, and from 1851 to 1866, president of Oberlin College.

Fisher, Geoffrey Francis (1887–1972)
Anglican priest and educationalist who became bishop of Chester (1932), London (1939), and finally archbishop of Canterbury (1945). His abiding interest was the work for Christian unity, being chairman of the World Council of Churches at its inauguration in 1948; he was the first archbishop of Canterbury to visit the Vatican, where he met with Pope John XXIII.

Fisher, St John (1469–1535)
In 1504 Fisher became chancellor of the University of Cambridge, where he had been in turn a student and a lecturer. He made strenuous efforts to raise the standards at the university. Appointed bishop of Rochester in 1504, he enjoyed a wide reputation as a scholar and a preacher and in both capacities worked to counter the Protestant influences spreading through England. As Catherine of Aragon's confessor he protested at Henry VIII's divorce plans; and for refusing the oath required by the Act of Succession he was arrested and imprisoned in the Tower of London. He was tried and convicted, and his elevation to the rank of cardinal by the pope did not save him from execution on 22 June 1535. He was acknowledged as a martyr by the Roman Catholic church and canonised in 1935.

Fisk, Wilbur (1792–1839)
American Methodist clergyman and educator whose wide reputation raised the quality and standing of Methodism in New England.

Flaget, Benedict Joseph (1763–1850)
American Roman Catholic Sulpician priest who, after serving in education and as a missionary, was appointed the first bishop of the old northwest of the United States. His many educational foundations and the standards they maintained were

legendary. He founded two orders of sisters to provide elementary education for girls.

Flemyng (Fleming), Richard (d. 1431)
Bishop of London (1420) who represented England at the church councils of Pavia and Siena and founded Lincoln College, Oxford.

Fletcher, John William (1729–1785)
An Anglican vicar who was an early supporter of the Methodist movement and renowned for his sanctity and his devoted pastoral work.

Forbes, Alexander Penrose (1817–1875)
While studying at Oxford he came under the influence of the Tractarians. He was first a vicar in Leeds, Yorkshire, then bishop of Brechin, where he worked to spread the Oxford Movement in Scotland.

Forbes, George Hay (1821–1875)
Brother of Alexander and also a High Churchman who proved to be, despite severe paralysis, a noted liturgist, patristic scholar and model priest of the Episcopalian church of Scotland.

Forsyth, Peter Taylor (1848–1921)
Scottish Congregationalist theologian whose early liberal thinking developed to a position of great originality, and interpreted the faith of the Reformation in modern terms. He was also an experienced pastor, serving in five pastorates. His seminal works were many, the most famous being *The Person and Place of Jesus Christ* (1909).

Fosdick, Harry Emerson (1878–1969)
American Baptist minister and writer who for some years (1918-1925) served as a Presbyterian preacher. From 1926

to 1946 he was the Baptist minister at Riverside Church, New York. His many books reflect a liberal-evangelical view of theology.

Foucauld, Charles Eugène de (1858–1916)

As a French calvary officer in Algeria, de Foucauld led a dissolute life, but on leaving the army undertook a dangerous expedition exploring Morocco. He was led back to the Catholic faith by the Abbé Huvelin and sought a life of austerity and solitude, first in the Trappist order, then in the Holy Land and finally at the oasis of Tamanrasset in the Sahara. His life of prayer was augmented with work in the Tuareg language, composing dictionaries, translations, etc. By the time of his assassination, despite much effort, he had failed to convert anyone. However, today, thousands of priests and religious brothers and sisters (the 'Little Brothers' and 'Little Sisters') live de Foucauld's rules of life, inspired by his writings and example.

Fox, George (1624–1691)

Born in Leicestershire, where his father was a weaver, at nineteen Fox left home and lived a wanderer's life for three years. In 1645, after long spiritual battles, he found the 'inner light' of the living Christ and experienced a lifelong call to bring people 'off' from false religion and the world. His preaching led to continual periods in prison, but his sincerity and enthusiasm attracted followers and in 1652 the Society of Friends (Quakers) was born. For the rest of his life Fox traveled widely, e.g., the West Indies, North America, Germany, Holland, appealing wherever he went to 'that of God in every man'. His *Journal,* a survey of his life, which conveys his magnetic personality, was dictated in 1675 and published after his death.

Foxe, John (1516–1587)

At Oxford, as student and fellow, he promoted the Reformation in England but fled the country on Queen Mary's accession. Abroad he continued his history of persecutions and martyrdom which when published came to be known as *Foxe's Book of Martyrs*. This monumental work, extolling the heroism of the Protestant martyrs, went through several editions in his lifetime. It was marred as an objective historical work by the bitterness of the time and the uncritical use of some sources.

Francis of Assisi, St (1181–1226)

Born Giovanni Francesco Bernardone, son of a rich cloth merchant of Assisi, Francis was a normal high-spirited rich young man of his time. After a serious illness and a conversion experience he devoted himself to the service of the poor. His close identification with them led to rejection by his father, at which Francis turned to the service of lepers and the repair of the church of San Damiano and then the church of the Portiuncula, near Assisi. Here he heard Matthew 10:7–19 as a personal call to follow literally Christ's way of renunciation. His preaching and example attracted followers, for whom he composed a rule of life. In 1212 he helped St Clare found a similar order for women. While Francis was on preaching tours to Spain, Eastern Europe and Egypt the Franciscan order grew rapidly, was structured, and then Francis left the leadership to others. While on Mt Alvernia, in 1224, he received the gift of the Stigmata, which he kept carefully hidden until his death. Francis's passionate love of God, his fellow man and nature have justly made him one of the most popular saints of modern times. His spirit is perfectly captured in his writings, for example in *The Canticle of the Sun*.

Francis of Paola, St (1416–1507)

A hermit whose early life was formed by contact with the Franciscans. About 1436, with companions, he founded the order of the Hermits of St Francis of Assisi (later known as Ordo Minimorum or Minims). Renowned for his holiness, he was sought by kings for spiritual guidance and many miracles were attributed to him. He was canonised in 1519.

Francis of Sales, St (1567–1622)

Bishop of Geneva and renowned spiritual counselor and writer who refuted the error of his time that spiritual perfection was not possible for ordinary secular Christians. He was one of the leaders of the Counter-Reformation, converting the Chablais from Calvinism to Catholicism. In 1610, with Jane Frances de Chantal, he founded the Visitandine sisters. His most famous spiritual books are *The Introduction to the Devout Life* and *Treatise on the Love of God.*

Frelinghuysen, Theodorus Jacobus (1692–1748)

Evangelist and leader of the Dutch Reformed churches in New Jersey. After pastoral work in Holland he sailed for America and ministered to the Dutch congregations in the New Brunswick area for thirty years. His evangelistic zeal and strict church discipline caused division, which was later healed. He is best remembered for his promotion of the First Great Awakening.

French, Thomas Valpry (1825–1891)

Anglican missionary sent by the Church Missionary Society to Agra, India. A good scholar and preacher, he was appointed the first Anglican bishop of Lahore in 1877. Although saintly, he was not an able administrator and resigned his see in 1887. Always of uncertain health, he died as a result of a missionary enterprise of his own to Arabia.

Friedrich, Johannes (1836–1917)

German church historian who opposed the definition of papal infallibility at the First Vatican Council; his refusal to acknowledge its decrees led to his excommunication. The Bavarian government gave him protection and for a while he was one of the leaders of the Old Catholic Movement in Germany.

Froude, Richard Hurrell (1803–1836)
Educated at Eton and Oxford where, as a tutor, he came under the influence of J.H. Newman. While health permitted, he worked with Newman and Keble in founding the Tractarian Movement. His posthumous writings, *Remains* (1838 and 1839), caused a sensation in the revelation of his own spiritual practices and his attack upon Reformed doctrines.

Fry, Elizabeth (1780–1845)
The daughter of a banker, Elizabeth was born of a Quaker family and in 1800 she married a strict Quaker. Eleven years later, while mother of a large family, she became a 'minister' of the Society of Friends. She devoted herself to the welfare of female prisoners at Newgate, but her prison work in earnest did not begin until 1817. The association she founded improved the lot of female prisoners in particular, and her energetic endeavours and travels bore fruit not only in Great Britain and Ireland, but throughout Europe.

Fuller, Andrew (1754–1815)
English Baptist theologian and minister who cooperated with John Ryland and John Sutcliff in assisting William Carey in the foundation and support of the Baptist Missionary Society, of which Fuller was the first secretary.

Fuller, Thomas (1608–1661)
Anglican scholar, writer and preacher who held various pastoral appointments but is remembered for his historical accounts of the period, particularly *Worthies of Britain* and *Church History of Britain* and his prolific, witty writing.

G

Gabriel Severus (1541–1616)
Greek Orthodox metropolitan and one of the most learned
Eastern theologians of the sixteenth and seventeenth centuries
who disputed with Catholic and Protestant theologians.

Gairdner, William Henry (1873–1928)
Anglican missionary of the Church Missionary Society who
went to Cairo in 1898 and studied Arabic and Islam. He
reorganised the Arabic Anglican church and pioneered Christian literature in Arabic.

Galen, Clemens August Graf von (1878–1946)
German Roman Catholic bishop and cardinal who offered the
most effective resistance, among German Catholic bishops, to
Nazism. From one of the oldest German noble families and
conservative in outlook, Galen opposed the Nazis from the
moment he became a bishop in 1933. He placed his life at risk
by his open opposition in several major incidents, but survived
to be made a cardinal a month before he died in 1946.

Gall, St (c. 550–645)
Irish missionary and companion of St Columbanus, who remained to convert Swabia (now Switzerland) when the latter
traveled to Italy.

Gallaudet, Thomas Hopkins (1787–1851)

Philanthropist, educator and founder of the first school for the deaf in the United States. After studying theology, Gallaudet studied methods for educating the deaf, in Europe. With Congressional support (1816) he founded the American Asylum for Deaf-Mutes, Hartford, Connecticut. He wrote textbooks for children and the deaf, but he is best remembered for his seminal *Plan of a Seminary for the Education of Instructors of Youth* (1825) and the changes in education that it prompted.

Gardiner, Stephen (c. 1490–1555)

Master of Trinity Hall, Cambridge, Gardiner was used by Henry VIII in the business of the annulment from Catherine of Aragon. In 1531 he became bishop of Winchester and opposed the Reformation doctrines. Imprisoned under Edward VI, he was restored to his see and became chancellor under Mary Tudor.

Garnet, Henry (1555–1606)

English Jesuit and superior of the English Mission in 1587. He became implicated in the prior knowledge of the Gunpowder Plot, which he may have received through the confessional. Arrested some months after the plot, he was executed for not revealing his knowledge of it.

Gasquet, Francis Aidan (1846–1929)

Monk of the Benedictine order, he became prior of Downside in 1878, where he enlarged the priory and the school. He worked on Roman commissions and was created cardinal in 1914. In 1919 he became Vatican librarian; his seminal books on medieval monasticism were influential, particularly *Henry VIII and the Monasteries*.

Geiler von Kaisersberg, Johann (1445–1510)

An exceptionally forceful preacher who began his career as a scholar and lecturer at Freibourg University. Personally retiring and acknowledged as a mystic, he became known as the German Savanarola, for from his pulpit in Strasbourg Cathedral he denounced the evils of the day and won a wide acclaim.

Gelasius—The name of two popes, the better known being:

Gelasius I, St (d. 496)
He devoted most of his energies to combating the Acacian heresy and asserting the primacy of the Roman see over that of Constantinople. The *Gelasian Sacramentary* has been wrongly attributed to him.

Gentili, Luigi (1801–1848)
Abandoning Roman social life, Gentili joined Antonio Rosmini-Serbati and his new Institute of Charity (Rosminians). In 1835, in England, he helped organise a new Roman Catholic college at Prior Park, Bath; there followed years of fruitful missionary work, particularly among Irish immigrants in the new industrial cities. He died of cholera caught while preaching in a Dublin slum. He is credited with founding the Rosminian order in England, and popularising devotions like the Stations of the Cross and the Forty Hours Devotion.

George, St
Patron saint of England who appears to have been an early martyr in the East, perhaps at Lydda, Palestine. Nothing for certain is known of his life, although his existence is generally accepted. Legends about him as a warrior saint became popular in about the sixth century, although the story of him rescuing a maiden from a dragon first appeared six centuries later. His popularity in England dates from the eighth century and returning crusaders popularised his cult.

Gerald, John (1564–1637)

English Jesuit missionary, trained in Rome, who from 1588 worked secretly in Norfolk, Suffolk and Essex. He was very successful, founding mass centres and making converts. In 1594 he was captured and imprisoned in the Tower of London for three years. In 1597 he escaped from the Tower (being the only prisoner in history to do so) and continued his missionary work. He returned to Europe and in 1607 wrote a vivid account of a life in hiding in Elizabethan England.

Gerhard, Johann (1582–1637)

German Lutheran theologian and highly regarded biblical and patristic scholar. Profoundly influenced in his early years by the Lutheran mystic Johann Arndt. His nine-volume *Loci theologici* (1610–1622) was the most important and influential Lutheran work of theology of the era.

Germanus, St (c. 378–448)

Elected bishop of Auxerre in 418, he visited Britain and fought Pelagianism; on a second visit he successfully led an army against the invading Picts and Saxons.

Germanus, St (496–576)

Patriarch of Constantinople. From the role of a humble cleric at the great church of Santa Sophia, he rose to become the patriarch. In this role he worked to refute monothelitism and became a key figure in the fight against iconoclasm. Only a few of his many writings survive, and in them he shows himself to be an ardent supporter of devotion to Mary, the mother of Jesus.

Gerson, Jean Le Charlier de (1363–1429)

French theologian, preacher and spiritual writer who had such a remarkable influence upon the church of the fifteenth century that he was given the title 'Doctor Christianissimus'. Gerson's life was devoted to the reform of the church from within;

his biggest success being personally responsible for the resolution of the Great Schism, when there were, at one time, three competing popes. He asserted the superiority of a general council of the church over an individual pope, and wrote of this in *De Unitate Ecclesiae* and *De Potestate Ecclesiae.* Gerson was influenced by nominalism in his theology, and his own mystical thought and writing, e.g., *The Mountain of Contemplation,* deeply influenced many later important spiritual writers.

Gertrude the Great, St (1256–1302) (to be distinguished from the Belgian abbess [626–659] of the same name)
Entrusted to the Benedictine convent of Helfta, Thuringia, at an early age, she remained there for the rest of her life; a conversion experience at twenty-five led her to a life of contemplation. Her book *Legatus Divinae Pietatis* was considered a spiritual classic. She is considered to be one of the first exponents of devotion to the Sacred Heart of Jesus, which she believed was revealed to her in the visions she experienced.

Ghéon, Henri (1874–1944) (writing name of Henri Leon Vangeon)
French Catholic playwright, biographer and writer whose modern, medieval-style mystery plays portrayed the lives of the saints. His many biographies of modern saints, e.g., Curé d'Ars, reached an international readership.

Gibbons, James (1834–1921)
Roman Catholic archbishop of Baltimore and second United States cardinal. Ordained in 1861, he served as a volunteer chaplain during the Civil War; consecrated bishop (1868) he attended the First Vatican Council. Widely and highly respected as archbishop of Baltimore from 1877, he became cardinal in 1886 and three years later the first chancellor of the Catholic University of America, Washington, D.C. He is especially remembered for his simple presentation of the Catholic faith in *The Faith of Our Fathers* (1876).

Gilbert of Sempringham, St (c. 1083–1189)

Parish priest of Sempringham, Lincolnshire, who founded the only English medieval religious order of sisters and brothers. The Gilbertines lived by an Augustinian rule and were distinctive in having double communities of men and women. At Gilbert's death there were nine of these communities in England.

Gillespie, George (1613–1648)

Leader of the Church of Scotland who negotiated with the Church of England for the freedom of his church to differ from the Anglican form of worship (1640). He drafted the church legislation sanctioning the Presbyterian form of worship (1645).

Gill, Eric (1882–1940)

English sculptor, engraver and essayist whose deep religious commitment, after his conversion to Roman Catholicism in 1913, was expressed through membership of the Third Order of St Dominic and his many works in lettering and stone—the most famous being the Stations of the Cross in Westminster Cathedral and the bas-reliefs of 'The Re-creation of Adam' in the council hall of the Palace of Nations at Geneva.

Gilpin, Bernard (1517–1583)

Gilpin was one of the most broad-minded upholders of the Elizabethan Church Settlement, refusing to espouse Calvinism outright or accept the decrees of the Council of Trent. He declined several posts of responsibility in favour of pastoral work, for which he was highly esteemed, and was often called 'the Apostle of the North' on account of his long missionary journeys in the north of England.

Gilson, Etienne (1884–1978)

French writer and lecturer in Thomist philosophy. His prolific writings on scholastics and scholasticism helped to introduce twentieth-century writers and thinkers to such medieval personages as St Bernard of Clairvaux, St Bonaventure, Duns Scotus, etc.

Gladden, Washington (1836–1918)

Congregational minister and a leader of the Social Gospel movement. With a journalist background, Gladden held pastorates at Springfield, Massachusetts (1875–1882) and Columbus (1882-1918). He worked to apply 'Christian Law' to social problems and is credited with being the first United States clergyman to support the development of trade unions. He is famed for his promotion of a simple practical gospel, well expressed in over 30 books, including *Applied Christianity* (1887) and *Social Salvation* (1901).

Gladstone, William Ewart (1809–1898)

One of the greatest Christian statesmen of the nineteenth century, four times prime minister of Great Britain (1868–1874; 1880–1885; 1886; 1892–1894). His evangelical upbringing was blended with the influence of the Oxford Movement and Gladstone first defended the establishment of the Church of England in *The State in its Relations with the Church* (1838)—a view he later reversed in *Chapter of Autobiography*—and its High Church doctrine in *Church Principles Considered in their Results* (1840). A strict moralist, Gladstone sought to apply his Christian principles to the conduct of domestic and foreign affairs.

Gomar, Francis (1563–1641)

Dutch Calvinist leader and professor of theology at Leyden, remembered for his rigid Calvinistic principles, which were evident in his bitter opposition to Arminius and all who followed him.

Goodrich, Thomas (1480–1554)

Bishop of Ely, biblical translator and supporter of Henry VIII's reforms of the English church, assisting the king in his matrimonial problems. Goodrich later conformed to Roman Catholicism under Mary Stuart.

Gordon, Charles George (1833–1885)

British general who was hailed as a national hero for his exploits in China, and as a result earned the title 'Chinese Gordon'. He developed his own mystical brand of Christianity and after the fall of Khartoum, Sudan, where he was governor and died at the hands of the rebels, the British public acclaimed him as a martyred warrior-saint.

Gore, Charles (1853–1932)

Anglican theologian, bishop and leader of the liberal school of thought in the Anglo-Catholic movement. Educated at Oxford he was the first principal of Pusey House, Oxford, and after the bishoprics of Worcester and Birmingham, he was translated, in 1911, to Oxford. Concerned with the foundation of the Community of the Resurrection, he served as its first superior (1892–1901). While he was widely known as a preacher and exegete, it was as a liberal theologian that he made his mark and his prolific works profoundly influenced the course of Anglican theology.

Goretti, Maria, St (1890–1902)

The twelve-year-old daughter of an Italian farmworker, she was stabbed to death by Alexander Serenelli, son of her father's partner, while resisting his attempts to seduce her. Pope Pius XII held her up as a model of modesty and purity and canonised her in 1950.

Gottschalk of Orbais (c. 803–c. 869)

Theologian, poet and monk of heterodox views who promoted an extreme form of predestination. Entered, by his parents, as a child into monastic life, he sought to leave in his twenties and the rest of his life was overshadowed by his failure to do so. His teachings were opposed by Rabanus Maurus and Hincmar and condemned by a succession of synods.

Grabmann, Martin (1875–1949)
German historian of medieval theology and philosophy; professor of Christian philosophy, first at Vienna (1913–1918) and subsequently at Munich. He was the first to show the development, extent and importance of scholasticism. His seminal writings stimulated later Thomist scholars like E. Gilson.

Grafton, Richard (c. 1513–1573)
London merchant who was an energetic supporter of the Reformation, but remembered as the printer of *Matthew's Bible* (1537) and the *Great Bible* (1539), also the first (1549) and second (1552) *Book of Common Prayer*. He suffered imprisonment and lost his title of 'King's Printer' under Queen Mary.

Gratian (uncertain dates, d. before 1159)
Little is known of his life. A Camaldolese monk, he lectured at Bologna and compiled what came to be known as *Decretum Gratiani*. This collection of nearly 3,800 texts touching all areas of church discipline became the textbook for the study of canon law for centuries. It became an important source for the Roman Catholic *Code of Canon Law* of 1917.

Gray, Robert (1809–1872)
First bishop (1847) and metropolitan archbishop (1853) of Cape Town (South Africa). The Colenso affair, commencing in 1863, when he excommunicated the liberal bishop John Colenso of Natal, brought him to the notice of the world. During his episcopacy he promoted the independence of the South African church, adding five sees.

Grebel, Konrad (1498–1526)

Principal founder of the Swiss Brethren, an Anabaptist movement which opposed the work of the Swiss Reformer Zwingli. The dispute centred upon adult baptism and in January 1525 Grebel performed the first adult baptism in modern history. This, and subsequent disobedience to civil authorities, produced harassment which pursued him to his death.

Gregory—There are sixteen popes of this name, those of interest being:

Gregory I, St (c. 540–604)

Often called 'Gregory the Great', he was one of the most influential of all the popes, receiving the title 'Doctor of the Church' in the eighth century. Of a Roman noble family, Gregory sold his vast property to help the poor and founded seven monasteries, becoming a monk in the Roman foundation. Later, while abbot, he passed, at the sight of British slaves in Rome, his much-quoted remark: 'Non Angli, sed angeli'. As pope he centralised administration, reformed the church and established its political independence in turbulent times. He sent St Augustine, with forty monks from his monastery, to convert England and began to call himself 'the servant of the servants of God', now a recognised papal title. His enthusiasm for the reform of the liturgy resulted in his name being given to church music, plainsong or Gregorian Chant. As an author his practical pastoral guide for bishops *Liber Regulae Pastoralis* (c. 591) became the manual for the medieval episcopate. His sermons and letters have proved of lasting importance and value.

Gregory VII, St (c. 1020–1085) (known as Hildebrand)

After a monastic education he was chosen by Pope Gregory VI as his chaplain; he then followed nearly thirty years of service to successive popes, being elected himself by popular acclaim on 30 June 1073. Gregory worked energetically for the reform and moral revival of the church. His desire to rid the church of secular interference and manipulation led to the condemnation of lay investiture and a long-drawn-out battle with European princes, particularly the emperor Henry IV, to enforce it.

Gregory of Nazianzus, St (329–389)

Son of the bishop of Nazianzus (also Gregory), he studied at Athens with Basil (St) and afterwards adopted a monastic way of life. After two years he returned to Nazianzus to help his father, reluctantly accepting orders and, in 372, consecration as bishop. He supported Basil's fight against Arianism and, after his death in 379, became leader of the orthodox party. His eloquent preaching at Constantinople restored the Nicene faith. He took a prominent part in the Council of Constantinople which assured victory for orthodoxy. Intrigues forced him to resign the see of Constantinople and retire to Nazianzus. His most famous theological works are his *Five Theological Orations* and his *De Vita Sua*. He is known as one of the Cappadocian Fathers.

Gregory of Nyssa, St (c. 330–395)

Brother of St Basil, who influenced the direction of his life; Gregory was well grounded in philosophy but entered the monastic life. Gregory of Nazianzus enlisted his help in the fight against Arianism; he was ordained priest, then bishop of Nyssa. A thinker of originality and a preacher of power and influence, he was a champion of orthodoxy and suffered considerable persecution for the Nicene cause. Gregory wrote numerous theological treatises, his greatest being his *Catechetical Discourse,* an exposition of the doctrines of the Trinity, incarnation and redemption, also the sacraments of baptism and the Eucharist. His reputation was such that the Second Council of Nicaea (680–681) hailed him as 'Father of the Fathers'.

Gregory Thaumaturgus, St (c. 213–270)

A disciple of Origen, who converted him to Christianity. His name 'Thaumaturgus' ('Wonderworker') originates from the legends of the wonders which accompanied his preaching and pastoral work as bishop of Neocaesarea. He guided his flock through the persecution of Decius and the invasion of the Goths (252–254). He wrote and preached against the heresies of Sabellianism and tritheism. He is credited, by Gregory of Nyssa, with the first recorded vision of the Virgin Mary. He has always been honoured as a father of the church by the Greek Orthodox church.

Grenfell, Sir Wilfred (1865–1940)

Medical missionary to Labrador who trained at the University of London and, influenced by Dwight L. Moody, initiated in 1892 a missionary service to the fishermen of Labrador. His autobiography *Forty Years for Labrador* (1932) tells of his dedicated desire to improve living conditions and the network of medical services he left on retirement.

Griesbach, Johann Jakob (1745–1812)

Rationalist Protestant theologian and New Testament scholar who was the first to make a systematic application of literary analysis to the Gospels. He originated the term 'Synoptic' to designate the first three Gospels and maintained that Mark was the latest of the three (the dependence theory). He also published a corrected Greek edition of the New Testament.

Grignion de Montfort, Louis Marie, St (1673–1716)

From early life he was dedicated to poverty and prayer and was ordained a priest in 1700. He founded two congregations of religious, to care for the sick and to preach missions. His own missionary preaching throughout Brittany brought persecution from the Jansenists. His *True Devotion to the Blessed Virgin Mary* (later, from 1842, to have a devotional impact upon the Roman Catholic church) and his popular preaching were tremendously successful, although critics charged him with emotionalism. He was canonised in 1947.

Groote, Gaert de (1340–1384) (also Gerardus Magnus)
Brilliant and rich teacher who renounced his life of luxury in 1374 and, under the influence of the mystic Jan van Ruysbroeck, became an outspoken missionary preaching against the laxity of the clergy. He drew around him followers who became the 'Brethren of the Common Life'. He was the father of 'Devotio Moderna' (the 'modern devotion'), which sought to root the spiritual life in daily life, favouring meditation rather than ritual. Groote's work contributed to the reform of the church and had a long-lasting impact upon the direction of spirituality.

Grosseteste, Robert (c. 1175–1253)
Little is known of his early life; at Oxford he was the most influential teacher of his time and chancellor of the university. After many clerical appointments he accepted the see of Lincoln (then the largest in England) in 1235 and proved a dynamic and demanding pastoral bishop. He fought against the practice of appointing clerics to sinecure pastoral posts for which they exhibited no care. As a scholar he was the most famous Englishman of his time, excelling at mathematics, astronomy and science. He made available in Latin philosophical works of Greek and Arab origin. His writings included commentaries on several of the biblical books.

Grou, Jean Nicholas (1731–1803)
French Jesuit professor at the Jesuit college of La Flèche who fled to England at the French Revolution and settled at Lulworth, Dorset. 'Père Grou' wrote on Plato and the Jesuit order but is best remembered for his acclaimed spiritual writings, e.g., *Meditations on the Love of God* and *Manual for Interior Souls*.

Grundtvig, Nikolai Fredrik Severin (1783–1872)
Danish preacher and poet, founder of a theological movement that revitalised the Danish church; he later accepted the title of bishop.

Guardini, Romano (1885–1968)
Italian-born German theologian of the Roman Catholic church whose influential writings advocated a return to personal asceticism as the way to genuine human freedom.

Guéranger, Prosper-Louis-Pascal (1805–1875)
French Benedictine monk who re-established the Benedictine order in France at the Abbey of Solesmes, which he made world-famous as the centre of a revival of interest in the Gregorian chant and the pioneer centre of the modern liturgical movement. Voluminous writer, his works on the liturgy, e.g., *Institutions Liturgiques* and *L'Anneé Liturgique,* were seminal for all subsequent liturgical study.

Gunkel, Hermann (1862–1932)
German Protestant theologian and Old Testament scholar who was one of the first to develop the method of form criticism.

Guthrie, Thomas (1803–1873)
Scottish Presbyterian minister with remarkable pastoral gifts; he supported the Free Church at 'the Disruption' (1843) by raising considerable funds. After 1847 his energies were devoted to his famous 'Ragged Schools' for the poor.

Guyon, Madame (Jeanne-Marie de la Mothe) (1648–1717)
From a neurotic youth and an early unhappy marriage, she progressed, as a result of her mystical teaching (heavily influenced by the works of Molinos), to be the central figure in a seventeenth-century French religious controversy. Her Quiet-

ism (total passivity and indifference of the soul, even to eternal salvation) was attacked by Bossuet and defended by Fenélon. Bossuet's charges of heresy were upheld by the Conference of Issy (1695) but this was not totally free of court/political intrigue. Madame Guyon's personal sincerity never seems to have been in doubt. Her chief mystical writings include *Moyen court et très facile de faire oraison* (1685) and *Le Cantique des Cantiques* (1688).

Gwyn, Richard, St (1537–1584)
After studying at both Oxford and Cambridge, Richard opened a school at Overton, Flintshire. Married with six children, he became a Roman Catholic and in 1579 was arrested for this. He escaped, but after recapture and torture was hanged, drawn and quartered at Wrexham in 1584, becoming the first Welshman to die for the Catholic faith under Elizabeth I. He was canonised by his church in 1970.

H

Halifax, Charles Lindley Wood (1839–1934)

Second Viscount Halifax, educated at Eton and Oxford, where he joined the High Church movement. He was associated with the foundation of the Cowley Fathers and, as president of the English church Union, he was involved with the many and varied ecclesiastical controversies of his time. His lively interest in reunion between the Church of England and the Roman Catholic church led to fruitless conversations at Rome (1894–1896) and the publication of his *Leo XIII and Anglican Orders* (1912). He arranged the Malines Conversations with Cardinal Mercier, but these ceased at Mercier's death; the documents relating to Malines he also published.

Hall, Joseph (1574–1656)

Bishop of Norwich, moral philosopher and English satirist of high repute who defended the episcopacy when it was attacked by Parliament, although he had been suspected by W. Laud of Puritan sympathies. Imprisoned in the Tower of London with the other bishops, on release he lived and died in poverty. One of his many works, *Heaven upon Earth,* was reprinted by John Wesley.

Hall, Robert (1764–1831)

English Baptist preacher and social reformer who was famous for his commanding oratory and defence of workers' rights, particularly the Leicestershire lace workers.

Haller, Berchtold (1492–1531)
Swiss schoolmaster and canon of Berne Cathedral who, influenced by Zwingli, became the leader of the Reform movement in Berne. He helped to develop a Protestant liturgy.

Hamilton, John (1511–1571)
Archbishop of St Andrews who vehemently opposed the spread of Protestantism in Scotland. He led a number of reforming synods which gave rise to the *Archbishop Hamilton's Catechism* (1552). After imprisonment for saying mass, he acted as adviser to Mary Queen of Scots but, after her fight, he was hanged at Stirling.

Hamilton, Patrick (c. 1504–1528)
While only thirteen years of age he was made abbot of Fern. Study in Paris introduced him to the writings of Luther, whom he later met. In 1527 he returned to Scotland where he was formally charged with heresy and burnt at the stake.

Hannington, James (1847–1885)
First Anglican bishop of East Equatorial Africa (1884) where he was sent by the Church Missionary Society. While leading a perilous expedition the next year he was murdered by natives of Uganda.

Harnack, Adolf (1851–1930)
After his doctorate, Harnack lectured at several German universities—Leipzig, Geissen, Marburg and Berlin. Historian, theologian and the most outstanding scholar of his time on the early church fathers, he is more commonly remembered for his contributions to the study of the Synoptic problem and New Testament studies. He wrote copiously on all the scholarly areas that interested him.

Hastings, James (1852–1922)

Presbyterian theologian and editor of several religious dictionaries and an encyclopaedia. In 1889 he founded *The Expository Times,* of which he was editor until his death.

Havergal, Frances Ridley (1836–1879)

Daughter of William Havergal, composer of sacred music, and a popular Victorian hymnwriter, her 'Take My Life and Let It Be' being still popular.

Headlam, Arthur Cayley (1862–1947)

Bishop of Gloucester and biblical scholar who disliked ecclesiastical parties in the Church of England and attempted to mediate between them. One of the most influential bishops of his time, he collaborated on the important International Critical Commentary on *Romans* and worked for church unity, particularly with his book *The Doctrine of the Church and Christian Reunion* (1920).

Heber, Reginald (1783–1826)

Ordained an Anglican priest in 1807, he dedicated his last years to the spread of Christianity as bishop of Calcutta. He was a hymnwriter of note; many of his hymns are still popular.

Hecker, Isaac Thomas (1819–1888)

Although of United States origin, he was ordained a Redemptorist priest in England (1849); he conducted missions with associates in America, where he later founded the Paulist Fathers, now a worldwide organisation, to work under local bishops. He also founded the Catholic Publications Society and two Catholic magazines.

Hegesippus (d. c. 180)

Jewish convert to Christianity who, after twenty years in Rome and visiting most of the important centres of Christianity, wrote the history of the first 150 years of the church; hence considered the father of church history.

Heiler, Friedrich (1892–1967)
German religious writer and scholar in the history of religion. Influenced by N. Söderblom, he converted from Catholicism to Protestantism, and later organised the German High Church movement and introduced an evangelical form of monasticism. His most important, long-lasting book was an analysis of prayer, *Das Gebet* (1918).

Helena, St (Helen) (c. 248–c. 328)
Wife of the emperor Constantius Chlorus; their son Constantine became emperor in 306, and due to his influence Helena became a Christian. In 326 she paid a visit to the Holy Land and founded basilicas on the Mount of Olives and at Bethlehem; according to a later tradition she at this time discovered the cross on which Christ had died.

Helwys, Thomas (c. 1550–c. 1616)
English Puritan leader who emigrated to Amsterdam and with J. Smith founded the first Baptist church there. Returning to London he founded the first General Baptist congregation in England. He was imprisoned for advocating religious tolerance.

Henderson, Alexander (c. 1583–1646)
Second only to John Knox as leader in the reformed Church of Scotland, he emerged from an Episcopalian background as a strong Presbyterian leader, particularly over resistance to the Prayer Book of 1637. He clashed with Charles I and with his draft of the Solemn League and Covenant of 1643, which contributed to the king's defeat. He was the author of numerous tracts, one of the most famous being *The Bishops' Doom* (1638).

Henry of Ghent (c. 1217–1293)

Scholastic philosopher and theologian, considered one of the most illustrious teachers of his time (accorded the title 'Doctor Solemnis'). He supported Augustinianism against St Thomas Aquinas and, as a secular priest, fought against the privileges of the mendicant orders. His theological teaching is extensively represented in his *Quodlibeta* and his unfinished *Summa Theologica*.

Henry Suso (c. 1295–1366)

German Dominican and one of the principal German mystics; he studied under Eckhart (1322–1325), for whom he retained a great admiration. Suso's spirituality shines through his *Little Book of Truth* (1327) and his masterpiece *Little Book of Eternal Wisdom* (1328). For defending Eckhart he lost his professorship but continued as a successful preacher and spiritual director. He died at Ulm after much persecution and slander. One of the most attractive and easiest to understand of the Rhineland mystics, his works were highly influential through the fourteenth and fifteenth centuries and admired by writers like Thomas à Kempis.

Henson, Herbert Hensley (1863–1947)

Anglican theologian and bishop of Durham who, through his many writings, tried to modernise Christian doctrine and proved to be a controversial figure. He was a strong establishment figure until Parliament rejected the Prayer Book revisions (1927–1928), when he became convinced that establishment was incompatible with the church's freedom.

Herbert, George (1593–1633)

Devotional poet and Anglican priest whose early life, with its classical training, pointed towards a public life; however, he studied theology and was ordained in 1630 and devoted the last years of his life to the pastoral duties of a country vicar at Bemerton. His fame rests upon his exceptional poetic gifts, since he was one of the first and finest of the Church of England's devotional poets. His prose work, *A Priest of the Temple,* presented the model of a pastoral priest; some of his poems are still in daily use as hymns.

Hermas (second century)
Author of *The Shepherd* (probably written 140–155), which was highly regarded by the Eastern church for its early teaching on, among other things, the need for repentance. Little is known of the life of Hermas, although accorded the title of 'Apostolic Father'. He appears to have been a freed slave-turned-merchant who repented of evil practices after a series of visions.

Herzog, Johann Jakob (1805–1882)
German Protestant theologian and church historian, pupil of Schleiermacher and Neander, who was responsible for much original research and edited a twenty-two volume reference work; the English abridged version, *The New Schaff-Herzog Encyclopaedia of Religious Knowledge,* appeared 1951–1954.

Hesychius of Jerusalem (d. c. 450)
A Greek monk renowned in the Eastern Orthodox church as a theologian, but particularly as a biblical commentator and preacher. Most of his writings, including a history of the church, have been lost, but he is said to have commented on the whole Bible and was highly regarded by his contemporaries.

Hilary of Poitiers, St (c. 315–367)
A convert from Neoplatonism, he was elected bishop of Poitiers and spent the rest of his life as a champion of orthodoxy against Arianism. Hilary was the most respected theologian of his time and was hailed as the 'Athanasius of the West'; he was declared a doctor of the church in 1851. Hilary's principal works were *De Trinitate* and *De Synodis.*

Hilda, St (614—680)

Of the Northumbrian noble lines, she was baptised by St Paulinus; after years as a noblewoman, at thirty-three she joined a convent and in 657 founded a double monastery for men and women at Whitby, becoming one of the foremost abbesses of Anglo-Saxon times; her abbey was renowned as one of the great religious and cultural centres of England.

Hildegard (1098—1179)

German abbess and mystic who experienced visions from an early age; known as the 'Sybil of the Rhine' for her powers of prophecy; from her convent at Rupertsberg she exerted a wide influence, even upon the emperor Barbarossa, kings and prelates. Her work *Scivias* (between 1141 and 1151) tells of twenty-six of her visions, but there were other theological and scientific writings. Long venerated as a saint, she was never formally declared such.

Hilton, Walter (d. 1396)

Devotional writer, of whose life little is known, who is considered one of the greatest English mystics of the fourteenth century. Hilton is thought to have studied at Cambridge and, after a period as a hermit, joined the Augustinian canons at Thurgarton Priory, Nottinghamshire. His spiritual writings exerted a great influence during the fifteenth century, and his most famous work, *The Scale of Perfection,* is still highly regarded.

Hincmar of Rheims (c. 806—882)

Archbishop, theologian and the most influential churchman of the Carolingian period. He defended the French church's independence against papal claims and defended the orthodox view of divine predestination in a controversy with Gottschalk.

Hippolytus, St (c. 170–236)

A controversial Roman priest and theologian who allowed himself to be elected as an antipope for a time, but was later reconciled with the papacy. He suffered and died during the persecution of the emperor Maximinus. His principal works were *A Refutation of All Heresies* and *The Apostolic Tradition*.

Hobart, John Henry (1775–1830)

American bishop of the Protestant Episcopal church whose emphasis upon 'evangelical truth and apostolic order' during the post-Revolutionary period of American history helped Anglicanism to expand in the new nation. A famed preacher, to promote a proper view of the church he wrote many manuals and founded the 'Protestant Episcopal Tract Society' in 1810, having founded what was to become the General Theological Seminary of New York in 1806.

Hodge, Charles (1797–1878)

Leading American Presbyterian theologian who spent most of his life lecturing in biblical studies at Princeton. Conservative in outlook, he resisted newer trends in his support of traditional Calvinism; his *Systematic Theology* was influential in this, and his New Testament commentaries stressed the verbal infallibility of the Bible.

Hofbauer, St Clement Mary (1751–1820)

Patron saint of Vienna. Ordained a priest of the Redemptorist congregation in 1785, he was authorised to establish Redemptorist houses throughout northern Europe. Centred for twenty years in Warsaw, he had considerable success. Driven from Warsaw by Napoleon, he settled in Vienna where he exerted a powerful pastoral influence. He was canonised in 1909.

Honorius—There were four popes of this name; of most interest is:

Honorius I (d. 638)
Modeling himself on Pope St Gregory the Great, Honorius gave great support to the Christianisation of the Anglo-Saxons, inducing the Celts to accept the Roman liturgy and date of Easter. The crux of his pontificate was his role in the Byzantine church's controversy over Monophysitism; about 634, replying to a letter from Sergius, patriarch of Constantinople, Honorius appears to give some support to the theory of 'one will' in Christ. He was posthumously condemned for his reply, but modern scholars debate his real understanding of the matter.

Hontheim, Johann Nikolaus von (1701–1790)
Roman Catholic auxiliary bishop of Trier, West Germany, theologian and historian who, concerned for Christian unity and the extent of papal power, wrote under the pseudonym of Justinus Febronius, proposing ideas which became known as Febronianism. His book *De Statu* and his theories were condemned by Rome in 1764; Hontheim later retracted in 1781.

Hooker, Richard (1554–1600)
Scholar and then fellow of Corpus Christi College, Oxford, after ordination to the Anglican ministry he served as rector in several places, finally at Bishopsbourne, near Canterbury. A theologian and an apologist of note, he successfully developed and defended Anglican theology against both the Roman Catholics and the Puritans. His book *A Treatise on the Laws of Ecclesiastical Polity* presents his theological thought that the Church of England is a threefold cord consisting of Bible, church and reason.

Hooker, Thomas (1586–1647)

Puritan minister who introduced innovations in his Chelmsford, Essex church and fled to Holland to avoid investigation; thence he traveled to the American colonies and eventually settled in Connecticut as a founder of Hartford. Hooker's progressive political ideas led him to be called 'the father of American democracy'.

Hooper, John (d. 1555)

Educated at Oxford, he expressed an interest in the continental Reformers which led to exile in Zurich, where he developed a personal friendship with the Reformers. On his return (1549) to England he was chosen for the see of Gloucester, then of Worcester. Noted for his extreme Protestantism and his zealous pastoral care, when Mary came to the throne Hooper was tried for heresy (1553) and burnt at the stake. His books, particularly *A Godly Confession and Protestation of the Christian Faith,* influenced later Puritan teaching.

Hopkins, Gerard Manley (1844–1889)

Educated at Balliol College, Oxford. While there he became a Roman Catholic and in 1868 joined the Jesuits. He was professor of Greek at Dublin from 1884; unknown to his superiors, he had returned to writing poetry, the deep intensity of which revealed his priestly concern for others and a degree of personal mysticism. One of the most individual and influential of the Victorian poets, his work was unknown in his lifetime; it was published for the first time in 1918 by his friend R. Bridges.

Hopkins, Samuel (1721–1803)

American theologian and writer who, as minister of the Newport Congregational Church, was one of the first to fight slavery. His belief in the need for social service is found in his major work *The System of Doctrines Contained in Divine Revelation* (1793).

Hort, Fenton J.A. (1828–1892)

Educated at Cambridge, where he later held various appointments, as a New Testament scholar he produced as a lifelong project, with Brooke Foss Westcott, one of the most important critical editions of the Greek New Testament.

Hoskyns, Sir Edwyn Clement (1884–1937)

Anglican biblical scholar and theologian who applied modern linguistic criticism to the New Testament. Hoskyns showed that the 'historical Jesus' of liberal Protestant theory was unhistorical and the origins of Christianity were much more complex than supposed. His best-known work, *The Fourth Gospel,* was published posthumously.

Houghton, St John (1487–1535)

After serving for four years as a parish priest, he joined the Carthusian order and was prior of the London charterhouse when Henry VIII ordered him to accept the Act of Supremacy. He was the first person tried for refusing the Act proclaiming the king as head of the English church, so he was dragged through the streets of London, hanged, drawn and quartered at Tyburn. He was canonised in 1970 by Pope Paul VI.

Howe, Julia Ward (1819–1910)

Famed for her 'Battle Hymn of the Republic', first published in 1862. She was a New York author and philanthropist who was especially concerned for equal educational and professional opportunities for women and for the welfare of Civil War widows.

Howard, St Philip (1557–1595)

Eldest son of the fourth Duke of Norfolk, he was baptised a Catholic but brought up a Protestant. A wastrel at Elizabeth I's court, after a conversion experience he returned to his neglected wife and his earlier Catholicism. Captured and imprisoned in the Tower of London, he was ordered to be executed but the sentence was never carried out and he died six years later in the Tower. He was canonised in 1970 by Pope Paul VI.

Hubert, Walter (d. 1205)
As bishop of Salisbury he accompanied Richard I on the Third Crusade and on his return raised the ransom when the king was imprisoned. Elected archbishop of Canterbury, he ruled England as justiciar for four years while Richard was away; in 1195 Pope Celestine III appointed him papal legate. King John chose him as his chancellor in 1199. Hubert's position in the church and state was unrivalled until Cardinal Wolsey in the sixteenth century.

Hughes, Hugh Price (1847–1902)
Welsh Methodist theologian and popular preacher who promoted liberal social reforms; founder of *The Methodist Times* (1885), in 1896 he became the first president of the National Council of the Evangelical Free Churches.

Hughes, John (1797–1864)
The first Roman Catholic archbishop of New York, he was of Irish birth and served, after his ordination in America, in several Philadelphia parishes before becoming bishop, and then, in 1850, archbishop. He founded *The Catholic Herald*, fought for state support of parochial schools and helped end the Draft Riots in 1863. As President Abraham Lincoln's personal agent he visited Europe to counteract pro-Southern support during the Civil War. He founded what is now Fordham University and helped found the North American College in Rome.

Hughes, Thomas (1822–1896)
Famed for his book *Tom Brown's Schooldays* (which ran to fifty editions), he was also a jurist, called to the Bar in 1848, and a social reformer. Influenced by F.D. Maurice he joined the Christian Socialists and was a founder-member and later princi-

pal (1872–1883) of the Working Men's College. His simple direct approach to Christianity is reflected in his tracts, e.g., *The Manliness of Christ* (1879).

Hugh of Cluny, St (1024–1109)

Abbot of the Benedictine Monastery of Cluny from the age of twenty-five until his death; as such, he was head of Cluny's extensive monastic network throughout western Europe. Under Hugh, Cluny reached the highest point of its power and international influence in its long history. He wholeheartedly supported the Gregorian reforms within the church and successive popes turned to him for advice and entrusted him with responsible missions. His integrity, generosity and saintliness influenced many contemporary international figures. Hugh supported the development of the Latin liturgy and championed orthodox doctrine at several church councils.

Hugh of Lincoln, St (c. 1140–1200)

When Henry II founded a Carthusian monastery at Witham, Somerset (1178), he asked for Hugh of Avalon, a French Carthusian already famed for sanctity, as the prior. In 1186 Hugh was appointed bishop of Lincoln and set a shining example of pastoral care. He opposed the king, but retained his friendship, in defence of his people's rights, and braved rioting mobs to defend the Jews of Lincoln. Internationally known for his courage, wisdom and justice, he was canonised twenty years after his death. Ruskin described him as 'the most beautiful sacerdotal figure known to me in history'.

Hugh of Saint-Victor (1096–1141)

Of noble birth, he entered the order of Augustinian Canons and about 1115 joined the Abbey of Saint-Victor, Paris. There, from 1133, the school flourished under Hugh's guidance. An eminent scholastic theologian, his works cover a wide field, including geometry and Scripture commentaries, but for Hugh everything was subordinated to the life of contemplation. It was this mystical tradition which made Saint-Victor famous in the twelfth century.

Huntingdon, Selina Hastings, Countess of (1707–1791)
In 1793 she joined the new Methodist society and on her husband's death devoted herself completely to spreading it among the upper classes. Her policy, as a peeress, of appointing numerous chaplains was disallowed by court and occasioned the founding of the body of Calvinistic Methodists known as 'The Countess of Huntingdon's Connexion'.

Huss, John (c. 1372–1415)
Educated at Prague University, where he later became rector, Huss was ordained and became a popular preacher and leader of the Czech national reform movement. Wycliffe's writings became an ever-increasing influence and he was excommunicated for upholding them. His chief work, *De Ecclesia* (1413), reflects his Wycliffite position. Huss appealed to a general council at Constance but was tried for heresy and died at the stake.

Hutchinson, Anne (1591–1643)
Originating from Lincolnshire, England, the daughter of a Puritan clergyman, Anne organised weekly women's groups in colonial Massachusetts, which met with opposition from the established ministers. Her emphasis upon an individual's intuitive way to God and her criticism of the local narrow interpretation of Puritanism led to her trial, conviction, excommunication (1637) and banishment. She is remembered as a religious liberal and one of the founders of Rhode Island where she and her followers settled.

I

Ignatius of Antioch, St (c. 35–c. 107)

Nothing certain is known of his life, except that he was bishop of Antioch (according to Origen, the second bishop; according to Eusebius, the third) and was taken under guard to Rome for martyrdom. On the way he wrote seven important letters which had exceptional influence upon the early church and are the source of early teaching upon the episcopacy. His letter to the church at Rome, to which he accords special respect, reveals a passionate devotion to Christ and a great desire to suffer martyrdom for him.

Ignatius of Loyola, St (1491–1556)

Born of a noble Spanish family, he sustained a leg wound in battle (1521) and was forced to remain inactive, a time during which he read the Bible and experienced a conversion. He resolved to live an austere life and to do penance for his sins. For a year, at Manresa, he lived such a life, had mystical experiences and began writing his *Spiritual Exercises*. He studied in Spain and at Paris for twelve years and while there gathered a group around him who became the first members of the Society of Jesus (the Jesuits). They took religious vows in 1534; several, with Ignatius, were ordained priests in 1537 and the Society was formally approved in 1540. Ignatius's paramount desire was to reform the Roman Catholic church from within;

the remainder of his life was devoted to this. He was canonised in 1622.

Inge, William Ralph (1860–1954)
Dean of St Paul's, London, and one of the best-known churchmen of his time. Educated at Eton and Cambridge, his fame derived principally from a long series of devotional and theological writings, including *Christian Mysticism* (1899) and *Faith and its Psychology* (1909).

Ireland, John (1838–1918)
First Roman Catholic archbishop of St Paul, Minnesota; head of a liberal group of clergy who promoted the integration of immigrant parishes into the life of the United States church and society. He helped to found the Catholic University of America at Washington D.C. (1889) and St Paul's Seminary in 1894.

Irenaeus, St (c. 130–c. 200)
Little is known of his life; he was acquainted with Polycarp, became a missionary in Gaul and, after a persecution at Lugdunum (Lyons), was chosen as bishop and contended with the heresy of Marcion. Irenaeus is the first great theologian; his work *Adversus Haereses* (180) was directed against Gnostic errors and is a witness to the apostolic tradition.

Irving, Edward (1792–1834)
Church of Scotland minister whose teachings became the foundation of the Catholic Apostolic Church or Irvingism. His later extreme eschatology lost him the impressive following he had enjoyed as a preacher in London.

Isaac the Great, St. (c. 345–439)
After marriage and, as a widower, the life of an Orthodox monk, he was appointed 'catholicos' (spiritual leader) of the Armenian Orthodox church. He fostered Armenian ecclesiasti-

cal independence and culture, producing the first translation of the Bible in Armenian; he is also credited with many Armenian hymns.

Isidore of Kiev (c. 1385–1463)
Greek Orthodox patriarch of Russia, theologian and humanist who worked for reunion between Greek and Latin Christendom, but the opposition of the Byzantine and Russian Orthodox churches drove him into exile.

Isidore of Seville, St (c. 560–636)
Succeeding his brother, Leander, as archbishop of Seville, Isidore put all his energy into spreading Catholicism in the face of barbarism and Arianism; to this end his immense knowledge found expression in his *Etymologiae,* an encyclopaedia used for many centuries; his other influential theological writings contributed to his being known as a doctor of the church within twenty years of his death; he was canonised in 1598.

J

Jacopone da Todi (c. 1230–1306)

Baptised as Jacopo dei Benedetti, born at Todi, in northern Italy, he was of noble family. On the sudden death of his wife (1268), he was converted from worldliness to a life of austerity, eventually becoming a Franciscan friar, advocating the most extreme poverty. A gifted poet, he was imprisoned and excommunicated for writing satirical verse against Pope Boniface VIII (1298), but freed by the next pope. He is remembered for more than a hundred mystical poems of great power and originality and for the hymn, the 'Stabat Mater', which was added to the Roman liturgy in the eighteenth century.

Jansen, Cornelius Otto (1585–1638)

Roman Catholic bishop of Ypres and founder of Jansenism. He studied at the University of Louvain, where he later became rector; his thorough study of the early church fathers, particularly St Augustine, led him to write *Augustinus* (1640) and lead a theological revival or reform movement, in opposition to the Roman Catholic Counter-Reformation theology and the Jesuits. His book and Jansenism were condemned after his death.

Jerome, St (c. 347–420)

His real name was Eusebius Hieronymus and he wrote under the name of Sophronius; educated at Rome, where he was baptised (366), he traveled widely. While living as a hermit in the Syrian desert for about four years, he learnt Hebrew; on his return to Rome, after ordination, he became secretary to Pope Damasus (382) but proved to be very outspoken. About 386 he settled in Palestine as leader of a new monastery at Bethlehem; the rest of his life was dedicated to study. One of the most learned of the early church fathers, his scholarship and writings, particularly his Latin translation of the Bible (the Vulgate), begun at the request of Pope Damasus, and his biblical commentaries profoundly influenced the Western church.

Jewel, John (1522–1571)
Anglican bishop of Salisbury who, influenced by Peter Martyr, became one of the intellectual leaders of the Reform movement in England. He opposed both the Roman Catholic and the Puritan positions and his masterly and celebrated *Apologia Ecclesiae Anglicanae* (1562) gave clarity and continuing strength to the Anglican position. Jewel proved to be a most caring and pastoral bishop and built the library at Salisbury.

Joachim of Fiore (c. 1132–1202)
Mystic, theologian and biblical commentator of whose life little is known, but whose influence was far-reaching. Called to the monastic life, he lived first as a Cistercian and then, in 1196, he formed his own local religious order. Of great personal sanctity, his writings on a trinitarian conception of history led to his optimistic hopes for the future and the spawning of revolutionary groups, like the Spiritual Franciscans.

Joan of Arc, St (1412–1431)
Second patron, and greatest heroine, of France. Joan was born of peasant family. A devout child, she first experienced visions at the age of thirteen; her voices revealed her mission to save France. Cleared by a panel of theologians, she convinced a doubting Dauphin and led the French army to victory at Or-

leáns (1429) and the crowning of Charles VII at Rheims. Captured by the Burgundians in a later campaign, she was sold to the British; a politically motivated church court condemned her to the stake as a heretic. A later court, in 1456, found her innocent and she was canonised in 1920.

Jogues, Isaac (1607–1646)

Jesuit missionary. Ordained in France for the Society of Jesus (1636) he was sent to Canada where he worked courageously among the Huron Indians. In 1642 he was captured by warring Iroquois, but escaped and became the first priest to visit New Amsterdam (N.Y.) on his way back to France. On his return, 1645, he was sent on a peace mission to the Mohawks at Ossernenon, who murdered him. He was declared a saint by Pope Pius XI in 1930.

John—There are twenty-three popes with this name; the most famous is without a doubt:

John XXIII (1881–1963)

One of the most popular and influential popes of all time. Angelo Giuseppe Roncalli originated from Bergamo, northern Italy, of a poor farming family. After ordination (1904) and a period as a bishop's secretary, he served in the First World War; afterwards he was called to Rome to serve in the Vatican Diplomatic Service. As vicar apostolic he served in Bulgaria (1925–1935), as apostolic delegate in Turkey (1935–1944) and as papal nuncio in Paris at the end of World War II. In 1953 he was created cardinal and patriarch of Venice. Elected pope in 1958, he proposed three aims: to call a diocesan synod of Rome, to convene an ecumenical church council, and to revise the body of canon law. The Second Vatican Council, which renewed the Roman Catholic church, was his greatest achievement, but he also contributed much to the development of church unity and wrote socially important encyclicals, especially *Pacem in Terris*. Although a diplomat, he was a pastor at heart and his simple, deep spirituality is reflected in his published diaries, *Journey of a Soul*.

John of Avila, St (1500–1569)

Known in Spain as 'the Apostle of Andalusia', he gave up a law career, sold his possessions and was ordained for missionary work (1525) in Mexico. However (1528), he was persuaded to preach throughout Andalusia and proved to be one of the greatest and most effective reforming preachers of his time. As author and spiritual director he influenced such people as Teresa of Avila, John of God and Francis Borgia. His writings, especially the spiritual classic *Audi Filia* (1530), reveal his own mystical experience and spirituality.

John Baptist de la Salle, St (1651–1719)

Born of a noble French family, he studied for the Roman Catholic priesthood (1678), but soon became involved in providing free schooling for the poor and the training of teachers. He distributed his fortune to the poor and gave himself completely to improving educational standards. He founded the Institute of the Brothers of the Christian Schools, a religious order of teachers, and established several teachers' colleges; his schools spread through Europe. Apart from his spiritual impact he was a significant pioneer in French education. He was canonised in 1900.

John Climacus, St (c. 579-c. 649)

A Byzantine hermit and later abbot of St Catherine's on Mount Sinai, his name (John of the Ladder) derives from his book *The Ladder of Divine Ascent,* which as a handbook on the ascetical and mystical life has been regarded as a spiritual classic.

John of the Cross, St (1542–1591)

One of the greatest Christian mystics and reformers, Juan de Yepes y Alvarez entered the Carmelite order in 1563 and was ordained priest in 1567. He met Teresa of Avila, who persuaded him not to leave the Carmelites for the Carthusians but to work with her for the reform of the Carmelite order. John set up a reformed Discalced Carmelite house (1568) and became spiritual director to Teresa's convent at Avila (1572). Violent dissent between the two forms of Carmelite life led to his imprisonment and great hardship (1576). He was finally banished to Andalusia, where he died. John's poetic sensitivity and Thomist theology, together with his deep mystical experience, produced Chritianity's great spiritual classics *Dark Night of the Soul, Spiritual Canticle* and *The Living Flame of Love.*

John of Damascus, St (c. 675-c. 749)
Sometimes called 'John Damascene', he succeeded his father as 'Logothete' or representative of the Damascus Christians to the Muslim caliph; soon after 730 he entered a monastery near Jerusalem. John played an important role in the eighth-century iconoclastic controversy, and the influence of his theological writings has reached through the middle ages to our own day; approximately 150 theological works, the most famous being *Fount of Wisdom* and *Sacra Parallela,* won him the title 'Doctor' of both the Greek and Latin church.

John of God, St (1495–1550)
Former shepherd and soldier converted to an ascetic way of life and great sanctity by John of Avila, he dedicated his life to the care of the poor and sick. He founded an order of nursing brothers later known as the Hospitaller Order of St John of God; in modern times the order has had the care of 225 hospitals worldwide.

John of Kronstadt (1829–1909)
Russian Orthodox theologian, known popularly as 'Father John', who as a priest-ascetic worked among the poor and promoted many pastoral and educational activities from his

parish of St Andrew, Kronstadt. Of several spiritual writings the best-known is *My Life in Christ*.

John of Odzun (650–729)

Learned theologian of the Armenian church who, in 718, became the catholicos (leader) of that church and encouraged orthodox Christology in the Eastern church. His principal work, in defence of the human nature of Christ, was *Against the Fantastic*.

John Paul I, Pope (1912–1978)

Albino Luciani was the first pope to take a double name, to emphasise the ongoing renewal work of the two previous popes. After pastoral work and teaching he was chosen patriarch of Venice, and cardinal (1973); while there his *Illustrissimi* was written. He died unexpectedly five weeks after his election to the papacy, on 26 August 1978.

Jones, Rufus Matthew (1863–1948)

One of the most respected of American Quakers, professor of philosophy at Haverford College (1904–1934) he wrote over fifty books, many of them on Christian mysticism; he also founded the American Friends Service Committee, a worldwide charitable organisation.

Joseph of Volokolamsk, St (1439–1515)

Theologian and monk who has been accorded the title 'Father of medieval Russia'. His monastic reforms emphasised community life and inspired a spiritual renewal in the Russian Orthodox church; he founded the celebrated monastery of Volokolamsk near Moscow.

Jowett, Benjamin (1817–1893)

Distinguished scholar with the reputation of being one of the finest teachers of his time. Educated at Balliol College, Oxford, where he was later Regius professor of Greek (1855) and master (1870). He was influenced by German philosophy and took a liberal stance in theology; this was reflected in *The Epistles of Paul* (1855) and his contribution to *Essays and Reviews* (1860).

Judson, Adoniram (1788–1850)
American Baptist missionary and linguist; one of the first missionaries to be sent abroad by the Nonconformist churches, he was ordained a Congregationalist minister but became a Baptist on arrival in India; in Rangoon (1813) he translated the Bible into Burmese and compiled a Burmese dictionary. His work in Burma was very successful, leading to a Christian community of about half a million.

Juliana of Liege, St (1191–1258) (Also known as Juliana of Mont-Cornillon)
Little is known of her early life. She became prioress of the Canonesses Regular of Mont-Cornillon (1222), where in 1209 she had a vision which encouraged her to work for a special church feast of the Blessed Sacrament. Pope Urban IV extended the celebration of Corpus Christi to the whole church in 1264.

Julian of Norwich (c. 1342-after 1413)
Celebrated English mystic of whom little is known (not even her real name), other than that she seems to have lived as an anchoress outside St Julian's Church, Norwich. According to her own account, she experienced in May 1373 a series of visions of the passion of Christ and the Holy Trinity which, after years of meditation, she recounted in her influential *Revelations of Divine Love,* a book which is quite unparalleled in English religious literature.

Justin Martyr, St (c. 100-c. 165)
Philosopher-apologist of the early church; he tried many pagan philosophies before embracing Christianity, and his writ-

ings, particularly the *Dialogue with Trypho the Jew* and two *Apologies,* represent the first encounter of Christian revelation with Greek philosophy and the first development of the idea of salvation history. Denounced as a Christian, he was scourged and beheaded.

Justus, St (d. c. 637)

Sent to England by Pope Gregory the Great to help Augustine, he was appointed by Augustine as the first bishop of Rochester. He eventually succeeded as the third archbishop of Canterbury (634) and dispatched St Paulinus to convert Northumberland.

K

Kagawa, Toyohiko (1888–1960)

Japanese social reformer and leader of labour and democratic movements that worked for the betterment of millions of Japanese. After conversion from Buddhism he studied modern social techniques at Princeton in the United States, and on his return to Japan dedicated himself to the improvement of social conditions. He founded the first labour union (1921), the National Anti-War League (1928) and the Kingdom of God Movement in 1930. Toyohiko was imprisoned in 1921 and 1922 for his labour activities and in 1940 as a pacifist. He wrote more than 150 books, several translated into English.

Keble, John (1792–1866)

Anglican priest, theologian and poet whose brilliant mind was evident in his educational success at Oxford, followed by a fellowship at Oriel at the age of nineteen. From 1817 to 1823 he was a tutor at Oriel, but from then on embraced pastoral work, being vicar of Hursley, near Winchester, for the last thirty years of his life. As a poet he is remembered for *The Christian Year* and numerous hymn lyrics; as a theologian it was his sermon 'National Apostasy' (1833) that set the Oxford Movement, or Tractarians, in motion. He led and guided the movement, with J.H. Newman and E.B. Pusey, writing nine of the *Tracts for the Times* and working on *A Library of the*

Fathers. A brilliant scholar, but self-effacing, he was much sought after for his spiritual guidance.

Kempe, Margery (c. 1373-c. 1440)
Mother of fourteen children, from Lynn, Norfolk, who was a visionary and mystic, and whose autobiography is one of the earliest in English literature. In her dictated *Book of Margery Kempe* (she herself was illiterate) she describes her pilgrimages to Jerusalem, Rome and Germany and her mystical experiences.

Ken, Thomas (1637–1711)
Anglican bishop of Bath and Wells, educationalist, hymn-writer and royal chaplain to King Charles II. He was one of the seven bishops who opposed James II's Declaration of Indulgence, but supported the king against William of Orange. This opposition led to his deposition from his see (1691) and he spent his last twenty years in ascetic retirement.

Kennicott, Benjamin (1718–1783)
English biblical scholar, educated at Oxford, whose fame rests upon his lifework of a critical study of the Hebrew text of the Old Testament. His research was published between 1776 and 1780 in two volumes.

Kentigern, St (c. 518–603)
(Also known as Mungo ['dear one'], little is known for certain of his life.) Brought up by St Serf, he lived at first as a hermit at Glasghu (Glasgow) and then worked as a missionary. Consecrated bishop of Strathclyde (c. 540), he preached in Cumbria and Wales and eventually returned to work in the Glasgow area; he is reputedly buried in Glasgow Cathedral.

Khomyakov, Aleksey Stepanovich (1804–1860)
Russian Orthodox lay theologian, poet and founder of the nineteenth-century Slavophile Movement. He attacked Ro-

man Catholic scholasticism and German idealism. His concept of the church as 'sobernost' ('togetherness'—symphony) was treated with suspicion during his life, but has been influential in twentieth-century theology.

Kierkegaard, Soren (Aabye) (1818–1855)
Danish religious philosopher and critic of rationalism who inspired the formation of existentialist philosophy. Originating from a wealthy but secluded background, Kierkegaard obtained a master's degree in theology (1840) and from his book *Either/Or,* in 1843, there followed a succession of philosophical works of great originality and influence. His later writings attacked the established church for its compromise, and his own ascetical life pointed to a sterner form of Christianity. His devotional works, e.g., *Christian Discourses* (1850), are less well-known.

Kilham, Alexander (1762–1798)
English Methodist minister who, after John Wesley's death, became leader of the Methodist New Connexion, a radical wing that was expelled (1796) by the Methodist Conference.

King, Edward (1829–1910)
Theologian and bishop of Lincoln with a reputation for pastoral care and great personal holiness. As a Tractarian, in 1888 he was involved in a famous prosecution over church rites; the court decided in his favour in 1890.

King, Martin Luther Jr (1919–1968)
Eloquent black Baptist minister who championed the civil rights movement in the United States from the mid-1950s. After theological training, including a Ph.D., he became a minister in Montgomery, Alabama (1954). He organised opposition to segregation on buses (1956), and in 1960 resigned his pastorate to devote himself completely to the civil rights movement, advocating nonviolent methods; this culminated

in the massive march on Washington (1963), President Kennedy's sympathy and the Civil Rights Bill. In 1964 he was awarded the Nobel Peace Prize, but his leadership was challenged by more militant forces and he was assassinated in 1968.

Kingsley, Charles (1819–1875)
Anglican clergyman; teacher, social reformer and novelist whose novels influenced social developments in Britain. A graduate of Magdalene College, Cambridge, and ordained in 1842, he became vicar of Eversley, Hampshire (1844), where he spent most of his life. As a founder-member of the Christian Socialist Movement he was more interested in re-educating his own social class than changing political structures. He was one of the first churchmen to support Darwin's evolutionary theories. He was disturbed by the Tractarian Movement, and his novels, such as *Westward Ho!* (1855) and *Hereward the Wake* (1866), have an anti-Catholic slant.

Kino, Eusebio (1645–1711) (Originally Chini, or Chino)
Jesuit missionary and explorer. He entered the Society of Jesus (1665) after an education in Germany and was sent to work in Mexico City (1681). He established missions in the Pimeria Alta region and from 1691, made up to forty expeditions into Arizona. It is claimed that he discovered the sources of the Colorado and the Rio Grande. He proved a lifelong friend and supporter of the Pima Indians.

Knox, John (c. 1513–1572)
Educated at Glasgow for the Roman Catholic priesthood, under the influence of George Wishart, he embraced the principles of the Reformation; by 1547 he was its acknowledged leader in Scotland. Chaplain to Edward VI, he fled to the continent on Mary's accession, but on his return to Scotland assumed a leadership of enormous political and religious influ-

ence. His famous tract *The First Blast of the Trumpet against the Monstrous Regiment of Women* (1558), written in Geneva, earned him Elizabeth I's hostility. He worked on the *First Book of Discipline* and wrote a *Treatise on Predestination* (1560), but his principal work was the *History of the Reformation of Religion within the Realm of Scotland*.

Knox, Ronald Arbuthnott (1888–1957)
Theologian, author, preacher and translator of the Bible. Born into an Anglican family and educated at Eton and Oxford, he became a Roman Catholic in 1917. Ordained in 1919 to the priesthood, from 1926 to 1939 he acted as chaplain to the Oxford students. The author of several popular religious books, e.g., *The Creed in Slow Motion*, he is however best-known for his translation of the Bible, commenced in 1939 and completed in 1949. This was followed by his New Testament commentaries (1953-1956). His own spiritual struggle appeared in his *Spiritual Aeneid* (1918).

Kolbe, Maximilian Maria (1894–1941)
Polish Franciscan priest and founder of religious communities called Niepokalanow, in Poland, India and Japan. Arrested by the Gestapo in 1941 for aiding Jews, he was imprisoned in Auschwitz. He volunteered to take a married man's place in the death cell and was finally killed by an injection of carbolic acid. The man he saved, Gajowniczek, was present when Pope John Paul II declared him a saint in 1982.

Kuhlman, Kathryn (1910–1976)
Evangelist and charismatic faith healer. Of nominal Christian background, from Concordia, Missouri, she experienced a call from God at thirteen and began to preach at sixteen. Ordained by the Evangelical Church Alliance, she had a second religious experience in 1946, which set her upon a healing ministry. At her 'miracle services' thousands claimed to have been healed

and she reached millions through her radio and TV programmes. Her best-known books are *I Believe in Miracles* (1962) and *God Can Do It Again* (1969).

Kuyper, Abraham (1837–1900)

Dutch theologian and statesman who was the leader of the Anti-Revolutionary Party. As a Dutch Reformed church pastor he founded the Free University of Amsterdam (1880) for the training of Calvinist pastors. His political party, in coalition, came to power in 1888 and he served as prime minister and minister of the interior (1901–1905).

L

Labouré, Catherine (1806–1876)
From a French farming family she joined the Sisters of Charity of St Vincent de Paul (1830) and immediately, at the rue de Bac Convent, Paris, she experienced a series of visions of the Virgin Mary (declared authentic by an examining commission in 1836), who asked for a medal of the Immaculate Conception to be struck. This medal, world-famous as the Miraculous Medal, was reproduced in the millions. From 1831 until her death, Catherine worked at menial tasks in the Hospice d'Enghien, but her evident sanctity led to her canonisation in 1947.

Labre, Benedict Joseph (1748–1783)
Known as 'the beggar of Rome'; of a French family, he tried unsuccessfully to enter religious orders, all of whom declared him unfit for community life. Instead, alone, he set out to visit all the major shrines of Europe. From 1774 he was a well-known figure in Rome, living rough in the Colosseum and worshiping daily in the churches. He was declared a saint in 1883.

Lacordaire, Henri Dominique (1802–1861)
French theologian and preacher. As a young French lawyer influenced by Rousseau he lost his Christian faith, but in

1824, after conversion, he trained at Saint-Sulpice for the priesthood. He worked for the separation of church and state (1830) with F. de Lamenais, but broke off on Lamenais's excommunication. He won great fame as a Paris preacher, particularly for his Lenten Conferences, later published as *Conférences de Notre Dame de Paris* in four volumes (1844–1851). He sought the renewal of the French church by re-establishing the Dominican order, which he had joined in 1838.

Lactantius (c. 240-c. 320)
Sometimes called the 'Christian Cicero', he is one of the most reprinted of the Latin church fathers and an outstanding apologist whose *The Divine Precepts* (304–311) was the first systematic Latin account of the Christian attitude to life. Before his conversion he had worked for the emperor Diocletian; later Constantine appointed him tutor to his son.

Legrange, Marie Joseph (1855–1938)
Theologian and outstanding Roman Catholic biblical scholar. He became a member of the Dominican order in 1879; he first taught before studying Oriental languages. His order sent him, in 1890, to Jerusalem to found the famous 'École Pratique d'Études Bibliques' and (in 1892) the influential *Revue biblique*. In 1902 he was appointed to the Roman Catholic Biblical Commission and in 1903 commenced his monumental Bible commentaries. He wrote several seminal books, including *Judaism before Jesus Christ* (1931).

Lake, Kirsopp (1872–1946)
Patristic and biblical scholar, educated at Lincoln College, Oxford. After ordination in the Anglican church, and two curacies, he became professor of New Testament at Leyden (1904-1914) and later in the United States, at Harvard University. He challenged and provoked by his writings, e.g., *Historical Evidence for the Resurrection of Jesus Christ* (1907). His later

work, in the five-volume *The Beginnings of Christianity: The Acts of the Apostles* and the series *Studies and Documents* (edited with his wife), has proved of lasting value.

Lamy, Jean Baptiste (1814–1888)

Pioneer missionary and first archbishop of Santa Fe, New Mexico. Born, educated and ordained in France, he was recruited for the American missions and, in 1850, appointed vicar apostolic of New Mexico. A tough, caring pastor, he coped with many hazards and problems; appointed bishop (1850), and archbishop in 1875, he traveled Europe, raised funds, recruited priests and sisters and built a thriving archdiocese out of virtually nothing. Highly regarded by all sections of the religious and secular community, he has been worthily commemorated in many forms.

Lanfranc (c. 1010–1089)

Benedictine theologian from northern Italy, archbishop of Canterbury and trusted counselor of William the Conqueror. Famed as a teacher and able administrator, in 1063 he became abbot of St Stephen's, Caen; in 1070, as archbishop of Canterbury, he conducted a successful reform and reorganisation of the English church but supported William's policy of replacing English prelates by Normans.

Lang, William Cosmo Gordon (1864–1945)

Archbishop of Canterbury. Of Scottish Presbyterian background, after studying for the Bar he was ordained for the Anglican church (1890). He worked as a curate in a Leeds parish then returned to Oxford as dean of Divinity. From suffragan bishop of Stepney (1901–1908) he went to York and twenty years later he was translated to Canterbury. He was involved in the abdication of Edward VIII and was a close friend and adviser to George VI. He retired as Baron Lang of Lambeth in 1942.

Langton, Stephen (d. 1228)

Considered one of the greatest of the medieval archbishops of Canterbury, he was a renowned theologian for twenty-five years in Paris, before being chosen as a cardinal and archbishop of Canterbury. He supported the barons in their struggle with King John, but later supported the regency against the barons. His voluminous writings included Bible commentaries and he was the first to divide the Bible into chapters and verses.

Las Casas, Bartolomé de (1474–1566)

Spanish missionary and opponent of slavery. In 1502 he went to Hispaniola (W.I.) to work among the Indians and from the start opposed slavery. In 1515 he returned to Spain to plead for improved conditions for Indian slaves. His project to found towns for freed slaves (the Paria experiment), 1520–22, failed and he retired from public life. He joined the Dominican order (1523) and wrote history, his most famed work being, *Historia da las Indias*.

Latimer, Hugh (1485–1555)

English priest, educated at Cambridge, who from 1525 was gradually converted to Reformation principles. His vigorous preaching won him acclaim, preferment under Henry VIII, and it contributed to the spread of the Reformation in England. After opposing the Act of Six Articles (1539) he was forced to resign the see of Worcester, to which he had been elevated in 1535, and was confined in the Tower of London. Although at freedom during Edward's reign, he was committed to the Tower again (1553) on Mary's accession. Sent to Oxford to dispute with Catholic theologians, he was found guilty of heresy, and finally died courageously at the stake on 16 October 1555.

Laud, William (1573–1645)

Archbishop of Canterbury. Educated at Oxford and ordained in 1601, he opposed Calvinistic theology from the beginning and tried to restore, as bishop (first of Bath and Wells, then London), something of the pre-Reformation liturgy of the English church. As religious adviser to Charles I his power increased, but he attracted the hostility of the Puritans and became increasingly unpopular. Attempting to impose Anglican liturgy on Presbyterian Scotland and, in 1640, a new set of canons, he was impeached before the Long Parliament, imprisoned, tried (1644-1645) and finally beheaded on Tower Hill, 10 June 1645.

Laval, Francois de Montmorency (1623–1708)
Born of one of France's most famous families, he was the first Roman Catholic bishop in Canada, and laid the foundation of his church's organisation there. As bishop of Quebec (1674) and member of the ruling council, he also had a powerful political influence. He founded the seminary at Quebec which later (1852) became Laval University.

Lavigerie, Charles (1825–1892)
French cardinal and archbishop of Algiers and Carthage who worked for the conversion of Africa by founding the White Fathers (1868) and fought against slavery, forming several antislavery societies.

Law, William (1686–1761)
Author of works on mysticism and Christian ethics. Educated at Cambridge, he refused the Oath of Allegiance and became a nonjuror; he was tutor to the Gibbon family from 1727 to 1737. From 1740 he lived in retirement, organising schools and almshouses, personally living a simple life of devotion and charity. He is best remembered for his *Treatise Upon Christian Perfection* (1726) and his spiritual classic *A Serious Call to a Devout and Holy Life* (1728). His ethical works have seldom found acceptance among Christian moralists.

Lawrence (Laurence), St (d. 258)

One of the seven deacons of Rome serving Pope St Sixtus II, Lawrence suffered martyrdom a few days after his patron, during the persecution of Valerian. It is reported that his death by roasting on a gridiron was so heroically and patiently borne that mass conversions to Christianity took place in Rome.

Lawrence of Brindisi, St (1559–1619)

A member of the Capuchin Friars Minor, a gifted linguist and preacher who won the title of doctor of the church (1959) for his work in resisting the rise of German Protestantism. He was canonised by his church in 1881.

Lawrence of Canterbury, St (c. 619)

One of the Benedictine monks who accompanied St Augustine to England (597) and succeeded him as archbishop of Canterbury in 604.

Lawrence of the Resurrection, Brother (c. 1605–1691) (originally named Nicholas Hermes)

After serving as a soldier, and leading a hermit's life, he entered the Carmelite order in Paris (1649), where he spent the rest of his life. In charge of the kitchen, amid the pots and pans, he developed a life of constant awareness of God's presence. His simple mystical writings, *Maximes spirituelles* (1692) and *Moeurs et entretiens du F. Lawrent* (1694), were edited by the Abbé de Beaufort and published after his death.

Leclerc, Jean (1657–1736)

Arminian theologian and biblical scholar who championed freedom of thought and supported advanced theories of exegesis and theological method. He made a lasting contribution to biblical studies with three vast encyclopaedias.

Lee, Ann (1736–1784) (also known as Mother Ann)

The illiterate daughter of an English blacksmith from Manchester, she joined the radical Shaking Quakers. In 1774, with followers, she emigrated to America and founded a settlement near Albany, New York, from which the Shaker movement spread throughout New England.

Leo—Thirteen popes share this title, the most noteworthy being:

Leo I, St (d. 461)

Given the title 'Leo the Great', he became pope in 440 against the background of the disintegration of the Roman Empire. Little is known of his life previous to this time. His papacy is noteworthy for the safeguarding of orthodox teaching and the advance of papal supremacy. In 449 his *Tome* was used to reject Eutychianism, an extreme form of the Monophysite heresy; his teaching was hailed as 'the voice of Peter' at the Council of Chalcedon (451). Leo's many letters and ninety-six sermons expounded his teaching on papal primacy and reveal the liturgical practices of the time. Politically he negotiated with the invading barbaric tribes. He was declared a doctor of the church in 1754.

Leo XIII (1810–1903)

After a career in the Catholic church's diplomatic service, he followed an authoritarian pope in 1878 and set out to pursue a more liberal programme. He brought the Kulturkampf in Germany to a finish and improved relations between the Vatican and Britain, Russia and Japan. His best-known contribution was his social teaching, enshrined in the letter *Rerum Novarum* (May 1891) and his encouragement to biblical study in *Providentissimus Deus* (November 1893). He did much to encourage ecumenism, although his letter *Apostolicae Curae* (1896) declared Anglican orders invalid. Other letters encouraged the devotional and spiritual life of the church.

Leslie, Charles (1650–1722)

Nonjuring Anglican divine and writer who, as an ardent Jacobite, accompanied the Pretender to Rome after the 1715 rebellion. He wrote many highly regarded apologetical works against the deist philosophy, the Quakers and Roman Catholicism.

Lewis, C.S. (1898–1963)

Educated privately, he served in the British Army in the First World War; afterwards, in 1918, he proved to be an outstanding scholar at University College, Oxford. From 1925 to 1954 he was a tutor and fellow of Magdalen College, Oxford; from 1954 to 1963 professor of medieval and Renaissance English at Cambridge. Lewis wrote nearly forty books, many of them on Christian apologetics, the most famous being *The Screwtape Letters* (1942) and his stories for children, the *Chronicles of Narnia* series. Also of note is his autobiographical *Surprised by Joy* (1955).

Liddon, Henry Parry (1829–1890)

Anglican priest and theologian who was ordained in 1852 and became vice-principal of the new seminary at Cuddesdon (1854) and vice-principal of St Edmund's Hall, Oxford, in 1859, where he was an energetic supporter of the Oxford Movement. As canon of St Paul's, London (1870), for the next twenty years he attracted great crowds with his preaching. Concerned for church unity, he encouraged the growth of the Old Catholic Movement. A great admirer of E.B. Pusey, he commenced his biography in 1882, posthumously published in four volumes (1893–1897). The religious centre, Liddon House, London, was founded in his memory.

Lightfoot, Joseph Barber (1828–1889)

At Trinity College, Cambridge (1847), he was a pupil of B.F. Westcott and later lectured in theology and biblical studies; from 1875 he was Lady Margaret Professor of Divinity at

Cambridge. He won international recognition for his work on the early Christian writers, his New Testament criticism and his famous commentaries. As bishop of Durham (1878) he promoted ecclesiastical and social reforms.

Liguori, St Alphonsus (1696–1787)

A brilliant student, he received doctorates in civil and church law at the age of sixteen. He began a career as a lawyer, but turned to the Roman Catholic priesthood in 1726. Alphonsus helped Sister Mary Celeste found a new order of nuns and himself founded (1732) the Redemptorist congregation of priests. Dissension tore at the new order, but Alphonsus continued his work of preaching missions and devoted himself to writing. Although appointed bishop (1762), he resigned his see in 1775. Besides the Redemptorist congregation he is best remembered for his extensive works of dogmatic and moral theology and his devotional writings. By the twentieth century these works had gone through eighteen thousand editions and been translated into sixty languages. Canonised by his church in 1839, he was declared the patron of moralists and confessors in 1950.

Lingard, John (1771–1851)

English Roman Catholic priest and historian whose famous eight-volume work *The History of England* (1819) has proved of lasting value. He helped found Ushaw College, Durham, and reopened the English College in Rome (1817).

Livingstone, David (1813–1873)

Born at Blantyre, Scotland, he was basically self-educated and joined the London Missionary Society in 1838, first intending to go to China. Arriving in South Africa (1840), he worked with Moffatt (whose daughter he married) and from Kuruman conducted missionary/exploratory journeys. He became devoted to Africa, undertaking his first major expedition in 1853, which won him international acclaim. He was the first white man to view the Victoria Falls (1855) and he sought the source of the Nile. More explorer than missionary, in his later travels he was sought and found exhausted in 1871 by Henry M. Stanley of the *New York Herald*. He was so loved by his African followers that after his death they carried his body to the coast, a journey of nine months, for eventual burial in Westminster Abbey.

Llull, Ramon (or Ramon Lull or Raymond Lully) (c. 1235–1316)

Lay missionary, mystic and poet. Educated as a knight, he acquired a knowledge of Islam from his upbringing on the island of Majorca. After a mystical experience he abandoned courtly life and devoted himself to the conversion of the Moors. He studied Arabic and Islamic culture to further his aim and succeeded in persuading state and church to establish institutions for the study of Oriental languages. He is best remembered as a mystic, a forerunner of the great Spanish mystics.

Loisy, Alfred (1857–1940)

Biblical scholar, linguist and philosopher of religion. Ordained a priest, he devoted himself to modernising the teaching of the Roman Catholic church and succeeded in founding Modernism, springing principally from his book *L'Évangile et L'Église*; this was condemned by Pope Pius X (1907). After the condemnation he parted with his church, but continued to write prolifically.

Lossky, Vladimir (1903–1958)

Lay theologian, expelled from Russia in 1922. In the United States and Paris he expounded and spread knowledge of Orthodox teaching. He opposed the teachings of Bulgakov and studied and wrote upon Meister Eckhart.

Louis IX of France, St. (1214–1270)

Crowned king at the age of twelve, he was guided by his mother, Blanche of Castile, and proved to be both pious and powerful as a monarch. Famed for his impartiality and mercy, he founded the Abbey of Royaumont and led the Sixth Crusade to the Holy Land. He brought the powerful barons under control, improved administration and worked for peace and harmony with England. In 1270 he sailed with another Crusade but died at Tunis. He was declared a saint by his church in 1297.

Lovejoy, Elijah P. (1802–1837)

American lay preacher and editor, from St Louis, Missouri, of the Presbyterian newspaper the *St Louis Observer*. He wrote forthright editorials against the evils of slavery and died when his newspaper offices were burnt down by a mob.

Lowder, Charles Fuge (1820–1880)

Anglo-Catholic pastoral priest who served first in Pimlico, London, then as a missionary in the East End. He founded the church of St Peter, London Docks, and converted thousands of East Londoners.

Lucaris, Cyril (1572–1638)

Greek Orthodox theologian and patriarch of Constantinople who sympathised with Calvinism and opposed Rome. He worked energetically for the reform of his own church and he presented the Codex Alexandrinus to King Charles I (1628). He was put to death on a political charge by the Sultan Murad.

Lucius—Three popes shared this name. The first (d. 254) was also honoured with the title of saint and he is the patron saint of Copenhagen, Denmark.

Ludlow, John Malcolm Forbes (1821–1911)
Educated in law and called to the Bar in 1843, he became a founder, with Maurice and Kingsley, of the Christian Social Movement. A member of the Church of England, he was largely responsible for the 1852 Industrial and Provident Societies Act and was cofounder of the Working Men's College.

Lunn, Sir Arnold (1888–1974)
World authority on skiing who invented the modern slalom race. Later in life he was converted to Roman Catholicism and became a vociferous apologist and writer. His own story was published as *Now I See*.

Luther, Martin (1483–1546)
Educated at the University of Erfurt; he joined the Augustinian Hermits in 1505, was ordained priest in 1507, and by 1515 he had become vicar of his order. In 1508 he was lecturing at the new University of Wittenberg in theology and Scripture. Reacting fiercely against the preaching of Tetzel on indulgences, he posted his celebrated Ninety-Five Theses on various church abuses (1517) and precipitated the Reformation movement. He refused to recant at the Diet of Worms (1521) and was placed under the ban of the Empire. He was rescued from physical harm by the Elector of Saxony, but returned to Wittenberg (1522) to restore order. Luther finally set aside his monastic habit in 1524 and married Catherine von Bora the following year. His many writings were mainly pamphlets and were principally to meet a particular need. His reply to Henry VIII's *Defence of the Seven Sacraments* lost him much support in England. From 1529 until his death, his disciples recorded the *Tischreden* which were table conversations with family and friends.

M

Macarius (1482–1564)

Metropolitan of Moscow, he began as a monk and became archbishop of Novgorod in 1526. After his elevation to metropolitan of Moscow and all Russia, he gave support to the autocratic monarchy to unite sacred and secular powers. He developed the idea of Moscow as the third 'Rome', replacing the first and Constantinople.

Macarius, St (c. 300-c. 390) (also known as Macarius of Egypt and Macarius the Great; not to be confused with St Macarius of Alexandria, a fourth-century Egyptian hermit)

Renowned for his sanctity, he founded a colony of monks which became one of the principal centres of Egyptian monasticism. He is regarded as one of the Desert Fathers and he had a considerable influence upon the development of the monastic life. The only authentic work to carry his name is *To the Friends of God*; later writings ascribed to him were influenced by his thought, but not written by him.

Macarius of Moscow (1816–1862)

Metropolitan of Moscow. Baptised Michael Bulgakov, he became a monk and after lectureships and elevation to the see of Tambov (1857), then Kharkov and Vilna, he became metropolitan in 1879. Considered one of the best Orthodox theologians of the nineteenth century, he wrote two influential theological works and a twelve-volume *History of the Russian Church*.

McAuley, Catherine Elizabeth (1787–1841)
Irish founder of the congregation of the Sisters of Mercy, dedicated to education and social service. She opened the first 'House of Mercy' on 24 September 1827, took first vows in 1831, and henceforth the Sisters of Mercy spread rapidly, becoming one of the largest congregations of religious sisters in the world.

McDonald, George (1824–1905)
Scottish novelist, poet and writer of Christian allegories. He became a Congregationalist minister but, after 1853, devoted himself to writing. He is still remembered for his children's books, especially *At the Back of the North Wind* (1871) and *The Princess and the Goblin* (1872).

McGuffey, William Holmes (1800–1873)
Educator, remembered for his famous series of elementary readers. From teaching in Ohio frontier schools at age thirteen, McGuffey progressed to president of Cincinnati College (1836–1839); Ohio University, Athens (1839–1843) and the chair of mental and moral philosophy, University of Virginia, Charlottesville. His school readers (122,000,000 sold) first appeared in 1836, 1837 and 1844.

Machen, John Gresham (1881–1937)
Presbyterian theologian and minister. Scholar and professor at Princeton Theological College whose fundamentalist opposition to a liberal revision of the Presbyterian creed led to his suspension from the ministry and his support for the foundation of the (later-named) conservative Orthodox Presbyterian

church (1936). He attacked liberal Protestantism in his *Christianity and Liberalism* (1923).

MacKay, Alexander Murdoch (1849–1890)
A Church Missionary Society missionary in Uganda, remembered for his engineering skills. He met with opposition and was expelled at a time of persecution. After expulsion from Uganda (1887) he translated the Bible into the Ugandan language.

McLeod, Norman (1812–1872)
Liberal minister of the Church of Scotland who worked to improve working-class conditions; the editor of the *Edinburgh Christian Magazine* (from 1849) and *Good Words* (from 1860). He was appointed chaplain to Queen Victoria (1857) and was elected moderator of the general assembly of the Church of Scotland in 1869.

McPherson, Aimee Semple (1890–1944)
Pentecostal evangelist of California and radio preacher who founded the International Church of the Foursquare Gospel. (In Britain known as the Elim Foursquare Gospel.) She won a large following, wealth and a certain notoriety; she died of an overdose of barbiturates.

Malachy, St (1095–1148)
Archbishop of Armagh who promoted reform in the Irish church and is regarded as one of the most influential Irish churchmen of the middle ages. He introduced both the Roman liturgy into Ireland and, through his friendship with St Bernard of Clairvaux, the Cistercian Order. On a second journey to Rome to receive the pallium, he died at Clairvaux.

Manning, Henry Edward (1808–1892)
From an evangelical Protestant background, at Oxford he turned to the Tractarian Movement. Ordained for the Angli-

can ministry in 1833, he married the same year. Disturbed by the Gorham Judgment, he was received into the Roman Catholic church in 1851. His wife having died, he was ordained to the Roman Catholic priesthood and founded the Oblates of St Charles. He rose rapidly in his church, becoming the second archbishop of Westminster, and later cardinal (1865). He was a staunch supporter of papal infallibility at the First Vatican Council and won national fame and respect for his successful mediation in the London Dock Strike of 1889.

Manning, James (1738–1791)
American Baptist minister who founded Brown University in Providence, Rhode Island and served as its first president. He also helped to found the Warren Association of New England Baptists.

Mannix, Daniel (1864–1963)
Roman Catholic priest who studied and lectured at Maynooth College and rose to be college president. Appointed archbishop of Melbourne in 1917, he was a forthright and controversial figure, e.g., demanding state support of church schools. After World War II he fought to prevent communist infiltration of the Australian trade unions. An energetic supporter of Catholic Social Action, he founded over 180 schools and a hundred parishes.

Margaret Mary Alacoque, St (1647–1690)
French nun and visionary. Bedridden as a child with rheumatic fever, she later refused marriage and entered the Visitation convent at Paray-le-Monial in 1671. There from December 1673, she received a series of visions of the Sacred Heart of Christ, in which she was told to promote devotion to the Sacred Heart of Jesus. Although her message was rebuffed for years, eventually it was heeded and seventy-five years after her death the devotion was officially approved by the Roman Catholic church. She was canonised in 1920.

Margaret of Scotland, St (c. 1045–1093)

Probably born in Hungary, she married Malcolm III of Scotland (1070). She instigated church reform, inspired many with her own personal devotion and made many benefactions. She was canonised by Pope Innocent IV in 1250.

Margunios, Maximus (d. 1602)

Greek Orthodox bishop and scholar who was an exponent of Greek culture and the foremost Orthodox theologian of his age. His attempts to bring union between the East and West aroused his fellow churchmen to suspect his orthodoxy.

Marillac, St Louise de (1591–1660)

French cofounder of the Daughters of Charity of St Vincent de Paul. From her youth she wanted to be a religious sister, but was advised to marry (1613). Widowed in 1625, she met Vincent de Paul and devoted the rest of her life to assisting him in his charitable work. In 1633 Louise became the first superior of the new foundation and traveled all over France founding hospitals and orphanages. By modern times her congregation was the largest in the Roman Catholic church.

Marmion, Columba (1858–1923)

An Irishman who lived all his life in France. He entered the Benedictine house of Maredsous in 1886 where, from 1909, he was abbot. Famous as a spiritual director, he was also a gifted writer. His best-known book, *Christ the Life of the Soul* (1918), sold over a hundred thousand copies.

Maritain, Jacques (1882–1973)

French Roman Catholic philosopher, respected worldwide for his interpretation of the thought of Thomas Aquinas, and the development of his own form of Thomism. A student of the Sorbonne, he held professorial chairs at the Institut Catholique, Paris (1914–1933), the Institute of Medieval Studies, Toronto (1933–1945), and Princeton (1948–1952). His numerous books applied Thomism to all branches of philosophy and religious experience.

Marquette, Jacques (1637–1675) (Known as Père Marquette)

Jesuit missionary and explorer. On arrival in Canada (1666) he helped to found missions at Sault Ste. Marie (now Michigan) and St. Ignace (1673). With Louis Jolliet he explored the Mississippi River and in 1674 was one of the first white men to camp on the site of modern Chicago. He attempted to found a mission among the Illinois Indians but died soon after, at the mouth of a river now named after him.

Marshall, Stephen (1594–1655)

Popular Puritan leader and minister who helped to formulate the Presbyterian expression of faith (1643) and worked on the Shorter Westminster Catechism (1647). He was an influential preacher, but was always a popular leader rather than a seminal thinker.

Martin of Tours, St (c. 316–397)

The first great leader of Western monasticism and the patron saint of France. Of a pagan family, Martin was forced to serve in the Roman army from the age of fifteen. Five years later he had his famous vision of Christ, after sharing his cloak with a beggar. He accepted baptism and afterwards seems to have served as a medical officer in the army; after release in 358 he set up a religious community at Ligugé. Elected bishop of Tours (371), he conducted church reforms and encouraged the spread of monastic communities throughout France. He died at Poitiers and his friend and biographer, Sulpicius Severus, tells how the men of Tours stole the body of their beloved bishop away in the night for burial at Tours.

Martensen, Hans Lassen (1808–1884)

Danish Protestant theologian who lived an academic life before becoming bishop of Seeland (1854). He developed and interpreted the Lutheran system of doctrine and presented this in his best-known work, *Den Christelige Dogmatik* (1866).

Martyn, Henry (1781–1812)

Anglican missionary who, after ordination as a deacon (1803), became a chaplain of the East India Company at Calcutta. While involved in missionary work he translated the Book of Common Prayer and the New Testament into Hindustani (1807). His devotion to missionary work won him hero status at the time in Great Britain.

Massillon, Jean-Baptiste (1663–1742)

French Roman Catholic priest who, having joined the Oratory (1681), was ordained in 1691 and rose to become the most famous French preacher of his time, often preaching before Louis XIV. Elected bishop of Clermont, he proved to be a model pastoral leader.

Mather, Cotton (1663–1728)

Son of Increase Mather (below) and a member of the celebrated Puritan family of New England, famed for their zeal, scholarship and involvement in controversy. Cotton was a Boston minister and author; ordained in 1685 he worked alongside his father in a ministry of preaching and writing. (He wrote and published over 400 books.) His special interest in science won him membership of the Royal Society of London.

Mather, Increase (1639–1723)

Born in Dorchester, Massachusetts, he was educated at Harvard and Trinity College, Dublin; afterwards he preached in England until Charles II became king (1660). Minister of North Church, Boston, he was also president of Harvard for six years (1661–1701). He is especially remembered for his opposition to the use of 'spectre evidence' in witchcraft trials.

Mathews, Shailer (1863–1941)
American leader of the Social Gospel Movement. He taught at Colby College, Waterville, Maine, and the University of Chicago. His many books and hundreds of articles, e.g., *The Messianic Hope in the New Testament,* promoted the social dimension of salvation.

Matteo da Bascio (c. 1495–1552) (or Matteo di Bassi)
After entering the Observant Franciscans (1511), he was eager to return to the early simplicity of St Francis of Assisi. He went barefoot, grew a beard and gathered a large following. His order of Friars Minor Capuchin (commonly called Capuchins) was approved by Rome in 1528. He acquired a reputation as a powerful preacher.

Maurice, (John) Frederick Denison (1805–1872)
Anglican theologian, author and founder of the Christian Social Movement. Originally of Unitarian background, he embraced the Anglican faith (1830) and accepted ordination (1834). While chaplain of Guy's Hospital, London, he wrote his *Kingdom of Christ* (1838), which established his reputation as a theologian, but also aroused considerable suspicion. He joined with Kingsley and Ludlow in founding the Christian Social Movement. His *Theological Essays* (1853) caused his dismissal from his theological professorship at King's College, London. Maurice founded and became the first principal of the Working Men's College (1854). While lecturing in moral theology at Cambridge (elected in 1866) he wrote his celebrated *Social Morality* (1869).

Mayhew, Jonathan (1720–1766)
Outspoken Boston, Massachusetts, preacher whose earlier fervour originated from the Great Awakening, but who later

distrusted religious emotionalism. Ordained pastor of Boston's West Church in 1747 (where he served until his death), he was famed for his preaching and his liberalism; his sermons were published in New England and London.

Mayne, Cuthbert (1544–1577)

The first of the English Roman Catholic priests trained in Europe to work secretly in Elizabethan England to be executed, in Cornwall, for his pastoral work (1576). After arrest and a trial at Launceston he was executed there on 29 March 1577. He was declared a martyr of the Roman Catholic church in 1970.

Machtild of Magdeburg (c. 1210–1285)

German mystic who became a béguine at Magdeburg and recorded the visions she experienced there (1250–1269). She remained at Magdeburg for forty years under the spiritual direction of the Dominican friars. In old age she retired to the convent at Helfta. (She is not to be confused with St. Mechtild of Helfta, who was a contemporary.) Her mystical experiences, which had a powerful influence upon the course of German medieval mysticism, are summarised in her book *The Flowing Light of Godhead*.

Melancthon, Philip (1497–1560)

Educated at Heidelberg and Tübingen, he became the first professor of Greek at the University of Wittenberg (1518) and developed a friendship with Martin Luther. He helped to systematise Luther's teaching; his *Loci Communes* (1521) was the first ordered presentation of Reformation doctrine to appear. He founded many schools and reformed several universities, translated the Bible and wrote commentaries that were highly regarded. Melancthon was a leading figure at the Diet of Augsburg (1530) and is credited with writing the *Confession of Augsburg*. Although he helped to lead the Reform movement after Luther's death, his standing was questioned by several controversies.

Melito of Sardis (second century)
Very little is known of his life but, through his writings, he exerted a powerful influence upon the church writers of the second and fourth centuries. Melito has been identified as an unmarried pastoral bishop of Sardis (Turkey). A prolific writer, he was virtually unknown until 1940; his masterly Easter treatise, *On the Pasch,* was discovered and first published in 1960.

Melville, Andrew (1545–1622)
Scottish scholar, educationalist and Presbyterian Reformer. After study in Scotland and France, in 1569 he studied in Geneva under the Reform leader, Theodore Beza. On his return to Scotland he reformed the educational system and helped Scottish universities to acquire an international reputation. He filled the vacuum caused by John Knox's death (1572) and gave the Reformed church its Presbyterian character. His outspoken opposition to King James VI (James I of England) led to imprisonment and exile.

Menno Simons (1496–1561)
Roman Catholic priest who rejected his church and became leader of the Dutch Anabaptists (1537). For twenty-five years, in constant danger as a heretic, he shepherded his communities, developing their teaching, which led to the formation of the Mennonite church.

Mercier, Désiré-Joseph (1851–1926)
Belgian educator, philosopher and cardinal. As a leader of the nineteenth-century revival of Thomism and the first professor of Thomism at the University of Louvain, he applied its principles to modern philosophical and scientific thought. Created

archbishop of Malines in 1906 and cardinal the following year, he was an outspoken leader of Belgian resistance to the Germans during the First World War. Enthusiastic for church unity, he was the Roman Catholic leader at the Malines Conversations (1921-1925).

Merry Del Val, Rafael (1865–1930)
Ordained to the Roman Catholic priesthood (1888), he was chosen by Pope Leo XIII for papal service; involved in momentous decisions, like the Schools Question in Canada (1890) and the Question of Anglican Orders (1896), he became cardinal and the Vatican's Secretary of State (1903) and implemented the anti-Modernist policy of Pope Pius X. His influence was also powerfully felt within the Roman Catholic church when he served as Secretary of the Holy Office.

Merton, Thomas (1915–1968)
United States journalist who, after a conversion, joined the Trappist Abbey of Gethsemane, Kentucky. He became the most influential proponent of traditional monasticism in modern times. His early autobiographical *The Seven Storey Mountain* gained him a wide readership and with his prolific writings he popularised Western spirituality. Before his sudden accidental death on 10 December 1968, he was exploring common ground with other forms of spirituality, notably in the Far East.

Meynell, Alice (1847–1922)
Poet and essayist. About 1872 she converted to Roman Catholicism, which was reflected in the many literary articles she wrote, and religion formed an important part of her poetry. She married Wilfrid Meynell in 1877 and bore him eight children. Her poetry, which appeared in collections, from *Preludes* (1875) to the posthumous *Last Poems* (1923), was so popular that she was considered as a possible Poet Laureate.

Michael Cerularius (d. 1058)

Patriarch of Constantinople who was fiercely opposed to the Western church and was so energetic in defence of the doctrinal, disciplinary and political independence of the Greek church that the Eastern Schism became a permanent separation.

Michelangelo (1475—1564)

His full name was Michelangelo di Lodovico Buonarroti Simoni. He was apprenticed to the painter Ghirlandajo (1488), from whom he learnt the basic skills which made him famous as one of the greatest artists of the Renaissance. His greatest sculptures include the *Pieta* (1499) in the Vatican, *David* (1504) at Florence, and *Moses* (1545), also in the Vatican. Pope Julius II commissioned him to paint the ceiling of the Sistine Chapel, on the themes of *Praeparatio Evangelica* (1508—1512) and the *Last Judgment* (1534—1541). At the time of his death he was the principal architect of St Peter's, Rome.

Middleton, Thomas Fanshawe (1769—1822)

Anglican missionary and first bishop of Calcutta. He held various pastoral posts, and was widely recognised for his biblical scholarship, before his consecration in 1814 to the vast see of Calcutta, which at the time included responsibility for the whole of India and Australia!

Miller, William (1782—1849)

Evangelical Adventist preacher. Miller's preaching was the origin of the Adventist denomination (later called Second Advent Christians and Seventh Day Adventists) beginning in 1831. He foretold the end of the world to be in 1843 with the Second Coming of Christ. His own personal following, the Millerite movement, went into decline after 1844.

Milton, John (1608—1674)

One of England's greatest poets. While at Cambridge (1625—1632), where he was highly regarded for his scholarship, he first wrote poetry in Latin, Italian and English. Disillusioned by the ways of the clergy, he gave up the idea of ordination and devoted himself to literature (1632–1638). Joining the Presbyterians in 1641, he attacked the clergy and defended the liberty of the press in his *Areopagitica* (1642). Milton gave his support to Oliver Cromwell, became an Independent and defended the government's action in executing Charles I. A prolific poet, his great epic *Paradise Lost* (1658–1665) and *Samson Agonistes* were written after he went totally blind in 1651. Milton's Christian beliefs, published posthumously in *De Doctrina Christiana*, were unconventional and individualistic.

Mindszenty, Josef (1892–1975) (originally Josef Pahm)

Hungarian primate and cardinal archbishop of Esztergom (1945). From his ordination in 1915, he was for over fifty years an implacable enemy of fascism and communism. He was imprisoned several times, twice in 1919, 1944 and 1948; the last was for refusing to permit the secularisation of Catholic schools by the communists and led to a sentence of life imprisonment. Freed and hailed as a great patriot during the uprising of 1956, he took refuge in the United States Embassy in Budapest when the communist government returned to power. President Richard Nixon persuaded him (1971) to leave Hungary for the Vatican. He died in Vienna, disappointed by the Vatican's policy of accommodation with communism.

Moffatt, James (1870–1944)

Writer and biblical scholar. Ordained to the ministry of the Free Church of Scotland (1896), he taught at Oxford and Glasgow before becoming professor of church history at Union Theological Seminary, New York (1927–1939). His translation of the New Testament appeared in 1913 and the Old Testament in 1924; he also edited a seventeen-volume *Commentary of the New Testament* (1928-1949).

Moffatt, Robert (1795–1883)
Missionary and Bible translator. A Scottish Congregationalist, he was sent to South Africa by the London Missionary Society in 1816. He eventually settled at Kuruman, where he developed, over forty-nine years, a major missionary centre and community. He traveled widely and translated the Bible, hymns and other literature into the native tongue. On a visit to England in 1839 he persuaded David Livingstone (later his son-in-law) to join him in Africa.

Mogila, Peter (1596–1646)
Russian Orthodox theologian and monk who became metropolitan of Kiev (1632). His writings and leadership strengthened the Russian church in its two-fronted controversy with Roman Catholicism and the Protestant Reformers. His most important work was *The Orthodox Confession of Faith* (1640), which brought order to Orthodox theology.

Möhler, Johann Adam (1796–1838)
Roman Catholic apologist, historian and theologian. He taught church history at Tübingen (1826–1835) and Munich (1835–1838). He sympathised with Protestantism and worked untiringly for church unity. His principal work, *Symbolik* (1832) (in English translation, *Unity in the Church*), prompted a theological revival in the church.

Molina, Luis de (1535–1600)
Spanish Jesuit theologian who taught at Coimbra (1563–1567) and Evora (1568–1583) and in 1588 published his work *The Union of Free Will and Divine Grace*, in which he tried to clarify the relationship between God's foreknowledge and man's free will. The book gave rise to a theological system called 'Molinism' and over three hundred years of fierce theological debate between the Jesuits and Dominicans.

Molinos, Miguel de (1628—1696)

After ordination in Spain (1652) and obtaining his doctorate in theology, he was sent to Rome (1663) as a spiritual director. There he became a celebrated confessor and gained great fame after the publication of his *Spiritual Guide* (1675). He advocated a perpetual union with God and taught that perfection was to be obtained by the total abandonment of the will. His extreme Quietism led to his arrest (1685), the examination of twenty thousand letters and a trial for heresy and immorality. He recanted the heresy but was imprisoned for life for the immorality.

Monica, St (c. 332—387)

Mother of St Augustine of Hippo and responsible for his conversion by her prayers and example. Widowed when forty, Monica followed Augustine to Rome (383) and on to Milan, where she was greatly influenced by St Ambrose and where Augustine was baptised. She became a popular saint in the middle ages, being regarded as the patron of mothers.

Monod, Adolphe-Théodore (1801—1856)

Reformed theologian of Swiss origin who was considered the foremost preacher of his time in France. He held pastorates at the Reformed Church, Naples (1826), the Free Evangelical Church, Lyons (1833), and the Church of the Oratoire, Paris (1847).

Montalembert, Charles (1810—1870)

French politician and Roman Catholic church historian (born in London) who helped to lead the struggle to free the church from state control in France. He joined Lamennais and Lacordaire in the publication of *L'Avenir*; the opposition of the Gallican church faction led to the closing of the newspaper and the condemnation of liberalism by Pope Gregory XVI (1832). Montalembert submitted, but continued in Catholic journalism and politics, where he championed Catholic principles.

Montecorvino, Giovanni da (1247–1328)

Franciscan missionary, from Italy, who worked in Armenia and Persia (c. 1280), then in the Madras region of India and there wrote the earliest Western account of the area. In 1294 he entered Peking, founding the first Christian mission in China. He opened several mission stations and was consecrated the first Roman Catholic archbishop of Peking in 1307. His missionary work was destroyed in the fourteenth century with the fall of the Mongol Empire.

Moody, Dwight Lyman (1837–1899)

American evangelist who began as a successful shoe salesman in Chicago; after conversion from Unitarianism to Congregationalism (1856) he worked with the YMCA, becoming President of the Chicago YMCA. The Moody Church was founded, and he conducted mission work in the slums. After meeting Ira D. Sankey they launched upon successful evangelistic tours. Moody made a first visit to Great Britain in 1867 and returned with Sankey for an extended term in 1873–1875, and again in 1881–1884. It was during the first of these tours that the *Sankey and Moody Hymnbook* (1873) appeared. He preached 'the old-fashioned gospel' message with literal interpretation of the Bible. At Northfield, Massachusetts, he conducted annual Bible conferences, founded a seminary for young women (1879) and one for young men (1881), and also founded what is now the Moody Bible Institute (1889).

Moore, George Foot (1851–1931)

American Presbyterian pastor and theologian who established a reputation as an Old Testament scholar with a remarkable knowledge of rabbinical source literature. He held academic posts at Andover Theological Seminary (1883–1902) and at Harvard. His most influential work was probably *Judaism in the First Century of the Christian Era*.

More, Hannah (1745–1833)

Popular religious writer and philanthropist. A bluestocking as a young woman, after the death of her friend David Garrick (1779) she turned to religion. Guided by William Wilberforce, she established schools in the west of England, worked to relieve poverty and wrote the *Cheap Repository Tracts* to educate and encourage the working classes.

More, Henry (1614–1687)

English philosopher of religion and poet. Educated at Cambridge and elected a fellow in 1639, he spent the whole of his life there. He was concerned to counter the secular philosophy of his day, corresponding with Descartes (published in 1659 as *The Immortality of the Soule*).

More, Sir Thomas (1478–1535)

Educated first in the classics, then in the law, he became a barrister in 1501. Attracted to the religious life at the London Carthusian charterhouse, he decided against celibacy and married in 1505, having entered Parliament the year before. Highly regarded as a scholar, his home at Chelsea became a centre for men of learning; More gave particular support to his friend Erasmus. He rose speedily after Henry VIII's accession, becoming a privy councillor in 1518, a knight in 1521 and eventually lord chancellor in 1529. His best-known work, *Utopia*, appeared in 1516. When Henry's intentions were clear, More resigned his post in 1532 and refused the oath on the Act of Succession eighteen months later. He was imprisoned in the Tower of London, where he wrote *Dialogue of Comfort against Tribulation*. On 6 July 1535 he was beheaded on Tower Hill, having been found guilty of treason for opposing the Act of Supremacy. In 1935 the Roman Catholic church canonised him as a martyr.

Morison, James (1816–1893)

Theologian and founder of the Evangelical Union. He trained for the ministry of the United Secession Church, but his preaching at Kilmarnock (1840) caused him to be accused of teaching against the Westminster Confession and he founded his own church. This later (1897) united with the Scottish Congregationalists to form the Congregational Union of Scotland.

Mornay, Philippe de (1549–1623)

French Protestant diplomat and writer. He wrote many political tracts in support of the Huguenots, for whom he also fought. A counselor of Henry of Navarre, he won a reputation of being the most outspoken publicist of the Protestant cause.

Morone, Giovanni (1509–1580)

Italian bishop of Moderna who served in the papal diplomatic service and, sympathetic to the Reformers' grievances, worked for a General Council to bring peace. Appointed cardinal in 1542, his reforming zeal led to suspicion and charges of heresy and, in 1557, imprisonment. The next pope, Pius IV, cleared him and Morone presided over the final session of the Council of Trent (1562), his diplomatic skill saving it from disaster. In his last years, as cardinal protector of England, he helped to administer the English College in Rome.

Morrison, Robert (1782–1834)

Presbyterian minister and first Protestant missionary to China. After ordination in 1807, the London Missionary Society sent him to Canton. With a colleague, William Milne, he translated the New Testament into Chinese (1813) and published a Chinese Grammar (1815). The whole Bible appeared in 1823. An Anglo-Chinese College was founded and was moved to Hong Kong in 1843. Morrison ended his days in China.

Morse, Henry (1595–1645)
After studying at Cambridge and for the law he became a
Roman Catholic in France in 1614. On a private visit to England he was imprisoned for four years for being a Catholic;
he returned to France, where he was ordained a priest in 1623.
Sent to England, he was almost immediately arrested and
spent three years in a York gaol. Although exiled, he returned
in 1633 and worked among the plague victims in London
(1636–1637). Again arrested and exiled, he returned once
more in 1643. Eventually captured and convicted at the Old
Bailey of being a Roman Catholic priest, he was hung, drawn
and quartered at Tyburn on 1 February 1645. In 1970 he was
declared a martyr by the Roman Catholic church.

Mott, John Rayleigh (1865–1955)
American Methodist layman. He was student secretary of the
International Committee of the YMCA (1888–1915) and assistant general-secretary of the YMCA in 1901. Mott was one of
the organisers of the World Missionary Conference which met
at Edinburgh in 1910, from which dates his involvement in the
ecumenical movement. He played an important part in the foundation of the World Council of Churches and was elected honorary president (1948). He served on the international scene in
various posts of responsibility, and was awarded the 1946 Nobel Peace Prize (shared with Emily Greene Bech) for his work in
international church and missionary movements. His many
writings included *The Future Leadership of the Church* (1909)
and *The Larger Evangelism* (1944).

Mott, Lucretia (1792–1880)
Quaker and pioneer reformer who founded the Women's
Rights Movement in the United States. She married a fellow
Quaker teacher and became a Quaker minister in 1821. The
couple were actively involved in the antislavery campaign.
With Elizabeth Stanton, in 1848 she held a convention at

Seneca Falls, New York, on women's rights and devoted the rest of her life to writing and lecturing for the cause.

Moule, Handley Carr Glyn (1841–1920)
A brilliant scholar at Cambridge, where he was elected fellow in 1865 and master of Marlborough College (1865–1867). In 1881 he became the first principal of the new evangelical theological college, Ridley Hall, Cambridge, and thereafter a leading light in English evangelicalism. He became bishop of Durham in 1901. He wrote many books, including _Veni Creator_ (1890) and _Christus Consolator_ (1915).

Mowinckel, Sigmund (1884–1965)
Norwegian biblical scholar who spent his whole teaching career at the University of Oslo (1917–1954). He made important contributions to Old Testament studies, but particularly to the study of the Book of Psalms. His _The Psalms in Israel's Worship_ (1962) is regarded as one of the major twentieth-century commentaries.

Mühlenberg, Henry Melchior (1711–1787)
German-born pastor and head of a celebrated family that led the Lutheran community in Pennsylvania for 150 years and contributed to public life, education and the army. In 1748 Henry organised the first Lutheran Synod in America.

Müller, George (1805–1898)
Although he was of German origin, most of his life was spent in England. Converted to Christianity at twenty, he joined the Plymouth Brethren and became a preacher. From 1832 he dedicated himself to caring for orphans on a large scale. The last seventeen years of his life were devoted to a world preaching tour.

Murray, John Courtney (1904–1967)
American Jesuit priest and theologian. Educated at Boston College, Woodstock and Rome; he taught theology at Woodstock Seminary and from 1941–1967 was editor of *Theological Studies*. He is best remembered for the formation of new principles of ecclesiastical political theology and for being the principal author of the Second Vatican Council's (1965) Declaration on Religious Freedom.

N

Nayler, James (c. 1618–1660)

Converted by George Fox to the Quaker teaching of the inner light (1651), he became Fox's deputy, preaching widely in northern England and leading the Society in London (1655). About that time, due to the influence of the Ranters, he was separated from Fox, imprisoned for blasphemy and only reconciled with Fox and the Society of Friends in 1660.

Neale, John Mason (1818–1866)

Anglican priest, author and hymnwriter. While at Cambridge he became a High Churchman, founded the Cambridge Camden Society with B. Webb (1839) and was ordained in 1842. Ill health bedevilled his pastoral work, but he founded the Sisterhood of St Margaret (1885), a religious community to care for the education of girls and tend the sick. He is best known for his hymns, many of which are still in popular use.

Neander, Joachim (1650–1680)

German pastor and hymnwriter. Converted to Christianity in 1670, he was attracted by the Pietist Movement and this and his love of nature shines through his many hymns. The popular 'Praise to the Lord, the Almighty' is just one which found its way into English translation.

Neri, St Philip (1515–1595)

Of Florentine origins, he went to Rome about 1533, where he tutored, studied and lived privately an austere life. Concerned for the care of the poor, convalescents and pilgrims, he founded a society to assist them (1548). Ordained in 1551, he joined a community of priests at the Church of San Girolamo, where later (1564–1575) he was the rector. So many boys and men came to his conferences that a special large room was built, called the Oratory, from which developed the Institute of the Oratory. (The Institute also encouraged music, hence 'oratorio'.) The congregation of the Oratory for Priests was approved in 1575 and Philip became the most sought-after figure in Rome, known for his gentleness and gaiety. He had numerous ecstatic experiences and was regarded as a saint long before being officially declared such in 1622.

Neumann, John Nepomucene (1811–1860)

Roman Catholic bishop of Philadelphia and the first American male to be canonised by the Roman Catholic church, by Pope Paul VI in 1977. After study in Prague and ordination in New York in 1836, he joined the Redemptorist Congregation of Priests and rose to become their United States superior. Devoted to education, he was a leader of the parochial school system in the United States. Appointed bishop of Philadelphia in 1852, he built many schools, churches and asylums in his diocese and, at the time of his death, was renowned for his holiness, charity and pastoral care.

Neumann, Therese (1898–1962)

A German stigmatic of Konnersreuth, Bavaria, on whose body appeared, from 1926, the marks resembling those on Christ's hands, feet and side. She also claimed to have visions of the Passion and the wounds were observed to bleed on most Fridays and during Lent. Examinations by the church authorities were inconclusive but, despite the local Roman Catholic bishop's caution, thousands flocked to visit her every year until her death.

Newman, John Henry (1801–1890)

Leader of the Tractarian Movement and later cardinal. Educated at Trinity College, Oxford, after ordination he became vicar at St Mary's, Oxford. A leading figure in the Oxford Movement from its beginning (1833), his sermons at St Mary's (published as *Parochial and Plain Sermons*) had a powerful influence upon its spread. He wrote twenty-four of the *Tracts for the Times* (1833–1841), the most famous and controversial being no. 90. His doubts about the Anglican church grew, and retiring from public life to a community he had founded at Littlemore (1842), he was finally received into the Roman Catholic church in 1845. His *Essay on the Development of Christian Doctrine* followed. Newman established the Oratory (see 'Neri, Philip') at Birmingham (1849); while serving as rector to the Catholic University, Dublin (1854–58), his *Idea of a University* was published. He was restored to national prominence with his *Apologia pro Vita Sua* (1864), which plotted his spiritual journey; but it was *A Grammar of Assent* (1870) which presented his mature thought. Newman was made a cardinal in 1879 by Pope Leo XIII.

Nicephorus, St (c. 758–829)

Greek Orthodox historian, theologian and patriarch of Constantinople who wrote and struggled in the cause of the Byzantine controversy over the veneration of images. Following in his father's footsteps, he supported the use of images in his *Apologeticus Minor* and *Apologeticus Major* (817). His works of history were highly regarded.

Nicholas, St (d. c. 350)

One of the most popular saints honoured in both the Eastern and Western churches; however, outside of tradition, nothing is known for certain of his life, except that he was probably bishop of Myra (fourth century), in modern Turkey. According to tradition he suffered during the Diocletian persecution and, as bishop, attended the Council of Nicaea. There was a shrine to him at Myra in the sixth century and Italian merchants seem to have removed the body to Bari in 1087. Other colourful traditions of his coming to the rescue of children, etc., were added later. Nicholas is the patron saint of several countries, including Russia and Greece, and of sailors and children. His modern popularity centres on his transformation, via the Dutch Protestant settlers in New Amsterdam (New York), into 'Sinter Claes', hence Santa Claus.

Nicholas—Five popes chose this name, the most noteworthy being:

Nicholas I, the Great, St (d. 867)
After years in papal service, he was elected pope in 858 and proved one of the most forceful of the early medieval popes. He was justly famed for his courage and firmness in dealing with emperors and kings. His support for the illegally deposed Ignatius, patriarch of Constantinople, led eventually to the Photian Schism; he upheld the dignity of marriage against King Lothair of Lorraine and King Charles the Bald of Burgundy. He sent missionaries to Scandinavia and Bulgaria. Nicholas was held in high regard for his personal integrity, care of the poor and pursuit of reform among the clergy.

Nicholas of Cusa (1401–1464)
Cardinal, scholar, mathematician, experimental scientist and influential philosopher. As a leading churchman he worked for reconciliation, e.g., of the Hussites with the church, and for reform; his _On Catholic Concordance_ (1433) was a complete programme for reform. He began as a supporter of the supremacy of a General Council, but in time reversed his opinion in favour of the supremacy of the papacy over the Council. In his greatest work _On Learned Ignorance_ (1440) he used mathemati-

cal principles to propound his philosophy. In breadth of learning and intellectual interests he was a forerunner of the Renaissance.

Nicholas of Flue, St (1417–1487)
Affectionately recalled in Swiss history as 'Bruder Klaus', after serving with distinction as a soldier (1439), cantonal councillor and judge, he consistently refused the post of governor. Happily married with ten children, at the age of fifty, with the approval of his family, he became a hermit at Ranft. He was famed for his holiness and wise counsel, which he used to avert a civil war between the Swiss cantons in 1481. He was canonised in 1947.

Nicole, Pierre (1625–1695)
Theologian and author whose controversial writings were, in the main, in support of Jansenism, a seventeenth-century movement within the Roman Catholic church. He taught at Port-Royal and cooperated with A. Arnauld. He opposed Calvinistic teaching and wrote against Molinos and Quietism. Among his many works, the most famous is the *Essays on Morality* (1671).

Niebuhr, Reinhold (1892–1971)
American theologian and writer. Ordained in 1915, he served at the Bethel Evangelical Church, Detroit, until 1928, when he accepted the post of professor of applied Christianity at Union Theological Seminary, New York City, where he remained until retirement. Firsthand experience of labour problems led him to advocate socialism, but he broke with the party in the 1930s. Theologically opposed to the liberalism of the 1920s, he was influenced by Barth and Brunner, but his own theology expounded 'a vital prophetic Christianity'. Niebuhr's best-known work was *The Nature and Destiny of Man* (1941–1943).

Niemöller, Martin (1892–1984)

The son of a pastor, he served Germany as a submarine commander in the First World War and after ordination (1931) pastored the Lutheran church in Dahlem, Berlin. He protested against Nazi interference in church affairs and founded the Pastors Emergency League, which developed into the Confessing Church. Arrested by the Gestapo, March 1938, he was imprisoned, eventually, in Dachau Concentration Camp. After the war he helped to rebuild the Evangelical church and served as head of its Foreign Relations Department (1945–1956). In 1961 Niemöller was elected as one of the presidents of the World Council of Churches.

Nightingale, Florence (1820–1910)

Born at Florence, Italy, after which she was named, she was educated largely by her father. From an early age she felt called by God to nursing; she studied, among other things, the approach of the Sisters of Charity of St Vincent de Paul and in 1851 undertook training with the Protestant deaconesses at Kaiserwerth, Germany. She offered to go to the Crimean War in 1854 and coped with conditions appalling in every way. Her devotion and expertise revolutionised nursing standards and became legendary. On her return to England (1856), the Nightingale School and Home for Nurses was founded (1860) in recognition of her services at St Thomas's Hospital, London.

Nilus of Ancyra, St (d. c. 430) (also called Nilus the Ascetic)

Greek Byzantine abbot and author of ascetical literature. A disciple and supporter of St John Chrysostom, he became a monk and eventually abbot of a monastery near Ancyra. He wrote many tracts on moral and monastic subjects; he refuted Arianism and wrote about a thousand letters of spiritual direction. His writings show him to be a master of Christian spirituality, and his influence on the direction of Eastern and Western monasticism was considerable.

Norbert, St (c. 1080–1134)

Archbishop of Magdeburg and the founder of the Premonstratensians (also called White Canons or Norbertines). Ordained as a subdeacon, he led a worldly life until a sudden conversion led him to accept ordination to the priesthood (1115). He became dedicated to preaching reform of life; renowned for his eloquence, he traveled throughout Europe. In 1119 Pope Calixtus II asked him to found a religious congregation at Premontre, France, to be dedicated to preaching. Chosen as archbishop of Magdeburg (1126), he exerted great influence in church affairs for the rest of his life. He was declared a saint in 1582.

Nowell, Alexander (c. 1507–1602)

Anglican priest, scholar and dean of St Paul's Cathedral, London, where his preaching often offended Elizabeth I. He wrote three Catechisms (1520) the *Large,* the *Middle* and the *Small*; the last, in substance, appears in the Book of Common Prayer and is still the official Catechism of the Church of England.

Oberlin, Johann (1740–1826)

A former teacher, he became a Lutheran pastor at Walderbach in the Vosges and dedicated his life to raising the living standards of all the people of the five isolated villages, regardless of their religion. He won an international reputation for his advanced thinking in social and educational methods. He transformed the area with schools, adult education, improved farming techniques, etc. His name was given to Oberlin House at Potsdam and to Oberlin College, Oberlin, Ohio.

O'Bryan, William (1778–1868)

A Methodist minister who founded, in Devonshire, England, the Bible Christian church (1815), which split away from Methodism. It spread to the United States (1846) via Canada. O'Bryan left and took up an itinerant preaching career in 1831. The Bible Christians joined the United Methodist church in 1907.

Ochino, Bernadino (1487–1564)

After an illustrious background in the Franciscan order, e.g., twice vicar-general of the Capuchins and sought after as an eloquent preacher, he became a Lutheran and accepted a pastorate at Augsburg. Invited to England by Cranmer, he enjoyed a clerical appointment at Canterbury. Renowned for his violent anti-Roman views, he wrote *The Usurped Primacy of the Bishop of Rome* (1549). He went to Zurich on Queen Mary's accession, but due to his unsound teaching in *Thirty Dialogues* (1563) he was expelled; he was also driven from Poland when he tried to settle there. He died of the plague while traveling in Moravia.

O'Connor, Flannery (1925–1964)
Roman Catholic writer and authoress. Born in Savannah, Georgia. It was always her ambition to be a writer and her first published story (part of her first novel) *The Geranium* won an award. Her writings include the novels *Wise Blood* and *The Violent Bear It Away*. Her personality comes across in the collected letters, *The Habit of Being* (1979).

Oecolampadius, John (1482–1531) (German name: Johannes Huszgen)
Lecturer, linguist, preacher and humanist. As a Roman Catholic he worked with Erasmus. His admiration of Martin Luther prompted him to join the Reform movement in 1522. At Basel he established a reputation as a lecturer and preacher and developed a friendship with Zwingli, whose teaching on the Eucharist he defended.

Ogilvie, John (c. 1579–1615)
A Scottish Calvinist, son of the baron of Drum-na-Keith, while studying abroad he became a Roman Catholic (1596). He joined the Jesuits and was ordained at Paris in 1610. Using the disguise of a horse trader he worked secretly among the persecuted Catholics of Edinburgh and Glasgow (1613–1615). Betrayed, he was imprisoned and tortured for several months. Refusing to acknowledge the spiritual supremacy of the king, he was condemned to death and hanged at Glasgow.

Oldham, Joseph Houldsworth (1874–1969)

Born in India, educated in Scotland and at Oxford, he was secretary of the YMCA in Lahore (1897–1901). While working for the Student Christian Movement, he was appointed organising secretary of the Edinburgh World Missionary Conference (1910). His dedication to Africa, and his assistance to missions and missionaries as the colonial powers withdrew, is generally considered his greatest achievement. He helped prepare for the launch of the World Council of Churches and held the post of secretary to the Council on the Christian Life (1939–1942) and the Christian Frontier Council (1942–1945).

Olier, Jean-Jacques (1608–1657)

Ordained a Roman Catholic priest (1633), he became a popular preacher conducting parish missions (1634–1639). He founded a seminary at Vangirard which transferred to Saint-Sulpice, Paris. A community of secular priests he founded there, called the Sulpicians, specialised in the training of priests. Saint-Sulpice became the model for other seminaries through Europe and further afield, e.g., Montreal, in 1657.

Oman, John Wood (1860–1939)

Presbyterian theologian, lecturer and principal of Westminster College, Cambridge (1907–1925). His teaching on the uniqueness and independence of the religious consciousness was expressed in his book *The Natural and the Supernatural* (1931).

Orchard, William Edwin (1877–1955)

Presbyterian minister who attracted large congregations to King's Weigh House Congregational Church, London. He became nationally known for his efforts to draw Protestants and Roman Catholics together. He led prolonged ecumenical negotiations with the Church of England which collapsed. Orchard became a Roman Catholic in 1932 and was ordained a priest in 1935. His many writings included the popular *The Temple* (1913).

Origen (c. 185-c. 254) (Latin name: Origenes Adamantius)

On the martyrdom of his father, Leonidas, at Alexandria (202) Origen was appointed head of the catechetical school there. He led an austere, ascetic life, traveled and studied pagan philosophy. From c. 218 to 230 he devoted himself to writing. On a visit (230) to Palestine he was ordained priest, but his own Alexandrian bishop declared it irregular and Origen settled at Caesarea (231), where he established a famous school. In the persecution of Decius (250) he was severely tortured, from which he never really recovered. Many of Origen's writings are lost. He was principally a biblical scholar, his *Hexapla* being a synopsis of several versions of the Old Testament. His greatest theological work was *On First Principles* (before 231), which reveals why he is regarded as one of the most influential theologians and biblical scholars of the early church.

Osmund, St (d. 1099)

Bishop of Salisbury (the old Sarum) and chancellor of England who followed William I to England. He helped compile the Domesday Book and is credited with the introduction of the Sarum Rite.

Oswald, St (c. 605–642)

King of Northumbria who appealed to Iona for monks to establish Christianity; St Aidan responded and received Oswald's support. He was killed in battle with King Penda of Mercia and ever afterwards was honoured as a martyr.

Oswald, St (d. 992)

Archbishop of York who established many monastic houses, particularly at Ramsey in Cambridgeshire. Also famed for his energetic reform of abuses and the education of the clergy.

Overbeck, Johann Friedrick (1789–1869)
German Romantic painter and leader of the Lucas Brother-hood, or the Nazarenes, who were devoted to depicting, in precise outlines and clear bright colours, Christian religious subjects, his major work being the 'Rose Miracle of St Francis' (1829) at Assisi.

Owen, John (1616–1683)
Puritan minister, writer and preacher. Originally a Calvinist, he became an independent, holding pastoral posts at Fordham and Coggeshall, Essex; his outstanding preaching before Parliament led to his appointment as dean (1651) and vice-chancellor of Christ Church, Oxford. After the Restoration he devoted himself to preaching and voluminous controversialist writing.

Ozanam, Antoine Frédéric (1813–1853)
Brilliant French scholar in law and literature; in his Catholicism he was influenced by Montalembert, Lacordaire and other liberal thinkers. His concern for social conditions led to the foundation of the Society of St Vincent de Paul (SVP), an association of lay people devoted to the service of the poor, and *Ère nouvelle*, the journal of the French Catholic Social Movement.

P

Pachomius, St (c. 290–346)

Of Egyptian origins, after serving in the emperor Constantine's North African army he became a Christian (c. 314) and embraced a hermit's life. About 320 he founded the first communal settlement, with a Rule of Life, for monks. His Rule, the first of its kind, influenced later more famous Rules, e.g., that of St Benedict. He was so popular an abbot that at his death there were eleven monasteries (nine male and two female) with a total of seven thousand monks.

Palestrina, Giovanni Pierluigi da (c. 1525–1594)

Originating from Palestrina (Italy), he moved to Rome as a boy and lived and worked there, filling a variety of musical appointments, rising eventually to composer of the Papal Chapel (1570) and choirmaster of St Peter's Basilica (1571). His motets and masses filled a vacuum in church music and he was influenced by and wrote music for St Philip Neri and his Oratory. Palestrina's deeply religious polyphony, welcomed by the Roman Catholic church, was enormously influential in the subsequent development of church music.

Paley, William (1743–1805)

Anglican priest, theologian and writer, educated at Christ's College, Cambridge, where he became a fellow in 1766. His most famous work, *View of Evidences of Christianity* (1794), became required reading for entrance to Cambridge, and his *Natural Theology* (1802) developed his theology of the teleological argument for the existence of God.

Palladius (c. 365–425)
After a period with monks in Egypt, under the direction of Evagerius Ponticus, he became bishop of Helenopolis and suffered exile for his faith. He is remembered for his famous Lausiac History, entitled *Friends of God* (c. 419), being the first history of early monasticism.

Papias (c. 60–130)
Bishop of Hierapolis of whom nothing is known beyond the remarks of Irenaeus, the second-century bishop of Lyons, that Papias was a disciple of the apostle John and a companion of St Polycarp. His work *Expositions of the Oracles of the Lord*, which now exists only in quotations in other writings, authenticates and casts light upon the Gospels of Matthew and Mark.

Parham, Charles Fox (1873–1929)
Pentecostal evangelist, founder and director of Bethel College, Topeka, Kansas. Influenced by the Holiness Movement, Parham's work was instrumental in the revival known as the Latter Rain, which later became the Pentecostal Movement.

Parker, Matthew (1504–1575)
Archbishop of Canterbury, of scholarly inclination, chosen (1559) by Queen Elizabeth I from relative obscurity. A moderate reformer, he strove to maintain the settlement of 1559, guiding the Church of England to a distinct identity apart from Roman Catholicism and Protestantism. Involved in the formulation of the Thirty-Nine Articles and the *Bishops' Bible*, he also wrote several scholarly works in English church history.

Parsons (or Persons), Robert (1546–1610)
After resigning a fellowship at Balliol College, Oxford (1568–1574), he became a Jesuit priest in Rome and returned secretly (1580) to minister to English Catholics. Forced to return to the Continent he directed the Jesuit Mission to England and established seminaries for English priests in Spain, at Valladolid and Madrid. He helped with the running of the English College, Rome (1597–1610), where he died.

Pascal, Blaise (1623–1662)
French mathematician, inventor, religious philosopher and theologian. Mathematically gifted as a child, Pascal was later responsible for the invention of the barometer and the first digital calculator (1644), the syringe and the hydraulic press (1647–1654). He experienced what he called a 'first conversion' when he 'discovered' the Jansenist teaching at Port-Royal (1646), and underwent his 'definitive' conversion in 1654, which led to regular visits to the Port-Royal community, his famous *Lettres provinciales* (1654) in defence of Jansenism and his posthumously published *Pensées*.

Paschasius Radbertus, St (c. 790–865)
French Benedictine abbot of Corbie, near Amiens, who is best known for his work *De Corpore et Sanguine Christi* (831), which became the dominant interpretation of the doctrine of the Eucharist for hundreds of years. He was also the author of commentaries on the Book of Lamentations and Matthew's Gospel.

Patmore, Coventry (Kersey Dighton) (1823–1896)
Roman Catholic poet and essayist who began writing poetry at an early age and was employed at the British Museum. His best-remembered poetry, containing a mystical view of divine love and married love, is in *The Unknown Eros and Other Odes* (1877). He translated *St Bernard on the Love of God* and wrote a long novel in five parts, *The Angel in the House* (1854–1863).

Paton, John Gibbon (1824–1907)

Presbyterian missionary to the New Hebrides who, after ten missionary years in Glasgow, Scotland, lived an austere and dangerous life on the island of Tanna. There his wife and child died. From 1866 to 1881 he was centred on Aniwa before moving to Melbourne.

Paton, William (1886–1943)

Presbyterian minister and writer. In 1911 he became secretary to the Student Christian Movement; from 1922 to 1927 he was general secretary of the National Christian Council of India, Burma and Ceylon. The author of several works on mission, he also edited the *International Review of Missions*.

Patrick, St (c. 389-c. 461)

The life of the apostle and patron saint of Ireland is shrouded in myth and legend. He is known from two short works, his *Confessio* and *Epistola*. Apparently, at sixteen he was captured from Roman Britain by Irish pirates and spent six years as a shepherd in Ireland. After escaping back to Britain he studied for the priesthood (some say in Gaul), probably being ordained c. 417. He returned to Ireland as a bishop c. 432 and spent the rest of his life traveling the length and breadth of the country, meeting a fierce opposition, but successfully converting the Irish. He probably set up his episcopal see at Armagh. Later traditions added embellishments of uncertain authenticity.

Patrick, Simon (1625–1707)

Originally a Presbyterian minister, he was ordained for the Anglican ministry in 1654, and after a succession of pastoral posts became a bishop, first of Chichester, then of Ely. A sincere Latitudinarian, he helped to found the Society for Promoting Christian Knowledge and the Society for the Propagation of the Gospel. He wrote many treatises and the notable *The Parable of the Pilgrim* (1664).

Patteson, John Coleridge (1827–1871)

Missionary bishop of Melanesia. Educated at Eton and Balliol College, Oxford, in 1855 he set out to work in the South Seas, where he was very successful, also founding a college for boys on Norfolk Island. Consecrated bishop in 1861, his murder by the natives of Nukapu caused great interest and concern in Great Britain.

Paul—Six popes chose this name, the most noteworthy being:

Paul VI (1897–1978)

Baptised Giovanni Battista Montini and ordained in 1920, he entered the Vatican diplomatic service and, over a period of thirty years, rose through various posts of responsibility. He was appointed archbishop of Milan in 1954 and cardinal by Pope John XXIII four years later. He succeeded John XXIII in 1963, guided the Second Vatican Council through its remaining sessions and then the task of carrying out its reforming decisions. His encyclicals appeared conservative, especially *Humanae Vitae* (1968), on birth control, and *Matrimonia Mixta* (1970), on mixed marriages. He was the first pope to travel abroad; for example he met Athenagoras, the Greek patriarch, on a pilgrimage to the Holy Land (1964) and traveled to the United States (1965) to plead for peace in an address to the United Nations General Assembly.

Paul of the Cross, St (1694–1775)

Originally Paolo Francesco Danei, he led an austere life of prayer and, in 1720, he began to have visions which inspired him to found a religious order, or congregation, devoted to the suffering of Christ on the cross, known as the Passionists. Faced with great difficulties, he worked as a missionary and was famed as a preacher and spiritual director. At his death he had founded twelve monasteries in Italy, but the Passionist order soon spread around the world. He was canonised in 1867.

Paulinus—There are four saints with the name Paulinus; that of most interest to English readers is:

Paulinus, St (c. 584–644)
Missionary of Northumbria. Sent to England in 601 to support and help the missionary work of St Augustine of Canterbury, he accompanied Ethelburga of Kent to York when she married Edwin of Northumbria in 625. A cathedral was begun at York and his missionary work was successful, but on the defeat of Edwin by Cadwallon he returned to Kent and occupied the see of Rochester.

Peake, Arthur Samuel (1865–1929)
Methodist lay biblical scholar, first to hold the Rylands Chair of biblical criticism and exegesis at Manchester University (1904). He was the author of several biblical works, including *The Bible, Its Origin, Its Significance and Its Abiding Worth* (1913), but is best remembered for his editorship of the *Commentary* that bears his name.

Peckham, John (c. 1225–1292)
Theologian, poet and archbishop of Canterbury. He joined the Franciscan order at Oxford (c. 1250), where he studied and later taught. From 1269 to 1271 he occupied the Franciscan chair of theology at Paris. After a period in Rome he was elected to Canterbury and immediately promoted church reform. Theologically he supported the Franciscan tradition, especially against the Dominicans; his works include Bible commentaries and his poetic work, *Philomena*.

Péguy, Charles (1873–1914)
French poet, philosopher and patriot. He gave up the study of philosophy to manage a bookshop in Paris which became an

intellectual centre supporting Christian Socialism: this was promoted by his journal *Cahiers de la quinzaine*. An ardent Roman Catholic and a socialist, his works, including two on Joan of Arc (1897 and 1910), express this. His last massive poetic work, *Eve* (1913), reflects meditatively on the human condition. While serving in the French army, he died at the Battle of Marne, 1914.

Pennington (or Penington), Isaac (1616–1679)

Originally a Puritan, educated at Cambridge, he heard George Fox speak and joined the Society of Friends (1657). For his Quaker beliefs he was imprisoned and lost his property. He wrote many books which, with his example, promoted the growth of the Society.

Penn, William (1644–1718)

Son of Admiral Sir William Penn, he was educated at Oxford, where he refused to conform to Anglicanism. In 1665 he joined the Society of Friends; for writing *The Sandy Foundation Shaken* (1668) he was imprisoned in the Tower of London, where he wrote the classic *No Cross, No Crown* (1669). Acquitted in a famous court case, he obtained authorisation (1682), founded the 'Free Society of Traders of Pennsylvania' and sailed for America, where the American Commonwealth of Pennsylvania was founded. The rest of his life was dedicated to developing this colony and defending Quaker principles and practices. Further works included *The Fruits of Solitude* (1692) and *Primitive Christianity* (1696).

Perkins, William (1558–1602)

English Puritan theologian, fellow of Christ's College, Cambridge (1584–1594), famed for his powerful anti-Romanist preaching and systematic exposition of Puritan theology. His works, highly regarded in the seventeenth century, included his *Reformed Catholike* (1597).

Peter Chrysologus, St (c. 400-c. 450)

Archbishop of Ravenna, Italy, who, supported by the empress Galla Placida, put through a vast building programme. A champion of orthodoxy, which earned him the title of 'Doctor of the Church' in 1729, he was renowned for his preaching (hence the Greek name 'Chrysologus', 'Goldenworded').

Peter Claver, St (1581–1654)

A Jesuit missionary to South America, he called himself 'the slave of the Negroes', dedicating thirty-eight years of his life to the total service of the slaves shipped from West Africa to Cartegena, South America's principal slave market. Despite fierce official opposition, Peter visited, defended, nursed and taught the black slaves. It is estimated that he instructed and baptised over three hundred thousand of them. He was declared a saint in 1888.

Peter Lombard (c. 1100–1160)

Theologian and bishop of Paris whose fame rests chiefly upon the authorship of *Sententiarum libri quatuor* (the *Sentences,* in four volumes), which is a clear systematic presentation of theology, especially on the sacraments. It became the standard theological textbook for hundreds of years and won him the title 'Master of the Sentences'.

Peter the Hermit (1050–1115) (also Peter the Little)

Influential preacher and monastic founder, who, after Pope Urban II called for a Crusade to liberate the Holy Places (1095), toured Europe preaching the Crusade. Eventually he entered Jerusalem with a victorious army and later returned to Europe (1100) as prior of the monastery at Neumoutier, which he had founded.

Peter of Verona, St (1205–1252) (also known as Peter Martyr)

Son of parents who were members of the Cathari sect, he studied at Bologna and joined the Dominican order. He gained a great reputation as a preacher, founded several religious centres to combat heresy and was appointed inquisitor for northern Italy by Pope Gregory IX (1251). He successfully preached among the Cathari, although some were forced into exile. Returning to Milan from a preaching tour, he was killed, with a companion, by two Cathari assassins.

Peter Martyr (1500–1562) (also Pietro Martire Vermigli)

Named after Peter of Verona, he was born in Florence and joined the Augustinian order. A Bible scholar, he was much in sympathy with the Reformers and fled to Zurich, Basel and Strasbourg, where he was appointed professor of theology. Invited to England, he was made Regius professor of theology at Oxford (1548) and was involved in the Book of Common Prayer of 1552. After a short imprisonment under Queen Mary he was allowed to return to his former post at Strasbourg (1554). He later removed to Zurich because of his views on the Eucharist.

Peter Nolasco, St (c. 1189–1258)

The precise details of his life are uncertain. Of a French family, he received his inheritance at age fifteen when his father died. He used his fortune to ransom Christian prisoners from the Moors. Between 1218 and 1234 he founded the order of Our Lady of Ransom (the Mercedarians), with St Raymond of Peñafort, to ransom Christians from the Saracens. (The order was later dedicated to hospital work.)

Peter of Alcantara, St (1499–1562) (original name: Pedro Garavito)

Ordained for the order of Observant Franciscans (1524), he emphasised the penitential aspects of St Francis of Assisi's teaching and became superior of several houses and provincial in Spain. His ideals of austerity were popular and c. 1557 he founded his own order, the Alcantarines, or Barefooted Friars Minor. Admired by St Teresa of Avila, whom he helped in her reform work, he was much in demand as a spiritual director. His friars spread to Italy, Germany and France.

Petrarch, Francesco (1304–1374)

Italian humanist and poet of international standing. His most famous poetry, which influenced all subsequent European Romantic poetry and is collected in the *Canzoniere,* was addressed to an idealised beloved, Laura. He traveled widely, copying classical manuscripts, but he also spent long periods in solitude. His religious poetry meditates upon the transitory nature of life.

Petri, Laurentius (1499–1573)

Swedish churchman and the first Protestant archbishop of Uppsala. He was responsible for the Swedish Bible of 1541. His *Kyrkoordning* ('Church Order') of thirty years later defined the church-state relations which led to the independence of the Swedish church.

Petri, Olaus (1493–1552)

Swedish churchman, and brother of the above, who played an important role in the reformation of the Swedish church. He rose to prominence in 1531 as chancellor to the king, but fell from favour by his later opposition. His preaching and his literature, including a Swedish New Testament, the Swedish liturgy, a hymnbook, etc., made him the leading exponent of reform in Sweden.

Philaret, Drozdov (1782–1867)

Russian Orthodox monk, theologian and metropolitan of Moscow. Well-known for his scholarship and his preaching, he was a skilled administrator and was considered an exemplary bishop. His best-known work, the *Christian Catechism of the Orthodox Catholic Eastern Greco-Russian Church* (1823), exerted a great influence upon nineteenth-century Russian theology.

Phillpotts, Henry (1778–1869)
Anglican bishop of Exeter and a conservative High Churchman who supported the Oxford Movement, he had a special interest in the liturgy and the monastic life. His refusal to institute George C. Gorham to the living of Bampford Speke gave rise to one of the most famous lawsuits of the nineteenth century.

Photius (c. 820–891)
Elected patriarch of Constantinople while still a layman and professor of philosophy (1858), he defended his church against the papacy. He is remembered for objecting to the insertion of the *Filioque* clause in the creed and for the schism which grew out of the break with Rome.

Pilkington, James (c. 1520–1576)
The first Protestant occupant of the see of Durham (1560) and a prominent leader of the Protestant party in the Church of England. He contributed to the revision of the Book of Common Prayer and, as Regius professor of divinity at Cambridge, promoted Protestant theology in and through the university.

Pire, Dominique (1910–1969)
Belgian Dominican priest and educator who won the Nobel Peace Prize (1958) for his energetic aid to displaced persons in Europe after World War II. In 1949 he founded the 'Aide aux Personnes Déplacée' and (1950–1954) four 'homes of welcome' in Belgium, as well as seven European 'villages' to help refugees. Later he worked for peace with the University of Peace, Huy, and his 'Islands of Peace' project in India.

Pius—There were twelve popes of this name. Noteworthy are:

Pius II (1405–1464)
Aeneas Sylvius Piccolomini was elected pope in 1458, having established a reputation as a humanist, scholar, poet and astute

politician. After the fall of Constantinople in 1453 he worked for a Crusade against the Turks' threat to Europe; however, he failed to unite the European princes.

Pius V, St (1504–1572)
An Italian Dominican, Antonio Ghislieri was an ascetic reformer who, from the post of inquisitor (1551) and grand inquisitor seven years later, then bishop of Nepi and Sutri (1556), rose to cardinal (1557). Elected pope in 1566, he inaugurated one of the most austere periods in the Roman Catholic church, eliminating Protestantism from Italy and putting the decrees of the Council of Trent into effect.

Pius IX (1792–1878)
Originally Giovanni Maria Mastai-Ferretti, he served as bishop of Spoleto (1827) and bishop of Imola (1832) before being chosen pope in 1846. His was the longest pontificate in history and marked a transition from liberalism to conservatism. His pontificate began with liberal reforms in the Papal States, but when these were lost in 1870, Pio Nono remained a virtual prisoner in the Vatican and became more conservative. He restored the Catholic hierarchy to England and Wales (1850), defined the dogma of the Immaculate Conception (1854) and issued the *Syllabus of Errors* (1864) and *Quanta Cura* (1864), which reaffirmed traditional Catholic beliefs. He summoned the First Vatican Council (1869–1870) that defined papal infallibility. He strengthened the spiritual authority of the papacy as its temporary power disappeared.

Pius X, St (1835–1914)
Born Giuseppe Melchiorre Sarto, of a poor Italian family, he rose through pastoral posts to cardinal patriarch of Venice (1893). Elected pope in 1903, he set his heart upon a spiritually orientated pontificate, but was compelled to issue two encyclicals against the French government over its confiscation of church property. Viewing Modernism as an insidious

new heresy, he issued the decree *Lamentabili* (1907) and the encyclical *Pascendi Gregis* (1907). He is best remembered for his pastoral concern, personal sanctity and as 'the Pope of frequent Communion', which he promoted and encouraged. Venerated as a saint in his own lifetime, he was canonised in 1954.

Pius XI (1857–1939)
Originally Ambrogio Damiano Archille Ratti, of scholarly background and interests, he taught, becoming the prefect of the Vatican Library in 1912. Nuncio to Poland (1919), he became a cardinal and archbishop of Milan (1921) and was elected to the papacy in 1922. He concluded the Lateran Treaty with Mussolini and issued several influential encyclicals, viz. *Divini Illius Magistri* (1929), on education, *Casti Connubii* (1930), on the dignity of marriage, and *Quadragesimo Anno* (1931), on social justice. He encouraged the Apostolate of the Laity through the Catholic Action Movement. While he encouraged missionary work he did not encourage the ecumenical movement.

Pius XII (1876–1958)
After ordination (1899) Eugenio Pacelli entered the Vatican Secretariat of State, and after serving in Bavaria (1917) and Berlin (1925) he was created a cardinal and Secretary of State to the Vatican (1929). Elected pope ten years later, he tried to prevent the Second World War with his *Five Peace Points,* but, having failed, he worked in neutrality for refugees and prisoners. He was a prolific writer, and some of his encyclicals were very influential, e.g., *Mystici Corporis Christi* (1943), on the church as the mystical Body of Christ, *Divino Afflante Spiritu* (1943), an encouragement and guide to the study of Scripture and *Mediator Dei* (1947), which encouraged reform of the liturgy. He reformed several liturgical practices, especially Holy Week. With the decree *Munificentissimus Deus* (1950) he defined the teaching on the Assumption of the Virgin Mary.

In the aftermath of the war he guided his church through reconstruction.

Plunket, Oliver (1629–1681)

Of a noble Irish family, he was educated and ordained in Rome, where he later lectured in theology. Appointed Roman Catholic archbishop of Armagh and primate of all Ireland (1668), he returned to a disorganised and dispirited Irish church. In the face of constant hardship he raised the standards of order, education and discipline. In 1673, under renewed persecution, he continued his pastoral work in secrecy. Betrayed (1679), he was imprisoned. Farcical legal proceedings led to his execution for treason at Tyburn, London. He was canonised as a martyr in 1975.

Pole, Reginald (1500–1558)

English cardinal and archbishop of Canterbury who was of royal descent through both parents, in recognition of which Henry VIII paid for his education at Oxford and Padua. He, however, broke with Henry over his antipapal policies (his two brothers and mother, Margaret, were subsequently executed by Henry for treason without evidence). Trained in humanism, he was the leader of those Catholic clerics who sought reform and reconciliation with Protestantism. A powerful figure in Mary Tudor's government, he pursued a reforming policy in the church, but Pope Paul IV cancelled his Legatine authority and accused him of unsound doctrine. He died, demoralised, twelve hours after Queen Mary.

Polycarp, St (probably c. 69-c. 155)

Greek bishop of Smyrna (modern Turkey) and a leading Christian figure in second-century Roman Asia. His importance lies in his intermediary position between the times of the apostles (St Irenaeus says he knew St John) and the great Christian writers of the end of the second century, as well as for his energetic defence of orthodoxy against the Marcian heresy, the Valentians and the Gnostics. His important *Letter to the Philippians* is a testimony to the New Testament texts from which he quotes. After a visit to Rome at the age of eighty-six, he was arrested and, refusing to sacrifice to the gods, was burnt to death.

Porres, St Martin de (1579–1639)

Dominican lay brother of Lima, Peru, who served in his monastic community as barber, infirmarian, etc., and who became famous throughout the city for his kindness, particularly his care of the sick and African slaves. He founded an orphanage and a foundling hospital. Canonised in 1962, he is the Peruvian national patron of social justice.

Prokopovich, Feofan (1681–1736)

Orthodox theologian and archbishop of Novgorod. After an Orthodox education he became a Roman Catholic and studied in Rome. Returning to Kiev (1701), he reverted to his Orthodox faith, becoming a monk and later an abbot. In 1716 he became an adviser to the Tsar and was eventually responsible for the legislative reform of the Russian church. As a theologian he is considered the father of Russian systematic theology, and his principal work is an exposition of the entire corpus of doctrinal theology.

Prosper of Aquitaine, St (c. 390-c. 463)

Monk and theologian of Marseilles, known for his defence of orthodoxy against the semi-Pelagian heresy and for his friendship and support of Augustine of Hippo. After Augustine's death (430) he went to Rome and won support for Augustine's teaching on grace and predestination; he also wrote in his defence, particularly *The Book of the Sentences of St Augustine*. Towards the end of his life he was secretary to Pope Leo the Great.

Provoost, Samuel (1742–1815)

The Anglican rector of Trinity Church, New York, who won the title 'patriot rector' for his loyalty to the American Revolution and overcame American diffidence towards the Anglican episcopacy. A chaplain to Congress (1785) and the United States Senate (1789), he was elected the first Episcopal bishop of New York in 1786.

Prynne, William (1600–1669)

An English lawyer and member of Parliament of unbending Puritan beliefs whose denunciation of the theatre (interpreted as an attack upon both Charles I and his theatrically inclined wife) and of archbishop Laud led to persecution by the government, imprisonment and disfigurement. A prolific writer and controversialist, he wrote against the Independents, the papists and the Quakers.

Pseudo-Dionysius the Areopagite (fl. c. 500)

Historical research has failed to reveal the identity of this writer who assumed the pseudonym of one of Paul's converts (Acts 17:34). He was probably a Syrian monk who wrote a series of treatises and letters for the purpose of uniting Neoplatonic philosophy with Christian theology and mystical experience. His influence has pervaded almost all theological thought from the Venerable Bede to the sixteenth-century Spanish mystics.

Pugin, Augustus Welby Northmore (1812–1852)

An architect and author who was the principal leader and inspirer of the English Roman Catholic Gothic revival. He was responsible for many new churches, including St Chad's Cathedral, Birmingham, and St George's Cathedral, Southwark. He also wrote extensively on church architecture, including *Contrasts* (1836) and *An Apology for the Revival of Christian Architecture in England* (1843).

Purcell, Henry (1659–1695)

English composer and organist at Westminster Abbey (from 1679) and the Chapel Royal (1682). Regarded as the most important English composer of his time, he is famous for both vocal and instrumental music. Besides secular music, he wrote many anthems for worship, his most famous sacred music being settings for the *Benedicite, Magnificat* and *Nunc Dimittis* and for his *Te Deum* and *Jubilate in D* (1694).

Pusey, Edward Bouverie (1800–1882)

Anglican theologian and leader of the Oxford Movement. Fellow of Oriel College, Oxford (1823), he studied in Germany and in 1828 was appointed Regius professor of Hebrew at Oxford. Associated with the Tractarian Movement from 1833, he wrote important tracts on baptism and the Eucharist; he assumed leadership of the movement when Newman withdrew. A fine preacher, he was suspended for two years as a result of his teaching on the Real Presence. In 1845 he helped to found in London the first Anglican Sisterhood. Known for his sincerity and humility, he built St Savior's Church, Leeds, at his own expense and cared for the sick in the cholera epidemic of 1866. His sermons were as influential as his many writings, which included *The Doctrine of the Real Presence* (1855) and *Daniel, the Prophet* (1864).

Quarles, Francis (1592–1644)

Anglican religious poet who is famous for his popular books *Emblemes* (1635) and *Hieroglyphikes* (1638). (Emblem books were popular devotional aids, highly regarded in seventeenth-century England.) Earlier he had produced many biblical paraphrases, such as *Job Militant* (1624).

Quesnel, Pasquier (1634–1719)

French theologian and writer who led the Jansenists and was the centre of continuing controversy in seventeenth-century France. His greatest work, *Nouveau Testament en francais avec des reflexions morales* (1692), was condemned by Pope Clement XI's bull *Unigenitus* (1708) and Quesnel spent the last years of his life defending his teaching.

R

Rabanus Maurus (c. 780–856)

Benedictine abbot of Fulda and archbishop of Mainz, recognised as one of the most influential churchmen and theologians of his age. He was accorded the title of 'Teacher of Germany' for his development of German language and literature. Elected abbot of Fulda (822), he developed the monastery into a renowned centre of learning and culture and a base for extensive missionary work throughout Germany. As archbishop of Mainz he convened synods to refute doctrinal error. His many works include several commentaries on books of the Bible and a vast twenty-two volume encyclopaedia of knowledge entitled *On the Nature of Things,* also known as *On the Universe* (842–847).

Rabaut, Paul (1718–1794)

Protestant minister of the French Reformed church who assumed leadership of the Huguenots on the death of Antoine Court. His patient restraint helped to achieve the Edict of Toleration of 1787.

Rad, Gerhard von (1901–1971)

German Old Testament scholar, educated at Tübingen University, who later lectured at Jena, Göttingen and, from 1949 to 1966, at Heidelberg. He specialised in the study of Old Testa-

ment theology and of the first books of the Bible, applying to
them the principles of literary analysis and form criticism.

Raikes, Robert (1736–1811)

English journalist, philanthropist and founder of Sunday
schools. From a concern for prison reform, Raikes turned his
attention to the unsupervised children on a Sunday of his
native Gloucester, and in 1780 he opened a Sunday school for
them. In spite of opposition he persevered and reported success in 1783 in his paper, the *Gloucester Journal*. There followed the Sunday School Society in 1785.

Rancé, Armand-Jean le Bouthillier de (1626–1700)

Abbot of La Trappe, France, whose early life as a priest was
very worldly; after a sudden conversion, in 1657, he entered
the Cistercian novitiate at Perseigne and became regular abbot
of La Trappe (which he had held as a benefice); he then devoted himself to the reform of the Cistercian order. His book
Treatise on the Holiness and Duties of the Monastic Life (1683), in
which he forbade study for monks, led to controversy with
other religious orders.

Raphael (1483–1520)

Painter and architect, one of the great masters of the Italian
High Renaissance style. After an apprenticeship and collabora-
tion with Perugino in Perugia (c. 1495–1504) he painted the
Crucifixion (1502) and *Espousals of the Virgin* (1504). Moving
to Siena and Florence he was influenced by Leonardo da Vinci
and Michelangelo; there followed the first of his famed series
of Madonnas. Pope Julius II summoned him to Rome, where
he executed many biblical scenes, including *St Peter Released
from Prison* and the celebrated *Sistine Madonna* (c. 1512). In
1514 he was appointed principal architect in the reconstruction of St Peter's Basilica.

Rapp, George (1757–1847)

German Lutheran lay preacher who emigrated to the United States in 1803 and, with about six hundred disciples, founded communities, in particular Harmony, Pennsylvania. Known as Rappites (or Harmonists), they founded Economy, Pennsylvania, in 1825; however, torn apart by internal disputes, the colony did not survive long after Rapp's death.

Rauschenbusch, Walter (1861–1918)

Minister, theologian and leader of the United States Social Gospel movement. Ordained (1886) for the Second German Baptist Church, New York, he became acutely aware of social problems and formed, with Williams and Schmidt, the Brotherhood of the Kingdom and launched the periodical, *For the Right*. As professor of church history at Rochester Theological Seminary he published *Christianity and the Social Crisis* (1907); his other writings include *Christianizing the Social Order* (1912) and *A Theology for the Social Gospel* (1917).

Raymond of Peñafort, St (c. 1185–1275)

Spanish Dominican friar and canon lawyer who studied and taught church law at Barcelona. He joined the Dominican order in 1222 and about that time wrote his celebrated *Summa de casibus poenitentia*. Pope Gregory IX commissioned him to codify the papal statutes; the resulting *Decretals*, published in 1234, remained operative for nearly seven hundred years. Appointed general of the Dominican order, he revised the constitutions. After resigning his post he devoted his time to promoting missionary work among Jews and Moors.

Reinkens, Josef Hubert (1821–1896)

German historical scholar and bishop. At the First Vatican Council (1869–1870) he opposed the definition of papal infallibility and, following his excommunication, was elected first bishop of the Old Catholic Church (1873). The rest of his life was dedicated to defending and promoting the Old Catholic cause.

Renan, Joseph Ernest (1823–1892)
French historian, philosopher and theologian. After a crisis of faith he left the seminary of Saint-Sulpice and the Roman Catholic church (1845). He wrote on the history of religious origins and after a visit to the Holy Land he wrote his famous *Vie de Jésus* (1863) which caused a sensation throughout Europe.

Revels, Hiram (1822–1901)
American minister of the African Methodist Episcopal Church who worked among blacks of the Midwest, Kentucky and Tennessee. In the post-Civil War period he became the first black member of the United States Senate (1870–1871).

Ricci, Matteo (1552–1610)
Italian Jesuit missionary to China. After an early education in classics and law he joined the Society of Jesus (1571) and showed a special interest in the sciences. Sent first to Goa (1578) and then to Macao (1582), he succeeded in gaining entrance to the interior of China, normally closed to outsiders, because he adopted the Chinese language and culture. His knowledge of the sciences won him entrance to the imperial city and he stayed in Peking, making many converts until his death. His skillful adaption of Christianity to the Chinese way of life led to protracted controversy and final disapproval in 1704 and 1715.

Richard of Chichester, St (c. 1197–1253) (also known as Richard of Wych)
After study at Oxford he became chancellor there (c. 1235) and then chancellor to his friend Edmund of Abingdon, at Canterbury. When Edmund died, Richard was ordained priest and elected bishop of Chichester (1244). After initial opposi-

tion from King Henry III he took possession of his see, proved to be a model bishop and won renown for his sanctity of life. He was canonised in 1262.

Richard of Saint-Victor (d. 1173)
Theologian of Scottish origins who went to study at the Abbey of Saint-Victor, Paris, and stayed to become eventually the prior (1162). Although he wrote the important treatise *De Trinitate* in six volumes, as well as many books of scriptural exegesis, he is best remembered for his influential works on Christian mysticism.

Richelieu, Armand Jean du Plessis (1585–1642)
French cardinal and politician, he is among the prime examples of the use of power for ecclesiastical and secular ends. Consecrated bishop of Lucan, he became adviser to Maria de Medici, the mother of Louis XIII, and Secretary of State in 1616. Exiled for a while, he wrote his famous catechism, *Instruction du chrétien* (1619). Restored to power, he became cardinal (1622), president of the Council of Ministers and actual ruler of France (1624). His major goals were the establishment of royal absolutism in France and the destruction of Hapsburg-Spanish power in Europe. He fought the Protestant Huguenots to achieve the first and cooperated with the Protestant German princes to achieve the latter.

Ridley, Nicholas (c. 1503–1555)
Educated at Cambridge, the Sorbonne and Louvain, he was ordained a priest about 1524 and ten years later showed sympathies with Protestant teachings. Appointed chaplain to Cranmer, archbishop of Canterbury, he rose rapidly in the church until he was appointed bishop of Rochester (1547), then of London (1550). He helped with the compilation of the Book of Common Prayer (1549) and the establishment of Protestantism at Cambridge University. He supported the claim of the Protestant Lady Jane Grey to the throne and was arrested

upon the accession of Mary Tudor. He was excommunicated and burnt at the stake at Oxford on 16 October 1555.

Ripalda, Juan Martinez de (1594–1648)
One of the most famous theologians of his time, a Spanish Jesuit, he lectured in theology at Salamanca and in moral theology at Madrid. His most important works were *De Ente Supernaturali* (1634–1648) and *Brevis Expositio Magistri Sententiarum* (1635).

Ritschl, Albrecht (1822–1889)
Lutheran theologian who lectured at the University of Bonn (1846-1864) and at Göttingen (1864–1889). His influential work *Die Christliche Lehre von der Rechtfertigung* (1870–1874), which presents most of his thinking, resulted in the 'Ritschlian School' of theologians, which stressed the role of 'community' in New Testament theology and ethics.

Robinson, Henry Wheeler (1872–1945)
Baptist Old Testament scholar and theologian. Principal of Regent's Park College (1920–1942), speaker's lecturer at Oxford and president of the Baptist Historical Society, his interest in Old Testament theology was reflected in many books, including *The Religious Ideas of the Old Testament* (1913) and *Inspiration and Revelation in the Old Testament* (1946).

Robinson, Edward (1794–1863)
American Bible scholar. After study in German universities he returned to the United States in 1830. Professor of biblical literature at Union Theological Seminary, New York, from 1837, he became renowned for his geographical study trips to the Holy Land. The publication of his researchers, e.g., *Biblical Researches in Palestine* (1841), led to him being considered the father of biblical geography.

Robinson, John Arthur Thomas (1919–1983)

Anglican bishop of Woolwich, theologian and New Testament scholar. He was educated at Cambridge, where he later lectured in theology (1953–1959 and again 1969–1983). He was a prolific writer, from his first success *In the End, God . . .* (1950) to his posthumously published *The Priority of John* (1985). While serving as bishop of Woolwich (1959–1969) he wrote his sensational *Honest to God* (1963), which stimulated a long-lasting debate; he also supported what was called 'the South Bank Theology', with which he was closely associated. His other works included *The Human Face of God* (1973) and *Wrestling with Romans* (1979).

Robinson, John (1575–1625)

Puritan minister who was originally ordained for the Anglican ministry, but joined the Separatist congregation at Scrooby, Nottinghamshire. The community was forced to move to Holland (1608), settling at Leiden, where Robinson built up and encouraged the members. He prepared them for their journey to America on the *Mayflower* (1620). Called 'the pastor of the Pilgrim Fathers', he was an able controversialist and his writings, such as *A Justification of Separation from the Church of England,* were influential and supportive to the Pilgrim Fathers.

Rogers, John (c. 1500–1555)

Educated at Cambridge, while serving as a chaplain to English merchants at Antwerp, Rogers met William Tyndale, whose influence drew him to Protestantism. After Tyndale's execution (1536) he edited the Bible translation published in 1537 as 'Matthew's Bible'. On his return to England (1548) he was given pastoral work in London and appointed divinity lecturer at St Paul's Cathedral. On Queen Mary's accession he was imprisoned for preaching Protestant doctrine and, after a year in Newgate Prison, in February 1555 he died, the first British Protestant martyr at Smithfield.

Rogers, Mary Joseph (1882—1955)
American founder of the Maryknoll Sisters of St Dominic (popularly known as Maryknoll Sisters). Her interest in foreign missions developed through working on *Field Afar,* the Catholic Foreign Mission Society of America's magazine. With companions she started a lay group called Teresians (1912), which evolved into the Foreign Mission Sisters of St Dominic. Mother Rogers founded the motherhouse at Maryknoll, New York, and at her death there were over eleven hundred Maryknoll Sisters who had served in all parts of Asia.

Rogers, William (1819—1896)
Anglican priest and educational reformer, known as 'Hang-Theology Rogers' because in his large network of schools in his London slum parish, he proposed that doctrinal training be left to parents and clergy. He tackled the problems of middle-class schools while rector of St Botolph's, Bishopsgate, London.

Rolle, Richard (c. 1300—1349)
English mystic, hermit and author of tracts on Christian mysticism. A Yorkshireman, he studied at Oxford, but broke off his studies at the age of eighteen to become a hermit, first on the estate of John Dalton of Pickering (North Yorkshire), but later in various places. His last years were spent near a convent at Hampole, where he acted as spiritual adviser to the nuns. He was highly regarded up to the Reformation for his sanctity and his many spiritual writings, which make reference to his own mystical experiences.

Rose of Lima, St (1586—1617)
Patron saint of South America and the Philippines, she lived her whole life in Lima, Peru. Noted for her beauty, she resisted all efforts to make her marry, having dedicated herself to virginity and an austere spiritual life, taking St Catherine of Siena as her model. Living the life of a recluse in a garden shed, she

suffered great opposition, but her sanctity attracted many to her for spiritual help. At twenty she joined the Third Order of St Dominic. Her short life ended after a long illness. She was canonised in 1671.

Rosmini-Serbati, Antonio (1797–1855)
Italian priest, philosopher, theologian and founder of the Institute of Charity or Rosminians. Ordained a priest in 1821, with the support of successive popes he dedicated himself to reconciling Catholicism with modern political and scientific thought. He also attempted to influence the nineteenth-century Italian nationalist movement. His Institute of Charity grew out of his dissatisfaction with the spiritual and educational state of the church. His philosophical works, contained in *The Origin of Ideas* (1830) and *Maxims of Christian Perfection* (1849), were examined and declared free of censure in 1854.

Rossetti, Christina Georgina (1830–1894)
Poetess and member of the famous Anglo-Italian family of letters, she was associated with the Pre-Raphaelite Brotherhood. A devoted Anglican, her poetry expresses her strong Christian faith. She is best remembered for *Goblin Market* (1862), *Princes' Progress and Other Poems* (1866) and the carol 'In the Bleak Mid-Winter'.

Rossetti, Dante Gabriel (1828–1882)
Elder son of the Rossetti family, and named after the Italian poet who influenced the family so markedly, he was both a poet and a painter. His poetic works include *The Blessed Damozel* (1850) and *The House of Life* (1881). He founded the Pre-Raphaelite Brotherhood (1848), which was devoted to a 'truth to nature' policy.

Rowntree, Joseph (1836–1925)
Quaker, philanthropist and social reformer. The head of the great cocoa business which had been founded by his father, he

pioneered better working conditions, higher wages and provision for old age. He founded the model village of New Earswick, promoted adult education and fought intemperance.

Rublev (also Rublyov), Andrei (c. 1360-c. 1430)

Honoured by the Russian Orthodox church as St Andrew, Rublev is best remembered for his famous icon, 'The Hospitality of Abraham' (also known as 'The Old Testament Trinity'). One of the greatest icon painters of the Russian church, he became a monk and learnt iconography from the famous artist, Theophanes the Greek.

Rufinus, Tyrannius (c. 345–410)

Priest, writer and translator. A friend of St Jerome, he studied Origen and became suspected of Origenism; although an original writer, he is best remembered for his translations from the Greek.

Ruskin, John (1819–1900)

Writer, art critic and social reformer who championed the Gothic revival, supported in *The Seven Lamps of Architecture* (1849). By his writings, e.g., *Unto This Last* (1862), and the foundation of the Guild of St George (1871) he promoted the dignity and moral destiny of men.

Ruysbroeck, Jan van (1293–1381)

Flemish mystic, originating from Ruysbroeck, near Brussels, he was ordained (c. 1317) and held the chaplaincy of St Gudule, Brussels (1317–1343). He retired to a hermitage in 1343, with several others, and founded a community of Canons Regular at Groenandaal. His influential writings spread rapidly and anticipated the fifteenth-century Devotio Moderna. His masterpiece *The Spiritual Espousals* (1350) is a guide for the soul in search of God.

S

Sabatier, Auguste (1839–1901)

French educator and Protestant theologian who helped to revolutionise the interpretation of the Bible by applying the principles of historical criticism and by promoting the development of liberal theology, which influenced not only French Protestantism but also prepared the way for the Modernist movement in the Roman Catholic church.

Sabatier, Paul (1858–1928)

Calvinist pastor, holding from 1885 to 1889, a pastorate in Strasbourg. An interest in St Francis of Assisi grew and he became an internationally acknowledged specialist, giving great impetus to Franciscan studies, especially by his *Vie de St Francois* (1893). He founded the 'Societa Internazionale di Studi Francescani' at Assisi (1902) and the 'British Society of Franciscan Studies' in London (1908).

Sabatier, Pierre (1682–1742)

Benedictine Bible scholar who, trained in historical methods, compiled over many years the exhaustive collection of pre-Vulgate Latin texts of the Bible. This was published posthumously in three volumes as *Bibliorum Sacrorum Latinae Versiones Antiquae.*

Salmon, George (1819–1904)
Theologian, writer and mathematician who, educated at Trinity College, Dublin, remained there to become fellow (1841), Regius professor of divinity (1866) and provost (1888). Strongly Protestant, he wrote *Cautions for the Times* and his *Introduction to the New Testament* (1885) was also popular.

Sancroft, William (1617–1693)
For refusing to take an oath of allegiance to the government of the Commonwealth he was dismissed as fellow of Cambridge. Rising swiftly through church appointments, he helped in the revision of the Book of Common Prayer (1662) and the rebuilding of St Paul's Cathedral, becoming archbishop of Canterbury in 1677. As leader of seven bishops who opposed James II's Declaration of Indulgence (1688) he was imprisoned in the Tower of London. After his acquittal, and the king's flight, he refused to recognise William of Orange and was deprived of his see (1690).

Sanday, William (1843–1920)
English New Testament scholar who, through his numerous books, was a pioneer in introducing to English students and the Anglican world the continental research in biblical criticism. His principal writings were the International Critical Commentary (with A.C. Headlam), *Romans* (1895) and *Outlines of the Life of Christ* (1905).

Sankey, Ira David (1840–1908)
The colleague of the American evangelist Dwight Moody, Sankey was the musician and accompanist on Moody's preaching tour. Together they produced the *Sankey and Moody Hymnbook* (1873).

Sarapion, St (also Serapion) (d. after 360)
Egyptian monk, theologian and bishop of Thmuis, on the Nile Delta. A key figure in early monasticism, with his friend

Athanasius he championed orthodox teaching against the Arians and wrote his celebrated treatise *Against the Manichees*. His other work of note is the *Euchologion,* which contains important collected prayers and liturgical texts.

Savile, Henry (1549–1622)
English mathematician and scholar who helped in the preparation of the Authorised Version of the Bible; he collected and published the works of St John Chrysostom and founded two Savilian professorships in astronomy and mathematics at Oxford University (1619).

Savonarola, Girolamo (1452–1498)
Florentine Dominican friar, preacher and reformer. At the Priory of San Marco, Florence (from 1482), he attracted great attention by his prophetic and reforming sermons. He boldly preached against the ruling Medici and, after their downfall in 1494, became leader of a democratic republic. After refusing to obey several papal summonses and preaching against the papal court, he was excommunicated in 1497. Savonarola ignored the excommunication and continued preaching; he lost popular support, was imprisoned, tried and hanged.

Savio, Dominic (1842–1857)
A student of John Bosco at Turin, while only a young boy he formed the Company of the Immaculate Conception to assist Bosco. Though young he had spiritual gifts beyond his years and reputedly received visions. He was canonised in 1954 and declared patron of choirboys.

Sayers, Dorothy L. (1893–1957)
English scholar and writer whose fame rests mainly upon her stories of mystery and detection. One of the first women graduates of Oxford University (1915), her first major work, *Whose Body?* appeared in 1923. Later in life she turned her attention to theological writing, e.g., *Creed or Chaos?* (1947) and her

much-admired, if a little controversial, series of plays for the BBC, *The Man Born to be King* (1941–1942).

Schaff, Philip (1819–1893)
American church historian, theologian and ecumenist who originated from Switzerland, was educated at Tübingen, Halle and Berlin. His works, especially *Creeds of Christendom* (1877) and his *History of the Christian Church,* in twelve volumes (1883-1893), set standards in the United States for scholarship in church history.

Scheeben, Matthias Joseph (1835–1888)
German Roman Catholic theologian, professor of dogmatic theology at a Cologne seminary, whose speculative work and erudite books, especially *Mysterien des Christenthums* (1865), were widely translated and admired.

Schleiermacher, Friedrich Daniel (1768–1834)
German Protestant theologian who is considered the founder of modern Protestant theology. Of Moravian background, his education began in a Moravian seminary but he moved to Halle University in 1787. After ordination (1794) he became pastor at the Charité Hospital, Berlin. His famous *Religion Speeches to Its Cultured Despisers* (1799) and his developing belief that religion is based on intuition and feeling, independent of dogma, led to the professorship of theology at Halle (1804). Moving to Berlin, he became pastor of Trinity Church and professor of theology at the new University of Berlin (1810). In his time widely regarded as a preacher, his theological thought appears fully in his *Der christliche Glaube*. Schleiermacher's emphasis upon feeling was a reaction to contemporary rationalism and immensely influenced subsequent Protestant theology.

Scheffler, Johannes (1624–1677)
Better known under his pen name Angelus Silesius. Of Polish Lutheran background, he became a Roman Catholic (1653)

and ordained priest (1661); afterwards he devoted his time to writing. Although he wrote many controversial tracts he is best known for his mystical poetry and songs, which celebrate, in vivid imagery, the soul's union with God. These were published under the titles *Heilige Seelenlust* (1657) and *Der Cherubinisch Wandersmann* (1675).

Schurer, Emil (1844–1910)
German New Testament scholar who held the biblical studies chair at Göttingen and is famous for his monumental five-volume work, *A History of the Jewish People in the Time of Jesus Christ* (1890-1891).

Schweitzer, Albert (1875–1965)
German theologian, philosopher, mission doctor and organist. Educated at Strasbourg University, he was a pastor in Strasbourg and a lecturer at the university following the publication of his *The Mystery of the Kingdom of God* in 1901. His influential work *The Quest of the Historical Jesus* (1906) established him as a world figure in theological studies. In 1905 he announced his plan to prepare for missionary work, and after qualifying as a doctor (1913) left with his wife for Lambaréné in French Equatorial Africa. There he founded a hospital, resited in 1924, to which a leper colony was added. Renowned as an organist and acclaimed for his interpretations of Johann Sebastian Bach, he never abandoned his musical or scholarly interests, writing up to his death. He was awarded the Nobel Peace Prize in 1953.

Schwenckfeld, Kasper (1489–1561)
Silesian Reformation theologian, writer and preacher who led the Reform movement in Silesia. Initially impressed by Martin Luther, he later parted company with some Protestant teachings, founding the movement called 'Reformation by the Middle Way'. He established societies which still survive in the United States as the Schwenckfelder Church.

Scofield, Cyrus Ingerson (1843–1921)

Fundamentalist Bible scholar. From a law practice he was converted (1879) to Christianity and became minister at the First Congregational Church, Dallas, Texas (1889–1895). His popularity as a conservative interpreter of the Bible grew and he influenced many at his Northfield Bible Training School. His Correspondence Course (1895–1915) grew into the Scofield Theological Seminary. His millenarian dispensational views are enshrined in the influential work, *The Scofield Reference Bible* (1909).

Scott, George Gilbert (1811–1878)

The most prominent church architect of the Victorian period, being the most successful exponent of the Gothic Revival style. In 1838 he designed his first church, St Giles, Camberwell, London; but his reputation was established after he was selected to work on the Martyrs' Memorial at Oxford (1841). His travels abroad widened his knowledge, which he applied to restoration work at Ely, Hereford, Salisbury and Gloucester cathedrals. In 1849 he was appointed architect to Westminster Abbey. His work of restoration was not without criticism and some controversy.

Scrivener, Frederick Henry Ambrose (1813–1891)

New Testament textual scholar, and headmaster of Falmouth School (1846–1856), who is remembered for his comprehensive study of New Testament manuscripts, published as *Plain Introduction to the Criticism of the New Testament* (1861), a reference book which went through many editions.

Seabury, Samuel (1729–1796)

After studying theology in America and medicine in Scotland, he was ordained for the Episcopal church of America in 1753, serving first as a missionary in New Brunswick. Loyal to the British government during the War of Independence, he was consecrated the first bishop of the Protestant Episcopal church of America by Scottish bishops, thus causing problems of a separate Episcopal line in the United States until 1789.

Sebastian, St (d. c. 288)
Little is known for certain of his life, although it is believed he was martyred during the persecution of the emperor Diocletian. According to legend, graphically portrayed by Renaissance painters, he was a Christian officer in Diocletian's army, condemned to be shot by archers for converting other soldiers.

Sellon, Priscilla Lydia (c. 1821–1876)
Founder of the first post-Reformation religious community in the Church of England. With E.B. Pusey's assistance, her charity work among the destitute grew into the 'Devonport Sisters of Mercy'. Schools and orphanages were founded and the sisters heroically nursed the sick in the cholera epidemic of 1848.

Selwyn, George Augustus (1809–1878)
Educated at Eton and St John's College, Cambridge, and consecrated the first missionary bishop of New Zealand in 1841. His heroic and inventive methods won him wide respect and he had a marked influence upon the subsequent development of the New Zealand church. On his return to England (1867) he was appointed to the see of Lichfield.

Seraphim of Sarow, St (1759–1833)
Originally Prokhor Moshnin, he took the name Seraphim on entering the Monastery of Sarow in 1777. After fifteen years in community, he withdrew to a hermit's life. After a further twenty-five years he returned to pastoral care, devoting the remainder of his life to spiritual direction. He was accorded the title 'Starets' (spiritual teacher) and acknowledged as one of the greatest spiritual counselors in Russian Orthodox history. His church declared him a saint in 1913.

Sergius (1867—1944) (originally Ivan Nikolayevich Stragorodsky)

Theologian and patriarch of Moscow under whose leadership the Russian Orthodox church rallied against Hitler's armies (1941) in a united effort with the Soviets. He thus obtained Soviet acknowledgement of the role and position of the Orthodox church in Russia.

Sergius—There were four popes of this name, the most noteworthy being:

Sergius I, St (d. c. 701)

Considered one of the most important seventh-century popes, he resisted moves to make Constantinople an equal see to that of Rome. He showed an interest in English affairs, baptising Caedwalla, king of Wessex (689); he also consecrated Willibrord bishop of the Frisians and ordered St Wilfred to be restored to his see of York (c. 700). He is further credited with introducing the *Agnus Dei* ('Lamb of God') into the Mass.

Sergius of Radonezh, St (1314—1392)

Originally Bartholomew Kirillovich, he took the name Sergius when he became a monk (1337). He founded the famous Monastery of the Trinity, which re-established the monastic life after the ravages of the Mongol invasions; it became the inspiration of seventy-five other monasteries and a centre and symbol of religious renewal. Sergius was famed for his ascetical life, his compassion for the needy and the help he gave in developing better methods of agriculture. He is credited with stopping four civil wars. Honoured as the greatest of Russian saints, he was canonised at some time before 1449.

Serra, Junipero (1713—1784)

The apostle of California, Serra was a Franciscan missionary priest whose work in North America won him acclaim. From missionary work among the Indians of Mexico he moved up into California (1769) and founded eight mission centres, including San Francisco in 1776. He was an energetic supporter of the rights of the native Indians.

Seton, Elizabeth Ann (1774–1821)
Born in New York City, educated by her father, she was involved early in life in social work, helping to found the Society for the Relief of Poor Widows with Small Children (1797). Herself widowed with five children in 1803, she converted from Anglicanism to Roman Catholicism in 1805, resulting in her ostracisation by family and friends. When she opened a school with companions, a religious community developed which was approved as the Sisters of Charity (the first American religious society) in 1812. Known as 'Mother Seton', she is credited with being the founder of the Catholic parochial school system of the United States. At her death Mother Seton's order had branched into twenty communities. She was the first American-born saint to be canonised, in 1975.

Seymour, William G. (d. 1923)
American black Pentecostal minister and evangelist. A former Holiness preacher and pupil of C.F. Parham, Seymour established the Apostolic Faith Gospel Mission at 312 Azusa Street, Los Angeles, which, from 1906, became a centre of Pentecostal fervour and pilgrimage.

Shaftesbury, Anthony Ashley Cooper, Seventh Earl of (1811–1885)
Educated at Harrow and Christ Church College, Oxford, he entered Parliament in 1826 and proved to be one of the most effective social and industrial reformers in nineteenth-century England. He was largely responsible for the Ten Hours Bill (1847), which limited the working day in textile mills, the Mines Act (1842) and the Factory Act of 1874. President of the Ragged Schools Union for thirty-nine years, he also served as president of the British and Foreign Bible Society. He was

the acknowledged leader of the evangelical movement with the Church of England; although opposed to ritualism, he supported, however, Catholic emancipation.

Sharp, James (1613–1679)
Church of Scotland minister who worked secretly for the Restoration and for the reintroduction of the episcopacy in Scotland. He was subsequently rewarded with the see of St Andrew's in 1661; however he was murdered by a party of Presbyterians, whose church he was working to suppress.

Sheed, Francis Joseph (1896–1981)
Roman Catholic lay theologian, apologist and writer. Born and educated in Sydney, Australia, on arrival in England he worked full time for the Catholic Evidence Guild and remained one of the best-known apologists for fifty years. With his wife Maisie Ward he founded the well-known Catholic publishing house Sheed and Ward. His many writings include *A Map of Life* (1933), *Communism and Man* (1938), and *Theology and Sanity* (1947). He is best remembered for opening up the specialist world of theology to lay people.

Sheen, Fulton J. (1895–1979)
United States Roman Catholic archbishop, preacher, writer and celebrated media personality. Ordained in 1919, his talents as a communicator took him to radio and TV work, including *The Catholic Hour* for NBC and hosting of *Life is Worth Living* (1951-1957). The recipient of many awards for media work, he was also the national director of the Society for Propagation of the Faith (1950–1966), bishop of Rochester, New York (1966–1969) and archbishop of Newport from 1969. His many books include, *Walk with God* (1965) and *That Tremendous Love* (1967).

Sheldon, Charles Munroe (1857–1946)
American Congregational preacher, founder of the Central Congregational Church, Topeka, Kansas, and inspirational writer. He is famous for his best-selling novel *In His Steps* (1897), which was the largest-selling book, apart from the Bible, in the United States for sixty years.

Sheldon, Gilbert (1598–1677)
Archbishop of Canterbury who was an active supporter of William Laud's reforms, particularly at his old college, Trinity, Oxford. The bishop of London in 1660, he was chosen archbishop of Canterbury in 1663.

Sheppard, Hugh Richard Lowrie (1880–1937)
Immensely popular (as 'Dick Sheppard') vicar of St Martin-in-the-Fields, London, who made his parish church the most lively and well-known in the British Empire. An enthusiast for church reform, the use of broadcasting by the church, and in his retirement, the cause of Christian pacifism. His best-known book was *The Impatience of a Parson* (1927).

Shorthouse, Joseph Henry (1834–1903)
Anglican man of business whose fame rests upon his novel *John Inglesant* (1881), which revived interest in the seventeenth-century community at Little Gidding. The book was widely admired by a wide cross-section of nineteenth-century Christians.

Simeon, Charles (1759–1836)
Vicar of Holy Trinity Church, Cambridge, and leader of the Evangelical Revival. He established the Simeon Trust to further this cause and helped to found the Church Missionary Society (1797), also assisting the newly founded British and Foreign Bible Society (1804). Renowned as a preacher, he also proved to be an able biblical commentator with his

seventeen-volume *Horae Homileticae,* which annotated the entire Bible for sermon material.

Simeon Stylites, St (c. 390–459)
The first known pillar hermit, or stylite. (He is not to be confused with a later, sixth-century stylite of the same name.) At first a monk, he was expelled from the community because of his excessive austerities and became a hermit. To avoid the attention of pilgrims he mounted first a low pillar then one of about fifty feet. He remained there until death but exerted an extraordinary influence upon the world of his time through those who flocked for counsel, those who imitated him and through his correspondence.

Simeon the New Theologian (949–1022) (also Symeon)
Byzantine monk, mystic and spiritual writer. Called 'New Theologian' to distinguish him from the fourth-century theologian and spiritual writer 'Gregory the Theologian' (in the West, St Gregory Nazianzen). Simeon became a monk at Studios and priest (980) and abbot of the Monastery of St Manas, near Constantinople. He was compelled to resign in 1009 because of his austere monastic policy. Considered the greatest of Byzantine spiritual writers, with deep mystical experience, his works include sermons, 'catecheses' and the *Hymns of the Divine Loves,* which describes his spiritual experiences.

Simon Stock, St (c. 1165–1265)
Born at Aylesford, Kent, he became a hermit ('Stock' may have originated from a legend that as a young hermit he lived in a tree trunk) and on a pilgrimage to Jerusalem joined the Carmelite order. He brought the order to England, promoted its expansion and became superior general of the order in 1247.

Simon, Richard (1638–1712)
Roman Catholic biblical scholar, regarded as the founder of Old Testament criticism. His *Histoire critique du Vieux Testa-*

ment, denying Moses as the author of the Pentateuch, resulted in his expulsion from his order, the French Oratory.

Sixtus—Five popes bore this name.

Slessor, Mary (1848–1915)
United Presbyterian missionary on the Calabar coast of West Africa. From work in an Aberdeen factory she went to a role of great influence in Africa. 'Ma Slessor' successfully brought tribal abuses, including human sacrifice and the murder of twins, to an end.

Smet, Pierre Jean de (1801–1873)
Courageous American Jesuit missionary and friend of the Indian tribes west of the Mississippi River. His pioneering efforts, involving journeys totalling some 180,000 miles in primitive conditions, to Christianise and act as mediator, won him the title 'Black Robe' from his beloved Indians. Towards the end of his life he was disillusioned by the exploitation of the Indians and continual violation of treaties by the government and its agents.

Smith, Bernard (1630–1708)
Familiarly known as 'Father Smith', he originated from Germany but established a reputation as a master organ-builder in Restoration England. Appointed king's organ-maker (1681), he thereafter built many important instruments, for example for St Paul's Cathedral, London.

Smith, Sir George Adam (1856–1942)
Scottish biblical scholar and preacher who helped to establish the acceptability of the higher criticism of the Old Testament. His many books include *The Early Poetry of Israel* (1916) and *Jeremiah* (1923). He was knighted in 1916.

Smith, Sydney (1771–1845)
Ordained to the Anglican ministry, he proved to be one of the foremost preachers of his time. Renowned for his wit and powers of persuasion, he supported parliamentary reform and Catholic emancipation.

Smith, William Robertson (1846–1894)
Scottish Semitic scholar and theologian whose writings, especially in the *Encyclopaedia Britannica* on the higher criticism of the Old Testament, caused him to lose his Free Church appointments. Moving to Cambridge, he was elected fellow of Christ's College (1885) and continued to exert great influence through his books, particularly *The Old Testament in the Jewish Church* (1881) and *The Prophets of Israel* (1882).

Smyth (Smith), John (1554–1612)
Se-Baptist and founder of the Great Baptists. Ordained for the Church of England ministry, he became a Puritan preacher, then a Separatist pastor, which led to exile in Amsterdam. Baptising himself (c. 1609), hence 'Se-Baptist', he set up the first modern Baptist church. In the year of his death a group of his followers traveled to England to establish the first Baptist church in Britain.

Soderblom, Nathan (1866–1931)
Ordained a Lutheran minister in 1893, he served first as a chaplain to the Swedish legation in Paris, then he became professor of theology at his old University of Uppsala (1901), later (1912–1914) at Leipzig. Appointed archbishop of Uppsala (1914), he traveled widely, developing his interests in comparative religion and ecumenism. Due to his efforts, the first Life and Work Conference met at Stockholm in 1925; he was awarded the Nobel Peace Prize in 1930 for his work for peace through church unity.

Southcott, Joanna (1750–1814)

A domestic servant who became a religious fanatic with a following of some forty thousand devotees; these were attracted by her allegedly inspired divine messages. She joined the Methodist Society in 1791 and wrote and sealed 'prophecies'. After her death, from brain disease, a box of these was left; finally opened in 1927, it contained nothing of value or interest.

Southwell, Robert (1561–1595)

Poet and Roman Catholic martyr, remembered not only for his saintly life but also for his religious poetry, which anticipated George Herbert and later poets. Ordained a Jesuit priest in 1585 in Rome, he returned to England as a missionary and became chaplain to the Howard family. He worked secretly until his betrayal in 1592; he was arrested while saying mass, severely tortured, and brought to trial three years later. Much of his poetry was written while in the Tower of London. He was hanged, drawn and quartered; soon afterwards collections of his religious poetry became widely available, appreciated by Protestants and Catholics alike. He was canonised in 1970.

Southworth, John (1592–1654)

Ordained a secular priest at Douai (1618) to work secretly as a Roman Catholic missionary in England, Southworth was arrested and condemned to death in 1627. He was released three years later, but was back in prison again in 1632. While there, he worked among the prison inmates who had the plague (1635–1636). Released again, he worked secretly until 1654, when, arrested on suspicion, he proclaimed he was a Catholic priest and was executed at Tyburn on 28 June. His body now rests in Westminster Cathedral, London; he was canonised in 1970.

Spalding, Martin John (1810–1872)

Roman Catholic archbishop of Baltimore, United States church historian and apologist. Raised on a Kentucky farm, after ordination (1834) his intellect, pastoral concern and ability led to progressive ecclesiastical appointments, until elected archbishop of Baltimore in 1864. During the Civil War he showed impartiality, providing chaplains and nursing sisters for both sides; and worked hard for reconciliation afterwards. His writings include *The History of the Protestant Reformation* (1860) and *General Evidences of Catholicity* (1847).

Spellman, Francis Joseph (1889–1967)

Cardinal archbishop of New York and military vicar to the United States Army and Navy Forces (1940–1967). Educated at Fordham University and North American College, Rome. From an assistant priest at Roxbury he rose to auxiliary bishop of Boston (1932–1939), archbishop of New York (1939–1967) and cardinal in 1945. An able administrator, he solved the problems of a debt-ridden diocese with energetic fundraising and an extensive building programme. Staunch believer in the Western Allied Forces as the upholders of Christian civilization, he won popularity with the troops in three wars, caring for their spiritual, physical and social needs in combat areas from Anzio to Da Nang.

Spener, Philipp Jakob (1635–1705)

Theologian, author and founder of Pietism. Answering a call to revivify the Lutheran church, he introduced his devotional gatherings ('collegia pietatis') and by preaching and correspondence encouraged personal spiritual growth. By the time of his death Pietism was well established in Germany, and its influence spread via England to the British colonies in America.

Spurgeon, Charles Haddon (1834–1892)

English Baptist minister of strong Calvinist and fundamentalist views who was extremely successful as a preacher, his sermons being translated into many languages and filling over fifty volumes. He preached first at sixteen (1850) and two years later had his own church at Waterbeach in Cambridgeshire; he moved to New Park Street Chapel, Southwark, London, where the crowds attending were so large that the Metropolitan Tabernacle at Newington Causeway, for six thousand, had to be built. Spurgeon edited a monthly magazine and founded a college for ministers (1856) and an orphanage (1867). Some of his extreme views led to a break with the Baptist Union in 1887. He wrote several books, including *Commenting and Commentaries* (1876) and *John Ploughman's Talk* (1869).

Stainer, Sir John (1840–1901)
Church organist and composer, he began his musical career as a choirboy at St Paul's Cathedral, London (1849), and at sixteen was organist at St Michael's College, Tenbury. Eventually he became organist at St Paul's Cathedral (1872), where he made important reforms in church music. Stainer founded the Musical Association (1874), was principal of the National Training School for Music (1880) and was knighted in 1888. His many compositions, including oratorios, cantatas (his best known, *The Crucifixion* [1887], being widely performed), anthems and hymns, many of which are still in regular use.

Stanislaus, St (1030–1079)
Bishop of Cracow (1072) who reproved the Polish king, Boleslav II, for his scandalous life. Murdered by the king, according to tradition, he was hailed as a saintly martyr by the people. Canonised in 1253, he has been patron of Poland since then. However, historians are uncertain about the true facts of his death, some suggesting that Stanislaus was executed for treason.

Stanley, Henry Morton (1841–1904)
Explorer and journalist who, on behalf of the *New York Herald,* made the famous discovery of Dr Livingstone in Central

Africa in 1871. He afterwards picked up Livingstone's work as an explorer, charting over two million square miles of the African interior; and as a missionary, corresponded with the Church Missionary Society, an activity which led to the beginning of missionary work in the Uganda area.

Staupitz, Johann von (1468–1524)

Vicar-general of the Augustinian order at the time of Martin Luther's revolt. As Luther's superior he counseled, advised and supported him until the reformer broke with Rome. Staupitz then withdrew his support, joined the Benedictine order and became abbot of St Peter's Abbey, Salzburg.

Stein, Edith (1891–1942)

Born of a rich orthodox Jewish family, she renounced her faith for atheism, studied phenomenology under Edmund Husserl and, impressed by the mystic St Teresa of Avila, converted to Roman Catholicism in 1922. She joined the Carmelite order in 1934 and took the name Sister Teresa Benedicta of the Cross. She continued writing, translating and lecturing on the application of phenomenology to Thomism. Moved suddenly from Cologne to Holland, to save her from Nazi persecution, she was eventually arrested in 1942 and died in the gas chambers of Auschwitz with her sister Rosa. Widely regarded as a modern saint and martyr, her philosophical writings are still published and studied.

Stephen—There were ten popes of this name, the most memorable being:

Stephen I, St (d. 257)

A Roman and pope from 254. Details of his life are known only through the correspondence which arose from his dispute with bishop St Cyprian of Carthage over baptism. He upheld the teaching authority of the bishop of Rome against Cyprian and three African Councils; he died during the emperor Valerian's persecution of Christians, before the matter could be resolved.

Stephen Harding, St (d. 1134)

An Englishman from Dorset who, after traveling widely, embraced the religious life at Molesme, France; he moved to Citeaux with companions and became abbot in 1109. The community was faced with extinction when unexpectedly (1112) Bernard of Clairvaux arrived with thirty companions; following this Citeaux became the centre of a large network of Cistercian monasteries.

Stern, Henry Aaron (1820–1885)

Anglican missionary of German-Jewish origins who dedicated himself, after his own baptism in 1840, to the mission to the Jews. He traveled widely and after ordination worked principally in Abyssinia among the Falasha Jews, the last years of his life being fruitfully spent in London. His writings include *Dawn of Light in the East* (1854).

Stone, Barton Warren (1772–1844)

American Presbyterian minister who was dedicated to seeking Christian unity; he founded the *Christian Messenger* to promote this and was one of the principal founders of the Disciples of Christ denomination (1832).

Stowe, Harriet Beecher (1811–1896)

Daughter of a well-known Congregationalist minister and married to a clergyman, she is remembered principally as the author of *Uncle Tom's Cabin,* which promoted popular feeling against slavery. She followed her success with many other novels, studies and religious poems.

Stratford, John (d. 1348)

Archbishop of Canterbury, and a native of Stratford-upon-Avon, of which town he was a benefactor. He was chancellor of

England and counselor of the young Edward III. He admired St Thomas à Becket and imitated him in standing up to the king over a peer's right to be judged by his equals in Parliament.

Strauss, David Friedrich (1808–1874)
German controversial Protestant philosopher, theologian and biographer who used dialectical philosophy in biblical interpretation. He is famous for his *Leben Jesu* (1835–1836), in which he denied the historical value of the Gospels and applied his myth theory to the life of Christ. Although he lost his own faith, his work heavily influenced liberal schools of biblical study and the search for the 'historical Jesus'.

Street, George Edmund (1824–1881)
Architect noted for his many English churches in the Gothic Revival style. His extensive travels through Europe influenced his commissions; he was diocesan architect to York, Winchester, Oxford and Ripon, and was also professor of architecture at the Royal Academy.

Streeter, Burnett Hillman (1874–1937)
Anglican priest, theologian and biblical scholar, remembered for the results of his study of the Synoptic problem. His most important work was *The Four Gospels* (1924). In a series of publications he dealt with many different modern problems from a Christian viewpoint.

Strossmayer, Joseph Georg (1815–1905)
Patriot and Roman Catholic bishop who led the Croatian national party in Yugoslavia. At the First Vatican Council he was a leading and vocal opponent of the move to define the infallibility of the pope.

Studd, Charles Thomas (1862–1931)
Protestant missionary of the China Inland Mission (popularly known as C.T.) who worked in China (1885–1894), India

(1900) and Central Africa (1910). He inspired the foundation of the Student Volunteer Movement and thought up the idea of a 'World Evangelisation Crusade', which spread to many countries.

Studdert-Kennedy, Geoffrey Anketell (1883–1929)
Anglican priest, remembered as the best-known military padre of the First World War and known affectionately by the soldiers as 'Woodbine Willie'. Rector of St Edmund, King and Martyr, Lombard Street, London, from 1922, he continued his preaching and published several popular books, including *The Hardest Part* (1918) and *The Wicket Gate* (1923).

Stumpf, Johannes (1500–1578)
One of the most important figures of the Swiss Reform movement, also remembered as a chronicler. A friend of Zwingli, he dedicated his life, after years as prior of the Knights of St John, to the work of building up the Reformation in Switzerland.

Suarez, Francisco de (1548–1617)
Spanish theologian and philosopher, the most important of the Jesuit order and one of the most prominent of scholastic philosophers. His *Defensio Fidei Catholicae* (1613), which opposed the divine right of kings, was burnt in England upon the steps of St Paul's Cathedral. He wrote other apologetical works and *De Legibus* (1612), on political theory. Credited with being the founder of international law, he was so highly regarded by successive popes that he was accorded the title 'Doctor Examinus'.

Sulpicius Severus (c. 363-c. 420)
Early Christian historian, ascetic and hagiographer, principal authority on Christian life in contemporary Gaul. A friend of Paulinus, bishop of Nola, and Martin of Tours, his life of the latter, *Vita S. Martini,* was highly influential on later hagiogra-

phy and his literary masterpiece *Dialogue* (404) reveals his interest in the development of monasticism.

Sunday, Billy (1863–1935) (full name William Ashley Sunday)
American revivalist preacher and evangelist. Prior to ordination as a Presbyterian minister, in 1903, he had been a professional baseball player and YMCA worker. He led more than three hundred revivals and claimed one million converts to Christ.

Surin, Jean Joseph (1600–1665)
French Jesuit spiritual writer and mystic whose influential book *Catéchisme spirituel* (1659) was suspected, for a while, of Quietism. His many other works reveal his deep spirituality, especially his belief in the need for purification and self-abnegation.

Suzuki, Bunji (1885–1946)
Japanese Christian who was active in issues of social justice and founded the Japanese Federation of Labour (1919). He helped to organise the new Social Democratic party and served several times in the Diet.

Swithun, (or Swithin) St (d. 862)
Priest of Wessex who, from chaplain and counselor to King Egbert of the West Saxons, went to Winchester as bishop in 852. He built several churches and was renowned for both his humility and his concern for the needy. The long-established superstition in England, associated with forty days of rain from his feast day, 15 July, is of unknown origin.

Sylvester—Three popes bore this name, the best known being:

Sylvester I, St (d. 335)

Pope at a crucial period of church history. Although little is known of his life, according to legend he converted and baptised the emperor Constantine. He allegedly received the 'Donation of Constantine' and during his reign he was represented at the Council of Nicaea, which condemned Arianism.

Sylvester II, (c. 940–1003) (Originally Gerbert of Aurillac)

Educated by the Benedictines, he became known for his learning, particularly in logic and mathematics. In 970 he met the emperor Otto I, whose son he tutored, and then progressed through a series of clerical offices to his election as pope in 999. The emperors Otto II and III regarded him as a loyal servant of the empire and as pope, Sylvester achieved a good working relationship with the emperor; he fought church abuses, opposed simony, upheld clerical celibacy and strengthened the church in Eastern Europe. Throughout his life he retained and deepened his reputation for scholarly achievement.

T

Tait, Archibald Campbell (1811–1882)
Archbishop of Canterbury who, as bishop of London and later (1868) as archbishop, opposed the spread of the Oxford Movement. While a fellow of Balliol College, Oxford (1834–1842), he had protested at Tract 90, but as a bishop he worked for reconciliation between the evangelical and High Church wings.

Tallis, Thomas (c. 1510–1585)
Little is known of his early life, although he was apparently organist at Waltham Abbey at some time before 1540. His unprinted compositions of vocal works for worship were circulating when he was appointed gentleman of the Chapel Royal. He is considered the most important gentleman English composer of sacred music before Byrd, with whom he had a monopoly of printed music for over twenty years. His first printed works appeared in 1560, but *Cantiones Sacrae* (1575) was the first publication, shared with Byrd, containing sixteen motets by Tallis. His *Responses,* made popular in the nineteenth century, are his best-remembered compositions.

Tauler, Johann (c. 1300–1361)
German Dominican mystic, influenced by Meister Eckhart and Heinrich Suso, who was immensely popular and exerted a

great influence upon the Gottesfreunde (devout Rhinelanders of like mind) by his preaching and example. His mystical teaching, which impressed Martin Luther and is found in his sermons, is solidly based upon the teaching of St Thomas Aquinas.

Tausen, Hans (1494–1561)
Roman Catholic monk and language scholar who converted to Lutheranism and for his work in establishing the Reformation in Denmark became known as the 'Danish Luther'. After the final triumph of the Reformation in Denmark (1536) Tausen accepted the Lutheran bishopric of Ribe.

Taylor, James Hudson (1832–1905)
Medical missionary who founded the China Inland Mission. In spite of ill health, he traveled extensively and courageously faced many problems in inland China. His books include *China: Its Spiritual Needs and Claims* (1865) and *Union and Communion* (1894).

Taylor, Jeremy (1613–1667)
Anglican bishop and spiritual writer. Ordained in 1633 after an education at Cambridge, he attracted the patronage of Archbishop Laud, then of the king himself; Charles I made him a doctor of divinity by royal decree. After serving as chaplain to the Royalist army, and a period of imprisonment, he retired to Wales, where much of his writing took place. Made bishop of Down and Connor, after the Restoration (1660) he helped to reconstitute the University of Dublin. He is remembered today for his devotional books, particularly the classics, *The Rule and Exercises of Holy Living* (1650) and *The Rule and Exercises of Holy Dying*.

Tekakwitha, Kateri (1656–1680)
The first North American Indian to be proposed by the Roman Catholic church for canonisation. Orphaned at four, she

was deeply impressed as a child by three Jesuit missionaries and later accepted baptism from Jacques de Lamberville. Persecuted by her people she fled to the Christian mission at Sault Saint-Louis, near Montreal. There her heroic suffering and sanctity won her the title 'Lily of the Mohawks'. She was beatified by Pope John Paul II in 1980.

Teilhard de Chardin, Pierre (1881–1955)
French Jesuit philosopher, theologian and palaeontologist. From an early age he showed an interest in geology, which continued through his preparation for ordination as a Jesuit priest (1911). Serving as a stretcher bearer in the First World War, he was decorated for bravery. He established a notable reputation for his palaeontological work in China, being involved in the discovery of Peking Man. Theological meditation upon evolution resulted in the manuscript *The Phenomenon of Man* (1956; English translation 1965), in which he presents a theology of evolution, with the theory that man is presently evolving toward a final spiritual unity. His devotional work *Le Milieu Divin* also reflects his philosophical theology. Both he and his writings were unknown outside scientific circles until after his death.

Temple, Frederick (1821–1902)
Archbishop of Canterbury and educational reformer. Ordained priest (1847) after teaching and serving as inspector of schools, he became headmaster of Rugby (1857–1869) and prominent in the education movement. Appointed bishop of Exeter (1869–1885), he did much for church schools and at London (1885–1897) came into conflict with the High Church wing. He was appointed archbishop of Canterbury in 1897.

Temple, William (1881–1944)
Archbishop of Canterbury and a leader of the ecumenical movement and labour and educational reforms. The second son of the above, he progressed from lecturer at Queen's College,

Oxford (1904–1910), headmaster of Repton (1910–1914), rector of St James', Piccadilly, London (1914–1917), and archbishop of York (1929–1942) to being archbishop of Canterbury (1942–1944). Prominent in national life, he gave enthusiastic support to the Faith and Order Movement, and influenced the formation of both the British Council of Churches and the World Council of Churches. An independent thinker and philosopher, his many works include *Mens Creatrix* (1917), *Nature, Man and God* (1934) and *Christianity and Social Order* (1942).

Tennent, Gilbert (1703–1764)

Presbyterian Revivalist preacher. Educated by his scholarly father, William, in Philadelphia. He went straight into Revivalist preaching, by 1729 with some success. Uncompromising in his spiritual demands and message, his preaching led to a split between the 'Old Side' (more conservative ministers) and the 'New Side' (a new faction led by Tennent). The latter formed the projudicature, the Synod of New York. In later life Tennent regretted the division and in 1758 the two sides were merged.

Teresa of Avila, St (1515–1582) (her religious name: Teresa of Jesus)

Spanish mystic, spiritual writer and founder of the Discalced Carmelites. She entered the Carmelite Convent, Avila, when twenty but suffered bad health. Within the convent she lived a lax life until she experienced a religious awakening in 1555. Her mystical experiences began soon afterwards, and in 1558 she resolved to reform the Carmelite way of life. This was achieved, in the face of fierce opposition, with official approval, at the Convent of St Joseph, Avila, in 1562. From this period date her *Life* and *The Way of Perfection;* both are outstanding spiritual classics, along with the later *The Interior Castle* (1588). From 1567, with the help of John of the Cross, who reformed the male Carmelites, Teresa, in spite of great difficulties, founded sixteen more convents. Her ascetic teaching has been regarded as the classical exposition of the contemplative life.

Tersteergen, Gerhard (1667–1769)
German Protestant spiritual writer and director. After a conversion experience (1687) he retired to a solitary life. After 1727, when he had founded his Pilgrim's Hut at Otterbeck, near Mulheim, he spent his life as a spiritual director and translator of devotional works. He is best remembered now for his hymns, some of which have been translated into English.

Tertullian, Quintus Septimus Florens (c. 160-c. 225)
Early Christian theologian and writer. Converted to Christianity c. 196, he emerged as a leader of the African church. Always a teacher, he developed as an apologist for Christianity and his many writings include apologetical and theological works. About 210, disturbed at the laxity of Christian life, he joined the Montanist sect; this too proved to be lacking in rigour, so he founded his own sect, which lasted until the fifth century in Africa.

Tetzel, Johann (c. 1465–1519)
German Dominican friar whose preaching and selling of indulgences reflected the church abuses of the period, caused great scandal throughout Germany and was the occasion of Martin Luther's Ninety-Five Theses in 1517. Tetzel replied, but soon after retired to Leipzig Priory, where he died.

Theobald (c. 1090–1161)
Benedictine monk and abbot of Bec, France, who became archbishop of Canterbury in 1138. He proved to be an exceptional administrator, strengthening the position of the church in England. He introduced the study of Roman law and, as an educator, he trained other leading churchmen for high office.

Theodore, St (c. 602–690)
A Greek from Tarsus, he was appointed by Pope Vitalian as archbishop of Canterbury. Arriving at Canterbury in 669, he established a school there and set about reorganising dioceses and reforming church government. His greatest achievement was to create a centralised church in England according to the Roman model. He also called the first synod of the whole English church (673).

Theodore of Mopsuestia (c. 350–428)
Controversial theologian and biblical exegete. Influenced by St John Chrysostom, he entered a monastery near Antioch, where he spent ten years. He became bishop of Mopsuestia (392) and started writing about 402. He wrote commentaries and theological works which had a big impact upon the Eastern church of the time.

Theodore Studites, St (759–826) (also known as Theodore of Studius)
Abbot of the Monastery of Studius who was a leading opponent of iconoclasm. He fought for church independence from imperial power, which caused him to be exiled twice. Through his work to reform monastic life, his monastery became a famous centre; his published works include homilies and nearly six hundred letters.

Theodoret (c. 393–466)
Controversial theologian and bishop of Cyrrhus. From a monastic background, as a bishop he was energetic in fighting heresy, writing several treatises of apologetics, the most famous being *Therapeutike*. He tried to shed more light on the Christological discussions of the time with his *On the Incarnation* (431) and *Eranistes* (446). This led to a famous conflict with Cyril of Alexandria and an eventual condemnation of some of Theodoret's teaching at the Council of Constantinople in 553.

Therese of Lisieux, St (1873–1897) (original name: Marie Francoise Thérèse Martin)

Carmelite nun. From a very pious home, at the age of fifteen, after much opposition, she entered the convent at Lisieux, where two of her own sisters were already nuns. Professed in 1890, she longed to go to the foreign missions, but ill health made it impossible. Neurotic as a child, in the convent she never exhibited anything but an unselfish pleasant manner. Her struggle to achieve this and her 'little way' to sanctity are recorded in her autobiography *Histoire d'une âme*, written in obedience. It was the huge popular success of this book, recording her courageous coping with the affliction of tuberculosis, that attracted a tremendous following. She was canonised in 1925 and named a patron of Roman Catholic foreign missions and copatron of France (1947).

Thierry of Chartres (c. 1100–1151)

Theologian, medieval philosopher and eminent teacher. He taught at Chartres (1121) and then at Paris (1124), John of Salisbury being one of his pupils; he was one of the first to introduce Arabian knowledge of science into the West. His unpublished *Heptateuchon* (book in seven volumes) and his commentary on Genesis reveal him as an exponent of the application of Platonist philosophy to the mysteries of the Christian faith.

Tholock, Friedrich August Gottreu (1799–1877)

German Protestant theologian who lectured at Berlin (1820–1826) and Halle University. He exerted great influence upon his students through pastoral care and in his works he reveals his Pietistic leanings, doing much to check the spread of rationalism in Germany.

Thomas à Kempis (1379/80–1471) (originally Thomas Hemerken)

Probable author of *The Imitation of Christ,* the devotional book which has been considered the most influential Christian work (excepting the Bible). He studied at the religious centre, Deventer, Netherlands, founded by the Brethren of the Common Life. In 1399 he joined the Augustinian Canons Regular community at Agnietenberg, where he spent the rest of his life, directing novices, writing, preaching and giving spiritual direction. His writings, of different kinds, are all permeated with the same devotional spirit of *Imitatio Christi,* which is the best representation of the 'Devotio Moderna', a religious movement founded by Gerhard Groote.

Thomas Aquinas, St (c. 1225–1274)

Foremost philosopher and theologian of the Roman Catholic church. Educated by (and destined by his family for membership of) the Benedictine Abbey at Monte Cassino, he chose, in the face of fierce opposition, to join the newly founded Dominican order. Furthering his education at the University of Paris, he was a pupil of the renowned Albertus Magnus, who introduced him to the thought of Aristotle. He taught at Paris and was appointed theological adviser to the Papal Curia (1259–1265). In 1272 he returned to Italy to found a Dominican house of studies at the University of Naples. He defended the application of Aristotelian principles to theology against the Franciscan scholar Bonaventure. At Naples he worked hard to produce his celebrated *Summa Theologica,* the classical systematisation of Latin theology. He died on his way to the Second Council of Lyons. Thomas's many theological and philosophical works, and biblical commentaries, reached a culmination in his two 'Summae', the first being *Summa contra Gentes,* the other being the *Summa Theologica.* His spiritual poetry lives on in several eucharistic hymns still used in the church's liturgy.

Thompson, Francis (1859–1907)

English Roman Catholic poet best remembered for his famous poem *The Hound of Heaven.* He left his training for the priesthood at Ushaw, for medicine; this too proved unsuccessful, and he lived in destitution in London for three years before he and his poetry were discovered by Wilfrid Meynell.

Thurneysen, Eduard (1888–1974)
Protestant theologian from Switzerland who successively held pastoral posts at Zurich, Bruggen (near St Gall) etc. He associated with Karl Barth in developing dialectical theology, himself supplying the pastoral dimension. His own works included *Das Wort Gottes und die Kirche* (1927).

Tikhon (1866–1925) (originally Vasily Ivanovich Belavin)
Patriarch of the Russian Orthodox church after the Revolution of 1917. He became a monk (1891) and rose swiftly in the church, serving as bishop for the Orthodox community, for two years, in New York (1905–1907). Returning to Russia, he was elected to the restored patriarchate of Moscow. Harassed by the Soviet government, he nonetheless wielded considerable moral authority.

Tillich, Paul (1886–1965)
Protestant theologian, educated at Tübingen and Halle (1904-1914). Ordained for the Lutheran ministry, he served as a chaplain in the First World War, after which he joined the Religious Socialists. While lecturing in theology and philosophy successively at Marburg (1924), Dresden (1925) and Frankfurt (1929), he developed his theology through many publications, including his major three-volume work *Systematic Theology* (1951–1963) and *Kirche und Kultur* (1924). Criticism of the Nazi movement led to him leaving Germany and settling in the United States, taking teaching posts at the Union Theological Seminary (1933–1955), Harvard (1955–1962) and the University of Chicago (1962–1965). He was a prolific writer and some of his books reached a large public audience, e.g., *The Courage to Be* (1952).

Tillotson, John (1630–1694)

Archbishop of Canterbury who reluctantly accepted the see (1691) and whose archiepiscopate was marked by his fierce opposition to Roman Catholics, Puritans and atheists. A famous preacher, he became the model for many later preachers.

Tischendorf, Constantin (1815–1874)

German biblical critic. Starting as a student at Leipzig University, and continuing as professor of theology, he devoted himself to the New Testament text, publishing eight editions of the Greek text (1841–1869). His invaluable contributions to biblical textual criticism included the search for manuscripts. His most famous find was of the *Codex Sinaiticus* at the Monastery of St Catherine in the Sinai Peninsula.

Toplady, Augustus Montague (1740–1778)

Author, hymnwriter and vicar of Broad Hembury, Devonshire, Toplady is remembered particularly for 'Rock of Ages', which first appeared in print in 1775. His most important prose work was *The Historic Proof of the Doctrinal Calvinism of the Church of England* (1774), which reflected his turning from support for John Wesley to extreme Calvinism.

Traherne, Thomas (1637–1674)

Ordained for the Anglican ministry (1660), he lived a pastoral life as rector and chaplain, having only one book published in his lifetime, the controversial *Roman Forgeries* (1673). His *Poetical Works* was discovered and published in 1903 and he was acknowledged as a religious poet of great originality of thought and depth of feeling. In 1908 his *Centuries of Meditations,* a collection of reflections on ethics and religion, was published.

Tremellius, John Immanuel (1510–1580)

Of Jewish origins, he was converted to Christianity (1540) and in 1541 became a Protestant. On leaving Italy, as a Hebrew scholar, he taught successively at Strasbourg, Cambridge, Heidelburg and Sedan. His greatest achievement was his translation of the Bible into Latin; this was the standard Protestant Latin translation for a long period.

Trench, Richard Chenevix (1807–1886)
Archbishop of Dublin and biblical scholar. As a writer he stimulated popular interest in New Testament studies with his *Notes on the Parables of Our Lord* (1841) and *Notes on the Miracles of Our Lord* (1846); he also wrote religious poetry. As archbishop he opposed the disestablishment of the Irish church.

Trimmer, Sarah (1741–1810) (See Kirby)
English authoress and mother of twelve children, she promoted the Sunday school movement with writing and the production of religious textbooks for charity schools. A woman of great piety and charity, she is best remembered for her children's book *The History of the Robins* (1786).

Truth, Sojourner (c. 1797–1883) (legal name: Isabella Van Wagener)
American black evangelist. Born and reared as a slave, she was set free by Isaac Van Wagener, whose name she took. Deeply religious from childhood, she had visions and believed herself called by God. From 1843 she adopted the name 'Sojourner Truth', and her personal magnetism made her a famous itinerant preacher. She energetically supported the abolition of slavery and the Women's Rights Movement.

Tunstall, Cuthbert (1474–1559)
Bishop of Durham (1530–1552 and 1553–1559) who reluctantly implemented the Reformation in England, demonstrating his conservatism in his treatise *De Veritate Corporis et Sanguinis Domini Nostri Jesu Christi in Eucharistia* (1554). He had proved valuable to Henry VIII in overseas diplomatic missions. Imprisoned under Edward VI, reinstated by Mary,

he was once again deprived of his see and imprisoned under Elizabeth I.

Tyndale, William (c. 1494–1536)

English Reformer, biblical translator and Protestant martyr. A student of Oxford and Cambridge, he was refused permission to publish an English version of the Bible, so he began the work in Cologne (1525) and completed it at Worms. His translation later became the basis of the Authorised Version. His other works include *Parable of the Wicked Mammon* (1528) and *Obedience of a Christian Man*. Arrested in 1535, and condemned for heresy, he was burnt at the stake.

Tyrrell, George (1861–1909)

English Roman Catholic theologian who advocated Modernism. Of evangelical origins, he converted to Roman Catholicism (1879) and joined the Society of Jesus (Jesuits) in 1880. He served at Stonyhurst College, Lancashire, and Farm Street, the principal Jesuit church in London. His friendship with Friedrich von Hugel and the influence of A. Loisy led to his Modernist publications; some of the many works were published under pseudonyms. He was expelled from the Jesuit order in 1906 and excommunicated by the Roman Catholic church. Pope Pius X condemned Modernism in his encyclical letter *Pascendi Dominici Gregis*.

U

Ullathorne, William Bernard (1806–1889)

Benedictine missionary to Australia and the first Roman Catholic bishop of Birmingham. After years as a cabin boy, he entered the Benedictine order in 1824 and volunteered to work in the convict penal colonies of Australia and Norfolk Island (1832–1842). His *Horrors of Transportation Briefly Unfolded* (1836) helped to bring the abolition of the transportation system. On his return to England he became vicar apostolic of the Western District of England (1846) and bishop of Birmingham in 1850. His most popular work, his autobiography *From Cabin Boy to Archbishop* (1856), was often reprinted.

Underhill, Evelyn (1875–1941)

Anglican mystical poet and exponent of mysticism. Educated at King's College, London, after a conversion experience (1907) she studied the mystics and her books *Mysticism* (1911), *The Mystic Way* (1913), *The Essentials of Mysticism* (1920) and others, helped to establish mystical theology as a reputable discipline for contemporary study. From 1924 she was much sought after as a spiritual counselor, retreat-giver and lecturer.

Uncles, Charles Randolph (1859–1933)

The first black Roman Catholic priest trained and ordained in the United States. Born at Baltimore, Maryland, he was ordained in 1891; with five other former Mill Hill Fathers he became cofounder of the Josephites (St. Joseph's Society of the Sacred Heart) for mission work among the American black community. Recognized as a scholar, he taught at the Josephite Seminary, Baltimore (1891–1925) then at Newburgh, New York (1925–1933).

Ursula, St (fourth century)

According to pious legend she was the leader of eleven, or possibly eleven thousand, virgins reputedly martyred at Cologne by fourth-century Huns (nomadic invaders from southeast Europe). The story is based upon an inscription found at Cologne; a later form of the legend suggests Ursula was a British princess killed on her way to Rome. The patron of many educational establishments, she is known today through the Ursulines, a congregation of religious sisters dedicated to education.

Ussher, James (1581–1656)

Archbishop of Armagh and a highly regarded scholar of his day. Memorable for his work on patristic texts, especially upon the writings of Ignatius of Antioch, and upon the chronology of the Old Testament. After the Civil War he worked for reconciliation between churchmen and dissenters.

V

Vadianus, Joachim (1484–1551)
Swiss poet and humanist who rose to be mayor of St Gallen (1526), where he also practised medicine and was a popular preacher. He was influential in establishing the Reformation in Switzerland.

Valdes, Juan de (c. 1490–1541)
Spanish humanist and religious writer who developed religious ideas similar to Erasmus; publication of these as *Dialogue on Christian Doctrine* (1529) caused him to flee to Italy from the Spanish Inquisition (1531). Although formally remaining a member of the Roman Catholic church, his ideas paved the way for the Reformation.

Valentine, St (third century)
The name of two legendary martyrs: a Roman priest who died during the persecution of the emperor Claudius (c. 269), and a bishop of Terni, Italy, martyred probably in Rome. It is possible that the legendary accounts have some basis in historical fact and may derive from one original person. The association of St Valentine's Day with a lovers' festival derives probably from the pagan Roman fertility festival of Lupercalia.

Valignano, Alessandro (1539–1606)

Italian Jesuit missionary who helped to introduce Christianity to the Far East. He trained missionaries, including Matteo Ricci, in Portuguese India (from 1574) and went personally to Japan, where he successfully converted several Japanese feudal lords. There he was highly esteemed, establishing a centre for the education of native priests; at his death there were over 115 Jesuits in Japan and an estimated three hundred thousand Christians.

Van Espen, Zeger Bernhard (1646–1728)

Belgian canon lawyer and supporter of Gallican theories who is remembered for his learned *Jus Ecclesiasticum Universum* (1700) and his judgement, in 1723, in the 'Chapter of Utrecht' case, in which he supported Jansenism, which led to his suspension and condemnation.

Van Eyck, Hubert (1366–1426) and Jan (1390–1441)

Flemish painters. Jan was probably pupil to his elder brother and settled at Bruges. Hubert started the famous *Adoration of the Lamb* altarpiece for the Cathedral of St Bavon, which was finished by his brother in 1432. This remarkable work is considered one of the masterpieces of Christian art.

Vane, Sir Henry (1613–1662)

English Puritan, usually called 'the Younger', to distinguish him from his statesman father. He traveled widely in Europe, then went to New England (1635), where he served as governor of Massachusetts for a year. Returning to England and entering politics, he worked against the episcopacy and was chief negotiator in arranging the Solemn League and Covenant with Scotland (1643). He opposed Cromwell's dictatorial methods, retired from politics and wrote several religious books, including the obscure *Retired Man's Meditations* (1655). At the Restoration he was imprisoned and executed for his parliamentary activities.

Vaughan, Henry (1622–1695)

Welsh poet, doctor and mystic. He practised medicine at Brecon and Newton-by-Usk and about 1650, after a spiritual experience, he produced religious poetry of great depth. His *Silex Scintillans* (1650) shows the influence of George Herbert. *The Mount of Olives* followed in 1652. Largely disregarded in his own day, his poetry had a great influence upon William Wordsworth.

Vaughan, Herbert (1832–1903)

Archbishop of Westminster and cardinal. Vice-president of St Edmund's Seminary, Ware, and founder of St Joseph's Missionary College, Mill Hill (1866). He championed the Ultramontanist cause prior to the First Vatican Council through his editorship of *The Tablet*. Appointed first to the see of Salford (1872), he was elevated to Westminster (1892) and made cardinal in 1893. As archbishop he commenced the building of Westminster Cathedral and was involved in the Education Bill of 1902.

Venantius Fortunatus (c. 530-c. 610)

Poet and bishop of Poitiers. As the result of a pilgrimage to the shrine of St Martin of Tours from Treviso, near Venice, he settled at Poitiers, France. He was impressed by the holiness of Radegunda, formerly a queen, who had founded a monastery there. He served the community as steward, then as chaplain, and finally became bishop of Poitiers. Although author of several lives of saints, he is remembered for his poetry which combines the style of the classical Latin poets with the mystical spirit of Christianity. His genius is best seen in the hymns still in use, the *Pange Lingua* and *Vexilla Regis*.

Veniaminov, Ivan Yevseyevich (1797–1879)

Russian Orthodox missionary. A married priest, Veniaminov was sent to Alaska (1822) to work among the Aleuts, Eskimos and Tlingit Indians. In 1840 he was consecrated their bishop, taking the name Innocent, and became the first Orthodox bishop to reside in the United States.

Venn, Henry (1725–1797)

One of the leading evangelical divines of his time and one of the first to have a parish, that of Huddersfield, where he had a reputation for piety and zeal. Author of the popular book *The Complete Duty of Man* (1736), he was also one of the founders of the Clapham Group.

Vermigli, Pietro Martire—See Peter Martyr.

Veronica, St

Renowned woman of Jerusalem who, according to legend, wiped the face of Christ as he carried his cross to Calvary. Although this incident is one of the Stations of the Cross, it has no foundation in Scripture. The origin of the legend may spring from a misapplication of a story in Eusebius of Caesarea's *Historia Ecclesiastica;* it seems to be of French origin.

Vianney, Jean-Baptiste (1786–1859) (also known as the Curé d'Ars)

Attracted early to the priesthood, he had severe difficulties with study; drafted into Napoleon's army, he deserted and after an amnesty (1810) he returned to the seminary. Eventually ordained (1815), he was first a curate at Ecully; he was appointed curé of Ars (1818), from where his fame as a model parish priest and saintly confessor with supernatural powers spread throughout Europe. By 1827 the remote village of Ars was a pilgrimage centre and from 1845 approximately twenty thousand visitors a year sought spiritual direction and confession from the curé. He was canonised in 1925 and declared patron saint of parish priests in 1929.

Victor—There were three popes of this name, the most significant being:

Victor I, St (d. 199)

Pope from 189 and believed to be an African by birth. He is memorable for imposing on the Eastern patriarchs the Roman date for Easter, strongly asserting papal authority. He also replaced Latin for Greek as the official language of the Roman church.

Victor III (1027–1087)

Benedictine monk (known as Desiderius) of the monastery of Monte Cassino who, as abbot (1058), promoted the abbey as a centre of learning and culture and radically rebuilt it. Chosen pope against his will, he was driven out of Rome by the emperor and became embroiled in problems with an antipope. He condemned lay investiture by the emperor and died at Monte Cassino, where he had taken refuge.

Vieira, Antonio (1608–1697)

Portuguese Jesuit theologian, missionary and master of classical Portuguese prose. Continually drawn to missionary work, his outstanding preaching drew him, however, to royal attention and several diplomatic missions. His befriending of converted Jews and Amazon Indians gained him enemies and his theology attracted the attention of the Spanish Inquisition. He played a positive role in both Brazilian and Portuguese history.

Vigilius (d. 555)

Pope from 537 to 555, and remembered for his part in the Three Chapters Controversy, a complex theological dispute which arose over the struggle with Monophysitism in the Eastern and Western churches. Vigilius succeeded Pope Silverius, who was forcibly removed by the civil authorities for his support of the Council of Chalcedon, which had condemned Monophysitism. Great imperial pressure was put upon Vigilius, whose *Constitution,* an attempt to resolve the problem, only resulted in a number of bishops deserting him, a schism which lasted 150 years.

Vilmar, August Friedrich Christian (1800–1860)
Lutheran theologian who rigorously opposed rationalism with his 'theology of facts', defending the retention of the early Christian creeds. He compiled a hymnbook and wrote many theological works, the most widely known being *Geschichte der Deutschen Nationalliteratur.*

Vincent de Paul, St (c. 1580–1660)
Of a French peasant family, he was ordained a Roman Catholic priest in 1600 but was captured by pirates (1605) and enslaved in Algeria for two years. Chaplain to Queen Margaret of Valois in Paris, he attracted much attention preaching and working among the city's poor. Tutor to the household of Count de Gondi, general of the galleys (1613–1625), he ministered to the galley slaves. In 1625 he founded the Congregation of the Mission (known as Vincentians or Lazarists), devoted to mission work among French peasants. Influenced by Francis de Sales, he founded, with Louise de Marillac, the famous Sisters of Charity and established hospitals, orphanages and seminaries to train priests for the missions. His whole life was devoted to the alleviation of human suffering. He was canonised in 1737.

Vincent Ferrer, St (c. 1350–1419)
Spanish Dominican friar and famous preacher. Professor of theology at Valencia, he became confessor to the antipope Benedict XIII (1394), but after five years he devoted his life to preaching missions to huge crowds, with great effect, throughout southern Europe. He tried to persuade Benedict XIII to abandon his claims and worked successfully to end the schism.

Vincent of Lérino, St (d. c. 450)

Theologian and monk of the Mediterranean island of Lérino, near Cannes, at that time a monastic centre of education and culture. Little is known of his life beyond his reputation for scriptural knowledge and theology, and for his work *Commonitoria* (c. 435), a reply to current heresies.

Vinet, Alexandre Rudolf (1797–1847)

French-Swiss Reformed theologian, moralist and literary critic who was influential in establishing the Reformation in Switzerland. An energetic defender of freedom of worship and the separation of church and state, he believed that conscience, not dogma, is man's basis for religion; these views found expression in his works, particularly *Mémoire sur les libertés des cultes* (1826).

Vitoria, Francisco de (c. 1485–1546)

Dominican priest and one of the greatest of Spanish theologians. He lectured in theology at the Universities of Paris, Valladolid and Salamanca, where he inaugurated a new school of theology. He is often regarded as 'Father of International Law' for his teaching on the conditions for a just war and his spirited defence of the rights of the Indians of the New World. His moral teaching was presented in his *Reflections*, based upon lectures given between 1527 and 1540.

Vladimir, St (956–1015)

First Christian ruler in Russia, considered 'Apostle of the Russians'. Steeped in paganism, he embraced Christianity to further his military conquests and ambitions but became an ardent promoter of his new faith, erecting many churches, promoting education and aiding the poor; however, his methods of spreading Christianity were sometimes heavy-handed.

Voetius, Gisbertus (1589–1676)

Dutch Reformed theologian of strong uncompromising convictions who stoutly defended the Calvinistic doctrine of predestination and condemned the rationalistic thought of the seventeenth-century French philosopher Descartes. He would allow no concessions to Roman Catholic thought, as his *Diatribe de Theologia* (1668) reveals.

Von Hügel, Baron Friedrich (1852–1925)

Roman Catholic philosopher, theologian and spiritual counselor. A naturalised British citizen, after a cosmopolitan education he lived most of his life at Hampstead (1876–1903) and Kensington, London (1903–1925). A conversion experience (1870) brought him to a deeper faith and with a keen interest in science, biblical criticism and philosophy he sympathised with the Modernist movement. He founded the London Society for the Study of Religion (1905) and wrote many works of lasting value, including *Eternal Life* (1912) and the posthumous *The Reality of God* (1931).

Voss, Gerhard Jan (1577–1649)

Dutch Protestant theologian and humanist who was suspected of Remonstrant teaching and involved in the disputes that arose. He was invited to England and, refusing a post at Cambridge, accepted one offered by archbishop Laud at Canterbury. All his works made a solid contribution to learning.

Wach, Joachim (1898–1955)
One of the foremost German Protestant theologians, he specialised in the modern science of religion. He lectured at Leipzig (1929-1935) and Chicago (1945–1955); in his works, which include *Sociology of Religion* (1944), he explored religious experience as well as the sociology of religion.

Wake, William (1657–1737)
Archbishop of Canterbury who engaged (1717–1720) in negotiations for reunion with the French Roman Catholic church, represented by the Gallican theologian, Dupin; the project ended with Dupin's death. He sympathised with the Nonconformists and advocated changes to accommodate them. His *Principles of the Christian Religion* (1700) proved very popular.

Waldenström, Paul Peter (1838–1917)
Swedish Free Churchman and theologian who was active in the Revivalist movement, editing *Pietisten*. He proposed theories contrary to traditional Lutheran theology; hence he founded a large sectarian movement in Sweden and took over direction of the Swedish Mission Society (1905).

Wallace, Lew (Lewis) (1827–1905)
Lawyer, diplomat, soldier and author. Although he is best remembered as the author of *Ben Hur* (1880) and other histori-

cal novels, e.g., *The Fair God* (1873) and *The Prince of India* (1893), Wallace served the Union cause in the Civil War and his country with distinction, as governor of New Mexico (1878–1881) and minister to Turkey (1881–1885).

Walther, Carl-Ferdinand Willhelm (1811–1887)
Conservative Lutheran theologian, of German origin, who settled in Missouri and worked to unite the various Lutheran groupings in the United States, becoming president of the Missouri Synod of American Lutheranism (1847).

Walton, Brian (1600–1661)
Bishop of Chester, remembered for his six-volume *Biblia Sacra Polyglotta,* or *London Polygot Bible,* which was begun in 1653 and never superseded. Walton lost his living and was imprisoned for supporting Laud, but the Restoration brought him recognition and the see of Chester.

Warburton, William (1698–1779)
Anglican bishop of Gloucester and controversialist. After ordination (1727) he held various livings before accepting the see of Gloucester. His works included many of literary criticism, and *The Alliance between Church and State* (1736) and his famous *The Divine Legation of Moses* (1737–1741). He attacked the new Methodist movement in *The Doctrine of Grace* (1762) and was an early, outspoken opponent of slavery.

Ward, Mary (1585–1645)
A Yorkshirewoman, she entered the Poor Clares religious order (1606) but left to found her own more active religious congregation in 1609. After opening houses in Liege, Cologne and Vienna, she was refused her request for papal approval (1629) and the congregation was suppressed. Later approval was given by Urban VIII and the houses reopened. The most famous in Britain is the Bar Convent at York, originally founded in 1642.

Ward, Wilfrid (1856—1916)
Son of W.G. Ward, he gave up training for the priesthood in favour of literary work. Biographer of his father, Cardinal Wiseman and Cardinal Newman, he also edited the *Dublin Review* and raised it to a high standard.

Ward, William George (1812—1882)
Anglican theologian, philosopher, fellow of Balliol College, Oxford, and keen supporter of the Oxford Movement. His book *The Ideal of a Christian Church* (1844) praised the Roman Catholic church, which he joined in 1845. Constantly engaged in controversial writing, he lectured at St Edmund's College, Ware, and supported the Ultramontanist party in the English Roman Catholic church.

Warham, William (c. 1450—1532)
Archbishop of Canterbury. Educated in civil law he rose rapidly, becoming master of the Rolls (1494) and, after ordination (1493), bishop of London (1502), lord chancellor and archbishop in 1504. A quiet intellectual, he had to continually give way to Cardinal Wolsey in ecclesiastical policy. Although he supported Henry VIII's divorce petition (1530) he was not in sympathy with the Protestant movement and resolutely opposed the king's anticlerical policies towards the end of his life.

Waterland, Daniel (1683—1740)
Anglican theologian and writer. Educated at Magdalene College, Cambridge, of which he became fellow (1704) and master (1713), he rose through other ecclesiastical preferments, but he is remembered as a learned theologian and author of several influential books, including *Eight Sermons in Defence of the Divinity of Our Lord Jesus Christ* (1720).

Watson, David (1933—1984)
Anglican priest, preacher and author. Educated at Cambridge, he was ordained (1959) and served as a curate at St Mark's,

Gillingham, Kent. After moving to York (1965) he dedicated himself to student work and led over sixty university missions. From 1974 David led many festivals worldwide, using a team of singers, dancers and musicians (from 1976) in corporate acts of worship. He wrote thirteen books, including his autobiography *You Are My God* and his last, *Fear No Evil*, which describes his struggle with cancer.

Watts, Isaac (1674–1748)
Nonconformist pastor and writer, also considered the father of English hymnody. While assistant (1699) and later full pastor at Mark Lane Congregational Chapel, London, he wrote his famous hymns, e.g., 'When I Survey the Wondrous Cross' and 'O God, our Help in Ages Past', which were published in *Horae Lyricae* (1706) and *Hymns and Spiritual Songs* (1707). He did much to establish hymn singing, previously suspect, as an essential part of Nonconformist worship. Ill health forced his resignation from pastoral work in 1712 and he lived the rest of his life at Abney Park, Stoke Newington. He wrote many books, including textbooks, but little, beyond his hymns, is remembered.

Weiss, Bernhard (1827–1918)
German New Testament scholar and theologian. Professor of New Testament exegesis at Kiel (1863–1877) and Berlin (1877–1908), his two important works are *Biblical Theology of the New Testament* (1868) and *The Life of Christ* (1882).

Weiss, Johannes (1863–1914)
Son of the above and a New Testament scholar of originality who laid the foundations for the development of form criticism. Professor at Marburg (1895) and Heidelberg (1908), his *Die Predigt Jesu vom Reiche Gottes* (1893) explored the eschatalogical dimension of the gospel and his many other works were equally influential.

Welch, Adam Cleghorn (1864–1943)

Scottish biblical scholar who was a pastoral minister and preacher, and became professor of Hebrew and Old Testament exegesis in New College, Edinburgh (1913–1934). A critic of Wellhausen, he is remembered particularly for his development of an alternative theory, published in five books, concluding with *The Work of the Chronicler* in 1939.

Wellhausen, Julius (1844–1918)

German biblical scholar and critic. After several posts he became professor in Semitics at Marburg (1885–1892) and Göttingen (1892–1913). His work of higher criticism, particularly upon the structure of the Book of Genesis, transformed Old Testament studies. His principal works were *Die Geschichte Israels* (1883) and *Das Evangelium Marci* (1903). His New Testament theories were not so readily accepted.

Wenceslas, St (c. 903–929) (also known by his Czech name Vaclav)

Prince-duke of Bohemia, martyr and patron saint of the Czechs. Raised and educated as a Christian by his grandmother, St Ludmila, after the death of his father and the violent anti-Christian regency of his mother Wenceslas became ruler. He promoted Christianity, encouraged missionary work and enjoyed a reputation for piety. His political friendship with Germany and his religion provoked his murder on his way to mass. Immediately there were stories of miracles and he was venerated as a martyr. His virtues are still extolled in the famous Christmas carol.

Wesley, Charles (1707–1788)

Anglican priest (1735), evangelist, and hymnwriter. Educated at Westminster School and Christ Church, Oxford, while at the latter he joined his brother John's study group, nicknamed 'Methodists' because of their methodical approach. He went to Georgia, North America, with John and founded Methodist

Societies there; on his return to England, and after a conversion experience, he began an itinerant preaching ministry. He established himself as the greatest of English hymnwriters, writing over 5,500, the first collection being published as *Hymns and Sacred Poems* (1739).

Wesley, John (1703–1791)

Anglican priest (1728), evangelist and founder of Methodism. Educated at Charterhouse and Christ Church, Oxford, while there he gathered around him a study group of serious Christians, nicknamed 'Methodists'. After an unsuccessful missionary trip to Georgia, North America, he became influenced by Moravian teaching, experienced a conversion and devoted the rest of his life to preaching. Churches were closed to him, so he preached in the open, traveling an average of eight thousand miles a year on horseback. Although he wanted the movement to remain with the Church of England, by 1784 the Methodists had removed themselves from it. John Wesley's journeys took him to Scotland and Ireland and at his death there were over seventy-one thousand members in Great Britain and over forty-three thousand in America.

Westcott, Brooke Foss (1825–1901)

Anglican bishop of Durham, best remembered for his theological works and his celebrated edition of the Greek New Testament, prepared with F.J.A. Hort (1881). Regius professor of divinity at Cambridge, he founded the Cambridge Clergy Training School (which became 'Westcott House'). As bishop he was concerned with social issues, mediating in the Coal Strike of 1892. In the same year his substantial theological work *The Gospel of Life* was published.

Weston, Frank (1871–1924)

Anglican bishop of Zanzibar (1908) who developed great empathy with his African people. Involved in the Kikuyu Dispute

(1913) he, however, worked for and inspired the drive for Christian unity at the Lambeth Conference of 1920.

Whately, Richard (1787–1863)
Anglican archbishop of Dublin, educator, logician and social reformer. Educated at Oriel College, Oxford, while there he wrote his satirical *Historic Doubts Relative to Napoleon Bonaparte* (1819). As archbishop of Dublin, in cooperation with the Roman Catholic authorities, he devised a nonsectarian programme of religious education which was later abandoned.

Wheelock, Eleazar (1711–1779)
American Congregational minister, educator and founder of Dartmouth College, established in New Hampshire at the new town of Hanover, which he helped to settle. A popular preacher, he played an important part in the Great Awakening.

White, William (1748–1836)
First bishop of the United States Episcopal church. Ordained an Anglican priest in England (1772) he returned to Philadelphia where he became rector of Christ Church. He led the foundation of the Protestant Episcopal church, independent of the Church of England, with its own bishops; he was himself the first presiding bishop of that church.

Whitefield, George (1714–1770)
Anglican priest and evangelist whose popular and powerful preaching supported the foundation of the Methodist movement and stimulated other dissident churches. His *Journal* began publication in 1739 and he prompted the foundation of nearly fifty colleges and universities in the United States.

Whitgift, John (c. 1530–1604)
Archbishop of Canterbury. Prominent at Cambridge, where he was educated as fellow, master of Trinity College and professor of divinity, he was first bishop of Worcester (1577–1583)

before going to Canterbury. He sought to strengthen and unify the Church of England, opposing both papal and Puritan influences. He founded almshouses and a school at Croydon, where he is buried.

Whitman, Marcus (1802–1847)
American Congregational missionary and physician who ministered to the Cayuse Indians of Waiilatpu, near Walla Walla. As a pioneer he helped to open up the Pacific Northwest; his valiant efforts failed and he and his family, with others, died in a massacre by the Indians in 1847.

Whittier, John Greenleaf (1807–1892)
American Quaker author, abolitionist and poet. At first just a journalist and poet, after 1832 he became a fervent antislavery advocate, using his poetry to good effect. His writing developed during the period 1843–1865, his Quaker poetry coming to the fore from 1866 to his death. His best-known poem, *Snow Bound* (1866), was followed by others, including *The Pennsylvania Pilgrim* (1872). Some of his poems, e.g., 'Dear Lord and Father of Mankind', became famous hymns.

Wilberforce, Robert Isaac (1802–1857)
Theologian of the Oxford Movement, second son of W. Wilberforce; his writings include *The Doctrine of the Incarnation* (1848). Close friend of Froude and Newman, he joined the Roman Catholic church in 1854.

Wilberforce, Samuel (1805–1873)
Anglican bishop, first of Oxford then of Winchester, and third son of William Wilberforce. He was considered a model bishop for his pastoral reforms and innovations, founding new churches, establishing religious communities and the first Anglican theological college at Cuddesdon (1854). He opposed Liberalism and attacked Darwinism, having a famous debate

with Thomas Huxley (1860) on the issue. In 1870 he initiated the revision of the Authorised Version of the Bible.

Wilberforce, William (1759–1833)
Politician, philanthropist and promoter of the abolition of the slave trade. He entered Parliament (1780) with his life-long friend William Pitt the Younger, and his parliamentary work was guided, after 1785, by his strict evangelicalism. He gained a reputation for radicalism, supporting the Roman Catholic political emancipation, and devoting much energy to bringing the slave trade, and then slavery, in British territories to an end. He was one of the founders of the Clapham Sect, and helped to establish the Church Missionary Society (1798) and the Bible Society (1803). His *Practical View of the Prevailing Religious System of Professed Christians* (1797) was widely popular and demonstrated his reputation as a leading evangelical.

Wilfrid, St (634–709)
Monk and bishop of York. He started his monastic life at the Celtic Lindisfarne (648) but later moved to Canterbury and studied the Roman form. Ever after he promoted Roman usage and papal authority, especially evident at the Synod of Whitby (664) and in the establishment of the Benedictine Rule at the Hexham monastery. A great builder at Hexham, Ripon and York, he improved the liturgy and, showing a lively missionary zeal, promoted the idea of Anglo-Saxons working as missionaries among the Germanic peoples. He is commonly considered to be one of the greatest English saints.

Wilkes, Paget (1871–1934)
Protestant missionary in Japan, where he traveled in 1897 under the auspices of the Church Missionary Society to work with B.F. Buxton. He founded the Japanese Evangelistic Band and dedicated his whole life to his missionary work.

Wilkins, John (1614–1672)

Anglican bishop of Chester, author and scientist who helped to found the Royal Society; as bishop he advocated tolerance for dissenters and wrote, among many works, *The Discovery of a World in the Moon* (1638).

William de la Mare (d. 1290)

English Franciscan theologian and philosopher who criticised the Aristotelian thought of Thomas Aquinas, against whom he wrote his *Correctorium Fratris Thomae*; this was approved for the whole Franciscan order in 1282.

William of Auvergne (1180–1249) (also known as William of Paris)

French scholastic theologian and philosopher who lectured in divinity at the University of Paris (1223) and was author of the monumental *Magisterium Divinale* (1223–1240).

William of Ockham (c. 1285–1349)

Originating from Ockham, Surrey, he trained in logic at Oxford and later lectured there. His radicalism eventually caused his philosophy to be examined but, although censured by papal authority, it was never condemned. He was embroiled in the dispute between the Franciscan order and the papacy, and his resultant excommunication caused him to attack the supremacy of papal power. A vigorous and independent thinker, Ockham was the most influential of fourteenth-century scholastic philosophers and the founder of nominalism.

William of Saint-Thierry (c. 1085–1148)

Monk, theologian and mystical writer. After entering the Benedictine monastery at Reims (1113), he became a specialist in Scripture and patristic writings; he devoted much of his life to synthesising the theology of East and West with these. Elected abbot of Saint-Thierry, near Reims, he was encouraged by his friend St Bernard of Clairvaux in his copious theological writing. To this period belong *On the Nature and Dignity of Love* and *On the Contemplation of God*. He retired to the Cistercian monastery of Signy, from where his more developed mystical writing comes, for example, *The Mirror of Faith* (1140) and the celebrated *Golden Letter* (1144).

Williams, Isaac (1802–1865)
Oxford-educated Anglican priest, poet and theologian, member of the Tractarian Movement, who contributed to *Lyra Apostolica* (1836) and the famous Tract 80, *Reserve in Communicating Religious Knowledge*. Losing the chair of poetry at Oxford (1842), he retired to concentrate upon his own poetry.

Williams, John (1796–1839)
Missionary sent out by the London Missionary Society to the Pacific (1817). He laboured among the islands, translating parts of the Bible into a local language until one day, landing at Dillon's Bay, Erromanga (1839), he was killed by cannibals. News of his death inspired much enthusiasm and support for missionary work in England.

Williams, Roger (1603–1683)
Pioneer and champion of religious toleration; founder of the colony of Rhode Island. After an Anglican ordination he sailed to North America (1630) in search of religious liberty. After many civil and religious disagreements he bought land from the Indians, later known as Rhode Island, which became a haven for Nonconformists and dissenters. He himself adhered to a Calvinist theology.

Williams, William (1717–1791)
Anglican minister who, by his preaching and poetry, did much to spread Methodism in Wales. He wrote more than eight hundred hymns and has been hailed as the first Welsh Romantic poet. His best-known hymn is 'Guide Me, O Thou Great Jehovah'.

Willibrord, St (c. 658–739)

Benedictine monk, archbishop and missionary. He was educated by the Benedictine monks of Ripon, Yorkshire, under the direction of St Wilfrid. Called to Ireland, he was ordained there. In 690, with companions, he was sent to evangelise West Frisia and he was consecrated archbishop of the Frisans in 695. Willibrord founded the monastery of Echternach and the success of his missionary work won him the title of 'Apostle of Friesland'. He is also patron saint of Holland.

Winchelsey, Robert (c. 1245–1313) (also known as Robert of Winchelsea)

Theologian and archbishop of Canterbury who championed ecclesiastical rights and found himself in constant opposition to both Edward I and Edward II.

Windthorst, Ludwig (1812–1891)

German Roman Catholic political leader of the Centre Party, which he founded to unify German Catholics and which struggled successfully against Bismarck's 'Kulturkamphf'. Twice minister of Justice (1851–1853 and 1862–1865) he had the 'May' Laws directed against the Catholic church gradually repealed (1888–1890); he is considered one of the greatest of German parliamentary leaders.

Winifred, St (d. c. 650) (also known as Gwenfrewi)

According to legend she was the beautiful daughter of a wealthy family living in north Wales. She refused the advances of Prince Caradog of Hawarden. Beheaded (or wounded) by him, she was healed by her uncle, St Beuno, and thereafter dedicated her life to God, becoming a nun and later abbess. A spring known as Holywell or St Winifred's Well marked the spot of her restoration (cure) to life, and this has been a great pilgrimage centre over the centuries. Patron saint of north Wales.

Winslow, Edward (1595–1655)

One of the *Mayflower* pilgrims who emigrated to New England; he was delegated to build relations with the local Indians, forming a friendship with Massasoit, their chief. He rose to become governor of the colony (1644–1645). What remains of his writings are of great interest, particularly the *Glorious Progress of the Gospel Amongst the Indians in New England* (1649).

Winthrop, John (1588–1649)

First governor of the Massachusetts Bay Colony. An English Suffolk squire unhappy with the anti-Puritan policies of King Charles I, he sold his estates and sailed west in the *Arbella* (1630). He led the community founded in the New World through the perils and early difficulties, being elected twelve times as governor of the colony.

Wipo (d. c. 1050)

Little is known of this priest and chaplain to the emperors Conrad II and Henry III who wrote poetry (most of which is lost); he is best recalled for his Easter hymn *Victimae Paschali Laudes*.

Wiseman, Nicholas Patrick Stephen (1802–1865)

First cardinal archbishop of Westminster. Of an Anglo-Irish family, he was educated in Rome and became rector of the English College there (1828–1840), also holding a position at the Vatican library. Appointed vicar apostolic, first of the Midland District then (1847–1850) of the London District, he was chosen as the first archbishop of Westminster and cardinal when the Catholic Hierarchy was re-established in 1850. An Ultramontanist, he faced opposition from the long-established English Roman Catholics, but won respect by his tact and constructive achievements; his writings include the widely read historical novel *Fabiola* (1854).

Wishart, George (c. 1513–1546)

Scottish Reformer. At Cambridge, where he had fled from a heresy charge, he met Hugh Latimer; further charges caused him to flee to the Continent. On his return to his native Scotland he preached Reformation doctrine, strongly influencing John Knox; arrested by the Earl of Bothwell, he was tried for heresy and burnt at the stake at St Andrew's.

Woodard, Nathaniel (1811–1891)

Anglican priest and founder of the 'Woodard Schools', which provided a middle-class public school education in an Anglican ambience. His ideas were outlined in the controversial *Plea for the Middle Classes* (1845) and furthered by the Society of St Nicolas, which he founded.

Woolman, John (1720–1772)

American Quaker preacher and campaigner against slavery. From 1743 he made long, arduous preaching journeys on foot, and in great simplicity, rallying Quaker communities against slavery. His *Journal* (1744) is recognised as a spiritual classic.

Wordsworth, Christopher (1807–1885)

Educator and bishop of Lincoln. Fellow of Trinity College, Cambridge, he was headmaster of Harrow (1836–1844), then held various appointments before accepting the see of Lincoln (1869). A conservative High Churchman, he compiled a Bible commentary, was respected for his writings on the early church fathers, and wrote many hymns, some of which are still in use.

Wordsworth, John (1843–1911)

Bishop of Salisbury, son of Christopher Wordsworth, he was a specialist in Latin and worked on a critical edition of the Vulgate New Testament (1911); he was appointed the first Oriel professor of the interpretation of Scripture in 1883. As bishop he worked for the reunion of the Church of England with the Swedish and Old Catholic churches; he also wrote in defence of Anglican orders.

Wordsworth, William (1770–1850)

Greatest poet of the English Romantic movement. Educated at St John's College, Cambridge, in his early twenties he rejected religious belief and espoused revolutionary ideals. A creative friendship with Samuel Taylor Coleridge produced the *Lyrical Ballads* (1798). He returned, with his sister Dorothy, to the Lake District (1799), where he lived the rest of his life. His autobiographical poem *The Prelude* (1805) was not published until after his death. Nature was his greatest inspiration, which brought him near to pantheism; but his devotion to the Church of England was deep and sincere.

Wulfstan, St (c. 1008–1095) (also known as Wulstan)

Bishop of Worcester and the last English bishop after the Norman Conquest. A Benedictine monk, he reluctantly accepted the office, but in his humility, austerity of life and able administration he proved to be a model bishop. He helped to suppress the slave trade between England and Ireland, assisted in compiling the Domesday Book and rebuilt Worcester Cathedral.

Wulfstan (d. 1023)

Monk and author of many sermons, treatises and codes of law; bishop of London (996–1002), archbishop of York (1002–1023) and bishop of Worcester (1002–1016). Little is known of his life prior to becoming bishop; his greatest achievement was his copious and influential writing. His most famous work is a call to reform, *Sermo Lupi ad Anglos* (he sometimes used the pen name 'Lupus'); as adviser to the kings Aethelred and Canute, he drafted their codes of law.

Wycliffe, John (c. 1330–1384)
Philosopher, theologian and reformer. Wycliffe was educated at Oxford, where he became master of Balliol (1360–1361). At the time Edward III appointed him rector of Lutterworth (1374) he came into the political service of the Black Prince and John of Gaunt; it was their families who appear to have shielded him from later ecclesiastical censure. As a philosopher he reacted against the current scepticism, and as a theologian he looked to the Bible and the fathers of the church; this was clear in his *De Ecclesia, De Veritate, Sacrae Scripturae* and *De Potestate Papae* (1377–1378). It was, however, his teaching on the Eucharist which brought condemnation of heresy down upon him. An energetic preacher, he inspired many followers who continued his teaching (taking popular expression in the Lollards) and his project of a Bible translation was seen through by his disciples.

Wyszynski, Stefan (1901–1981)
Archbishop of Warsaw and primate of Poland who was imprisoned (1953–1956) by the Communist authorities for protesting at the false accusations directed at the Polish hierarchy.

Xavier, St Francis (1506–1552)
Of Spanish origin, he was one of the original founder-members of the Society of Jesus (Jesuits), having met Ignatius of Loyola at the University of Paris (1525). Ordained a priest in 1537, he left for the missions three years later. He spent these highly successful years (1542–1545) in Goa, then traveled to the Malay Archipelago, and eventually traveled on to Japan, where he founded a Christian community. In 1552 he returned to Goa, then set out for China, but died before arriving. He is generally considered the greatest Roman Catholic missionary of modern times, credited with over seven hundred thousand conversions; hence he is often called the 'Apostle of the Indies' and 'of Japan'. He was canonised in 1622 and declared 'Patron of Foreign Missions'.

Ximenez de Cisneros, Francisco (1436–1517)
Cardinal archbishop of Toledo. A Spanish secular priest who became an austere Franciscan and, through the office of chaplain to Queen Isabella (1492), became first a reformer of his religious order and then, reluctantly, archbishop of Toledo and chancellor of Castile with heavy political responsibilities and involvements. He was a zealous patron of education, founding the University of Alcala and re-establishing the Mozarabic rite in the Spanish church.

Y

Yonge, Charlotte Mary (1823–1901)

English novelist who dedicated her life and talents to the service of the church. For seventy-one years she taught Sunday school in her village of Otterbourne and from 1851 edited *The Monthly Packet,* an uplifting magazine for girls. She is best remembered for her support for the Oxford Movement, especially through her novels, including *The Heir of Redclyffe* (1853), her first, and *Heartsease* (1854), *The Young Stepmother* (1861) and many others.

Z

Zaccaria, St Antonio Maria (1502–1539)
Italian physician who became a priest and founded the Congregation of Clerks Regular of St Paul (also known as Barnabites) to revive spirituality in the church (1530). He dedicated the remainder of his life to reform and missionary work in Vicenza, Italy. He was canonised in 1897.

Zahn, Theodor (1838–1933)
German New Testament and patristic scholar who successively held professorships at five different German universities and whose work was notable for its erudition and thoroughness. He did pioneer work on the New Testament canon, edited a commentary on the New Testament and contributed many valuable books on the study of the fathers of the church.

Zinzendorf, Nikolaus Ludwig, Graf von (1700–1760)
After studying law at Wittenberg University he entered politics, but left in 1727 as his religious interests, particularly the Herrnhut community on one of his estates, grew. Ordained a Lutheran pastor (1734) and a bishop of the Moravian Episcopal Church ('Unitas Fratrum') in 1737, he traveled widely, establishing Moravian communities in the Netherlands, the Baltic States, England, the West Indies and North America. He sought to create an ecumenical Protestant movement. He

was equally opposed to rationalism and rigid Protestantism, proclaiming a 'religion of the heart'. His emphasis upon the role of the emotions found lasting expression in the later Protestant theology of Schleiermacher.

Zwingli, Ulrich (1484–1531)

Leader of the Protestant Reformation in Switzerland. Educated at the Universities of Vienna (1498) and Basel (1502), he was ordained priest in 1506 and became pastor at Glarus (1506–1516), then at Einsiedeln. In 1518 he accepted the post of Peoples' Preacher at the Great Minister in Zurich. Well-read in humanism and the early Christian writers, with a knowledge of New Testament Greek, his preaching began to reflect the new Reformation teaching. He published and defended his sixty-seven theses in 1523, receiving much local support. He opposed the Anabaptists and disagreed with Luther on the theology of the Eucharist. His movement spread to some other cantons, but violent conflict developed (1531) between these and cantons that remained Catholic. Zwingli, acting as chaplain with a force from Zurich, was killed in battle.